Christina Latham-Koenig
Clive Oxenden
Paul Seligson

ENGLISH FILE
Elementary Student's Book

Paul Seligson and Clive Oxenden are the original co-authors of
English File 1 and *English File 2*

Contents

			Grammar	Vocabulary	Pronunciation
	1				
4	A	My name's Hannah, not Anna	verb be +, subject pronouns: *I, you*, etc.	days of the week, numbers 0–20, greetings	vowel sounds, word stress
6	B	All over the world	verb be ? and –	the world, numbers 21–100	/ə/, /tʃ/, /ʃ/, /dʒ/; sentence stress
8	C	Open your books, please	possessive adjectives: *my, your*, etc.	classroom language	/əʊ/, /uː/, /ɑː/; the alphabet
10	**PRACTICAL ENGLISH** Episode 1 Arriving in London				
	2				
12	A	A writer's room	*a / an*, plurals; *this / that / these / those*	things	final *-s* and *-es*; *th*
14	B	Stars and Stripes	adjectives	colours, adjectives, modifiers: *quite / very / really*	long and short vowel sounds
16	C	After 300 metres, turn right	imperatives, *let's*	feelings	understanding connected speech
18	**REVISE AND CHECK 1&2**				
	3				
20	A	Things I love about Britain	present simple + and –	verb phrases	third person *-s*
22	B	Work and play	present simple ?	jobs	/ɜː/
24	C	Love online	word order in questions	question words	sentence stress
26	**PRACTICAL ENGLISH** Episode 2 Coffee to take away				
	4				
28	A	Is she his wife or his sister?	*Whose...?*, possessive *'s*	family	/ʌ/, the letter *o*
30	B	What a life!	prepositions of time (*at, in, on*) and place (*at, in, to*)	everyday activities	linking and sentence stress
32	C	Short life, long life?	position of adverbs and expressions of frequency	adverbs and expressions of frequency	the letter *h*
34	**REVISE AND CHECK 3&4**				
	5				
36	A	Do you have the X Factor?	*can / can't*	verb phrases: *buy a newspaper*, etc.	sentence stress
38	B	Love your neighbours	present continuous	verb phrases	/ŋ/
40	C	Sun and the City	present simple or present continuous?	the weather and seasons	places in London
42	**PRACTICAL ENGLISH** Episode 3 In a clothes shop				
	6				
44	A	Reading in English	object pronouns: *me, you, him*, etc.	phone language	/aɪ/, /ɪ/, and /iː/
46	B	Times we love	*like* + (verb + *-ing*)	the date; ordinal numbers	consonant clusters; saying the date
48	C	Music is changing their lives	revision: *be* or *do*?	music	/j/
50	**REVISE AND CHECK 5&6**				

			Grammar	Vocabulary	Pronunciation
	7				
52	A	At the National Portrait Gallery	past simple of *be*: *was* / *were*	word formation: *paint* > *painter*	sentence stress
54	B	Chelsea girls	past simple: regular verbs	past time expressions	*-ed* endings
56	C	A night to remember	past simple: irregular verbs	*go*, *have*, *get*	sentence stress
58	**PRACTICAL ENGLISH** Episode 4 Getting lost			
	8				
60	A	A murder story	past simple: regular and irregular	irregular verbs	past simple verbs
62	B	A house with a history	*there is* / *there are*, *some* / *any* + plural nouns	the house	/eə/ and /ɪə/, sentence stress
64	C	A night in a haunted hotel	*there was* / *there were*	prepositions: place and movement	silent letters
66	**REVISE AND CHECK 7&8**				
	9				
68	A	What I ate yesterday	countable / uncountable nouns; *a* / *an*, *some* / *any*	food	the letters *ea*
70	B	White gold	quantifiers: *how much* / *how many*, *a lot of*, etc.	food containers	/ʃ/ and /s/
72	C	Quiz night	comparative adjectives	high numbers	/ə/, sentence stress
74	**PRACTICAL ENGLISH** Episode 5 At a restaurant			
	10				
76	A	The most dangerous road…	superlative adjectives	places and buildings	consonant groups
78	B	CouchSurf round the world!	*be going to* (plans), future time expressions	holidays	sentence stress
80	C	What's going to happen?	*be going to* (predictions)	verb phrases	the letters *oo*
82	**REVISE AND CHECK 9&10**				
	11				
84	A	First impressions	adverbs (manner and modifiers)	common adverbs	word stress
86	B	What do you want to do?	verbs + *to* + infinitive	verbs that take the infinitive	sentence stress
88	C	Men, women, and the internet	articles	the internet	word stress
90	**PRACTICAL ENGLISH** Episode 6 Going home			
	12				
92	A	Books and films	present perfect	irregular past participles	sentence stress
94	B	I've never been there!	present perfect or past simple?	more irregular past participles	irregular past participles
96	C	The *English File* questionnaire	revision: question formation	revision: word groups	revision: sounds
98	**REVISE AND CHECK 11&12**				

100	Communication	124	**Grammar Bank**	165	**Irregular verbs**
111	Writing	148	**Vocabulary Bank**	166	**Sound Bank**
116	Listening				

G verb *be* +, subject pronouns: *I, you*, etc.
V days of the week, numbers 0–20, greetings
P vowel sounds, word stress

1A My name's Hannah, not Anna

Hi, I'm Mike. What's your name?

Hannah. Nice to meet you.

1 LISTENING & SPEAKING

a 1 2))) Look at the pictures. Listen and number them 1–4.

b Listen again and complete the gaps.

1 **A** Hi, I'm Mike. What's your ¹_____?
   B Hannah.
   A ²_____?
   B Hannah!

2 **A** What's your phone ³_____?
   B It's 7894 132 456.
   A ⁴_____. See you on Saturday. Bye.
   B Goodbye.

3 **A** ⁵_____, Mum. This is Hannah.
   B ⁶_____. Nice to meet you.
   C Nice to ⁷_____ you, Anna.
   B ⁸_____ name's Hannah.
   C Sorry, Hannah.

4 **A** Hi, ⁹_____. You're early!
   B Hello, Mrs Archer. How are ¹⁰_____?
   C I'm very well, ¹¹_____ you, Anna. And you?
   B ¹²_____, thanks.
   A It's Hannah, Mum.

c Complete the gaps with a word from the list.

| Fine   Hi   I'm...   Thanks   Bye |

Hello = _____
My name's… = _____
Very well = _____
Thank you = _____
Goodbye = _____

d 1 3))) Listen and repeat some phrases from the dialogue. Copy the rhythm.

e 1 4))) In groups of three, practise the dialogues with the sound effects. Change roles.

f Introduce yourself to other students.

Hello, I'm Antonio. What's your name? *Carla. Nice to meet you.*

2 GRAMMAR verb be +, subject pronouns

a Complete the sentences with *are*, *is*, or *am*.

I'm Mike.	= I _____ Mike.
My name's Hannah.	= My name _____ Hannah.
You're early.	= You _____ early.
It's 7894 132 456.	= It _____ 7894 132 456.

b ▶ **p.124 Grammar Bank 1A.** Learn more about verb *be* + and subject pronouns, and practise them.

c (1 6)) Listen and repeat the pronouns and contractions.

d (1 7)) Listen. Say the contraction.))) *I am* *I'm*

e In pairs, try to remember the names in your class. Say *He's / She's* _____.

f Stand up and speak to other students.

Hi Carla. How are you? Fine thanks. And you?

3 PRONUNCIATION
vowel sounds, word stress

a (1 8)) Listen and repeat the words and sounds.

fish	tree	cat	egg	train	bike
it	he	am	very	they	I
this	we	thanks	well	name	Hi
	meet				Bye

b ▶ **p.166 Sound Bank.** Look at the example words and spellings for the sounds in **a**.

> 🔍 **Word stress**
> Multi-syllable words have one stressed syllable.
> **so**|rry   good|**bye**   **Sa**|tur|day

c (1 9)) Listen and under<u>line</u> the stressed syllable in these words.

air|port   com|pu|ter   e|mail   ka|ra|te
ho|tel   mu|se|um   sa|lad   te|nnis
pas|ta   in|ter|net   bas|ket|ball   sand|wich

d Write the words from **c** in the chart.

food	technology	sports	places

e In pairs, write more words that you know in each column. How do you pronounce them?

4 VOCABULARY
days of the week, numbers 0–20

a Look at the picture. Can you remember what Mike and Hannah say?

b ▶ **p.148 Vocabulary Bank** *Days and numbers.* Do parts 1 and 2.

c (1 12)) Listen and say the next day or number.

))) *Monday, Tuesday* *Wednesday*

d What's your phone number? What day is it today? And tomorrow?

5 LISTENING & SPEAKING

a (1 13)) Listen. Where are they? Write 1–6 in the boxes.

☐ airport	Gate number _____
☐ sandwich bar	_____ euros _____ cents
☐ hotel	Room _____
☐ museum	Closed on _____
☐ taxi	_____ Manchester Road
☐ school	Classes on _____ and _____

b Listen again. Write a number or a day in each space.

c (1 14)) Listen and respond.

))) *Hello. Nice to meet you.* *Nice to meet you.*

G verb *be* ? and −
V the world, numbers 21-100
P /ə/, /tʃ/, /ʃ/, /dʒ/; sentence stress

Where are you from?
I'm from Ireland.

1B All over the world

1 VOCABULARY the world

a Can you name three countries in English?

b ▶ p.149 **Vocabulary Bank** *The world*.

c ◁))1 17 Listen. Say the nationality.

))) Scotland → Scottish

d In pairs, do the quiz.

> **Useful phrases**
> *I think* it's in Italy.
> *I think* it's Russian, but *I'm not sure*.

THE WORLD QUIZ

1 Where are these capital cities?
 a Canberra _____
 b Prague _____
 c Warsaw _____
 d Ankara _____
 e Edinburgh _____

2 What country is the money from?
 a the dollar _____
 b the yuan _____
 c the rouble _____
 d the pound _____
 e the yen _____

3 What country is the food from?
 a *tapas* _____
 b *goulash* _____
 c *pasta* _____
 d *tacos* _____

4 What nationality are the flags?
 a 🇯🇵 _____
 b 🇦🇷 _____
 c 🇨🇭 _____
 d 🇧🇷 _____

5 ◁))1 18 What national anthem is it? Write the nationality.
 a _____ c _____
 b _____ d _____

6 ◁))1 19 What language is it? Write a–d in the boxes.
 ☐ Turkish   ☐ Russian
 ☐ Chinese   ☐ Irish (Gaelic)

> **Languages**
> The word for a language is usually the same as the nationality adjective, e.g. in Italy the language is Italian.

2 PRONUNCIATION /ə/, /tʃ/, /ʃ/, /dʒ/

> **The /ə/ sound**
> The /ə/ sound is the most common vowel sound in English. The /ə/ sound has many different spellings, e.g. H*e*llo, S*a*turday, Brit*ai*n

a ◁))1 20 Listen and repeat the words and sounds.

| c*o*mputer | **A**m*e*rican   **A**rg*e*ntinian |
| | Scotl*a*nd   Switz*e*rland |

b ◁))1 21 Listen and repeat the sound pictures and sentences. Practise with a partner.

1 chess — **Ch**arles is **Cz**ech, not Fren**ch**.

2 shower — **Sh**e's Poli**sh** or Ru**ss**ian. I'm not **s**ure.

3 jazz — We're **G**erman and they're **J**apanese.

c ▶ p.166 **Sound Bank**. Look at the example words and spellings for the sounds in **a** and **b**.

3 GRAMMAR verb be ? and –

a 1 22))) Cover the dialogues. Listen to three interviews in London. Which countries are the people from?

b Read the dialogues. Complete with *I'm, I'm not, are, aren't, is,* or *isn't.*

1 A Are you English?
B No, _____ English. _____ Scottish.
A Where _____ you from in Scotland?
B _____ from Glasgow.

2 A Where _____ you from?
B _____ from Australia, from Darwin.
A Where's Darwin? _____ it near Sydney?
B No, it _____. It's in the north.
A _____ it nice?
B Yes, it _____. It's beautiful.

3 A Where _____ you from?
B We're from Columbus, Ohio, in the USA.
A _____ you on holiday?
C No, we _____. We're students.

c Listen and check.

d ▶ p.124 **Grammar Bank 1B**. Learn more about verb be ? and –, and practise it.

e 1 24))) Listen and respond with a short answer.

))) Is Sydney the capital of Australia? No, it isn't.

f With a partner, write three questions beginning *Is…?* or *Are…?* Ask them to another pair.

4 PRONUNCIATION & SPEAKING
sentence stress

> 🔍 **Sentence stress**
> In sentences we stress the important words.
> **Where's** she **from**? She's from **China**.

a 1 25))) Listen and repeat. Copy the rhythm.
1 A **Where** are you **from**?
  B I'm from **Dublin**.
2 A Are you **American**?
  B No, I'm **not**. I'm Aus**tralian**.

b Practise the dialogues in 3 with a partner.

c ▶ **Communication** *Where are they from?* **A** p.100 **B** p.106.

d Ask people in the class *Where are you from?*

5 VOCABULARY numbers 21–100

a Look at the signs. Can you say the numbers?

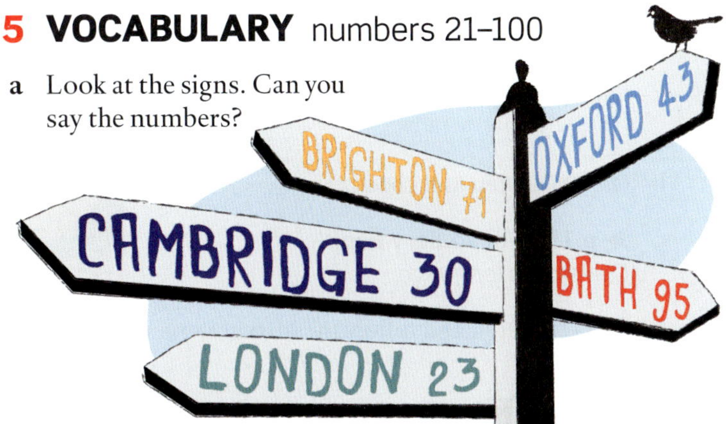

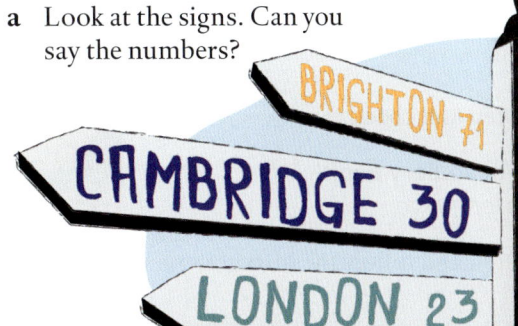

b ▶ p.148 Vocabulary Bank *Days and numbers.* Do part 3.

c 1 27))) Listen and write the numbers.

d Write ten numbers from 21–100. Dictate them to a partner.

6 LISTENING

a 1 28))) Listen and repeat the pairs of numbers. What's the difference?

1 a 13 b 30   5 a 17 b 70
2 a 14 b 40   6 a 18 b 80
3 a 15 b 50   7 a 19 b 90
4 a 16 b 60

b 1 29))) Which number do you hear? Listen and circle a or b above.

c Play *Bingo.*

7 1 30))) SONG *All Over the World* 🎵

G possessive adjectives: *my, your,* etc.
V classroom language
P /əʊ/, /uː/, /ɑː/; the alphabet

1C Open your books, please

How do you spell your surname?

B-E-Z-E-R-R-A.

1 VOCABULARY
classroom language

a Look at the picture of a classroom. Match the words and pictures.

- ☐ board /bɔːd/
- ☐ chair /tʃeə/
- ☐ computer /kəmˈpjuːtə/
- ☐ desk /desk/
- ☐ door /dɔː/
- ☐ picture /ˈpɪktʃə/
- 8 table /ˈteɪbl/
- ☐ wall /wɔːl/
- ☐ window /ˈwɪndəʊ/

b ◁)) 1 31 Listen and check.

c ▶ p.150 Vocabulary Bank *Classroom language.*

d ◁)) 1 34 Listen and follow the instructions.

2 PRONUNCIATION
/əʊ/, /uː/, /ɑː/; the alphabet

a ◁)) 1 35 Listen and repeat the words and sounds.

əʊ phone	ph**o**ne	cl**o**se	m**o**bile
uː boot	b**oo**t	sch**oo**l	d**o**
ɑː car	c**a**r	cl**a**ss	**a**nswer

b ◁)) 1 36 Look at these common abbreviations. Can you say any of them in English? Listen and check.

**OK BBC MTV
CNN USB DVD
BMW ATM**

c ◁)) 1 37 Complete the alphabet chart with B, C, D, K, M, N, O, S, T, U, V, W. Listen and check.

eɪ train	iː tree	e egg	aɪ bike	əʊ phone	uː boot	ɑː car
A H J ___	___ ___ E G P ___	F L ___ X Z	I Y	___	Q ___	R

d ◁)) 1 38 Listen and (circle) the letter you hear.

1 E A I 2 G J 3 K Q 4 C S
5 V P B 6 M N 7 V W 8 U Y

e Practise saying the phrases below with abbreviations.

a **P**ersonal **C**omputer   a **V**ery **I**mportant **P**erson
the **U**nited **K**ingdom   the **U**nited **S**tates of America
the **E**uropean **U**nion   a **P**ortable **D**ocument **F**ormat
a **D**isc **J**ockey   the **N**ational **B**asketball **A**ssociation

a PC

3 LISTENING & SPEAKING

a ◉ 1 39))) A student goes to London to study English. Listen to the interview and complete her form.

First name	D _ _ _ _ _
Surname	B _ _ _ rr _
Country	
City	
Age	
Address	Avenida Princesa Isabel
Postcode	
Email	dbezerra@mail.com
Phone number	55
Mobile phone	

b ◉ 1 40))) Listen. Complete the receptionist's questions.

1 What's your _____ name?
2 _____ your surname?
3 _____ do you spell it?
4 Where are you _____?
5 _____ old are you?
6 _____ your address?
7 _____ your postcode?
8 What's your _____ address?
9 What's your _____ _____?

c Listen again and repeat the questions. Copy the rhythm.

d Ask your partner the questions. Write down their answers.

> 🔍 **Spelling: names and addresses**
> RR = double R   @ = at   . = dot

4 GRAMMAR possessive adjectives: *my*, *your*, etc.

a Complete the gaps with *I*, *you*, *my*, or *your*.

1 Where are _____ from?
  _____ 'm from Rio.
2 What's _____ name?
  _____ name's Darly.

b ▶ **p.124 Grammar Bank 1C.** Learn more about possessive adjectives and practise them.

c ◉ 1 42))) Listen. Change the sentences.

))) I'm Richard.   (My name's Richard.

5 SPEAKING

➤ **Communication** *What's his / her real name?* **A** p.100 **B** p.106. Find out if some actors' and singers' names are their real names or not.

6 WRITING

➤ **p.111 Writing** *Completing a form.* Complete an application for a student visa and write a paragraph about you.

Practical English Arriving in London

1 VOCABULARY in a hotel

a Match the words and symbols.

1 2 3

4 5 6

- [ ] Reception /rɪˈsepʃn/
- [ ] the lift /lɪft/
- [ ] a single room /ˈsɪŋɡl ruːm/
- [ ] a double room /ˈdʌbl ruːm/
- [ ] the bar /bɑː/
- [ ] the ground floor /(ɡraʊnd) flɔː/ (first, second, third, etc.)

b (1 43))) Listen and check.

2 INTRODUCTION

a (1 44))) Watch or listen to Jenny and Rob. Mark the sentences **T** (true) or **F** (false).

1 Rob lives and works in London.
2 He's a writer for a magazine.
3 The name of his magazine is *London 20seven*.
4 Jenny is British.
5 She's an assistant editor.
6 It's her second time in the UK.

b Watch or listen again. Say why the **F** sentences are false.

3 CHECKING IN

a (1 45))) Watch or listen to Jenny checking into a hotel room. Answer the questions.

1 Complete Jenny's surname: ZI__LI__SK__.
2 What's her room number?

b Watch or listen again. Complete the **You Hear** phrases.

))) You Hear	You Say 💬
Good evening, madam.	Hello. I have a reservation. My name's Jennifer Zielinski.
Can you _____ that, please?	Z-I-E-L-I-N-S-K-I.
For five nights?	Yes, that's right.
Can I have your passport, please?	Just a second…Here you are.
Thank you. Can you sign here, _____? Thank you. Here's your _____. It's room 306, on the third floor. The _____ is over there.	The lift? Oh, the elevator.
Yes. Enjoy your stay, Ms Zielinski.	Thank you.

> **British and American English**
> *lift* = British English *elevator* = American English
> z = /zed/ in British English, /ziː/ in American English
> **Greetings**
> *Good morning* = > 12.00   *Good afternoon* = 12.00 > 18.00
> *Good evening* = 18.00 >   *Good night* = Goodbye (when you go to bed)
> *Madam* = a polite way to greet a woman
> *Sir* = a polite way to greet a man

c (1 46))) Watch or listen and repeat the **You Say** phrases. Copy the rhythm.

EPISODE 1

d Practise the dialogue with a partner.

e Work in pairs. Read your role and look at the dialogue in **3b**. What do you need to change?

  A (book open) You are the receptionist. It's 11.00 a.m. B's room is 207 on the second floor. Begin with *Good morning sir / madam*.
  B (book closed) You arrive at the hotel. Use your name and surname.

f Roleplay the dialogue. Then swap roles.

g (1 47)) Look at the information in the box. Listen and repeat the *Can…?* phrases.

> **Can you…?** = Please do it
> Can you sign here?
> Can you spell that?
>
> **Can I have…?** = Please give me (your passport, etc.)
> Can I have your passport, please?
> Can I have my key, please?

h You are in a hotel. How do you ask the receptionist to give you…?

  • your key   • your passport
  • a map of London   • a pen

4 JENNY TALKS TO ROB

a (1 48)) Watch or listen and mark the sentences **T** (true) or **F** (false).

  1 Jenny has a coffee.
  2 She is in London on business.
  3 The waitress is German.
  4 Jenny phones Rob Walker.
  5 Jenny is tired.
  6 Their meeting is at 10.00.

b Watch or listen again. Say why the **F** sentences are false.

c (1 49)) Read the information in the box. Listen and repeat the *Would you like…?* phrases and the responses. Practise offering drinks and responding.

> **Would you like…?**
> Would you like a coffee?   Yes, please.
> Would you like another tea?   No, thanks.
>
> We use *Would you like…?* to offer somebody something.
> We respond *Yes, please* or *No, thanks*.

d Look at the **Social English phrases**. Who says them: **J**enny, **R**ob, or the **w**aitress?

> **Social English phrases**
> I'm here [on business].   This is [Rob. Rob Walker].
> I'm from [New York]. What about you?   That's perfect.
> No problem.   It's time for bed.
> Is that [Jennifer]?

e (1 50)) Watch or listen and check. Do you know what they are in your language?

f Watch or listen again and repeat the phrases.

> **Can you…?**
> ☐ check into a hotel and spell your name
> ☐ ask somebody to do something / to give you something
> ☐ offer somebody a drink, and accept or refuse

G *a / an*, plurals; *this / that / these / those*
V things
P final *-s* and *-es*; *th*

2A A writer's room

What's this in English?
It's a purse.

1 VOCABULARY things

a Look at a photo of Roald Dahl, the author of many famous children's books and stories for adults. Do you know any of his books?

b Look at the photo of his room. Tick (✓) or cross (✗) the things you can see in the picture. Do you think the room is tidy?

☐ a table
☐ a lamp
☐ a computer
☐ a chair
☐ pencils
☐ photos
☐ a window
☐ a printer
☐ a phone
☐ pieces of paper

c ▶ p.151 **Vocabulary Bank** *Things*.

2 GRAMMAR *a / an*, plurals

a Complete the chart.

Singular	Plural
a pen	pens
____ umbrella	____
____	watches
____	diaries

b ▶ p.126 **Grammar Bank 2A part 1**.
Learn more about *a / an* and plurals, and practise them.

3 PRONUNCIATION final *-s* and *-es*

a ◀)) 53 Listen and repeat the words and sounds.

s	snake	books lamps tickets
z	zebra	photos keys pens
/ɪz/		glasses watches purses

b ◀)) 54 Read the rule. Circle the words where *-es* is pronounced /ɪz/. Listen and check.

> 🔍 **Final *-es***
> Final *-es* after *ce*, *ch*, *sh*, *s*, *ge*, and *x* = /ɪz/, e.g. *watches, glasses, purses*

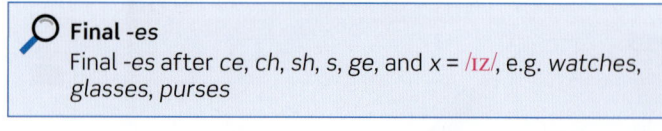

1 classes   3 headphones   5 pieces   7 pages
2 files   4 boxes   6 tissues   8 mobiles

4 LISTENING & SPEAKING

a ▶ **Communication** *What's on the table?* p.100.

b (1 55)) Listen to three people say what things they have on the table or desk where they work. Are their tables tidy?

c Listen again and tick (✓) the things they have.

	1	2	3
a computer / a laptop	☐	☐	☐
a printer	☐	☐	☐
a lamp	☐	☐	☐
a phone	☐	☐	☐
books	☐	☐	☐
a dictionary	☐	☐	☐
a diary	☐	☐	☐
photos	☐	☐	☐
pieces of paper	☐	☐	☐
pens	☐	☐	☐
DVDs	☐	☐	☐
tissues	☐	☐	☐

d Talk to a partner about the table where you work or study. Say what things you have. Say if the table is tidy or not.

I have a laptop and a printer. I have… It isn't tidy.

e Play *What is it?* with your partner. **A** close your eyes. **B** give things to your partner and ask *What is it? What are they?*

5 GRAMMAR
this / that / these / those

a (1 56)) Look at pictures 1–4 and complete the dialogues. Listen and check. Practise the dialogues.

b Read the dialogues again. What's the difference between…?
1 *this* and *these*
2 *this* and *that*
3 *these* and *those*

c ▶ p.126 **Grammar Bank 2A part 2.** Learn more about *this / that / these / those* and practise them.

6 PRONUNCIATION *th*

a (1 58)) Listen and repeat the words and sounds.

	mother	this	that	these	the	they

	thumb	thanks	thing	thirty	three	Thursday

b (1 59)) Listen and repeat the phrases. Practise saying them.
1 this Thursday
2 thirty-three
3 those things
4 Thanks for that.
5 These are the keys.
6 What are those things there?
7 I'm thirty-three this Thursday.

c Work in pairs. Put four of your things on your table (singular or plural). Ask your partner.

For the things on your table:
What's this in English? — *It's a watch.*

For things in the classroom (point):
What are those in English? — *They're pictures.*

1 What's this?
It's _____ _____ _____.

2 What are these?
They're _____.

3 What's that?
It's _____ _____.

4 What are those?
They're _____.

G adjectives
V colours, adjectives, modifiers: *quite* / *very* / *really*
P long and short vowel sounds

2B Stars and Stripes

Is she attractive?
Yes. She's very tall, with red hair.

1 VOCABULARY colours, adjectives part 1

a What colour is the American flag? Write the missing letters.

 It's **r__d**, **wh____t**, and **bl____**.

b Complete the other colours.

bl__ck **y__ll__w** **gr__y** **p__nk**
__r__ng__ **br__wn** **gr____n**

c Practise with the flags. Ask and answer.

What colour is it?

d What colour is *your* flag?

e ▶ p.152 Vocabulary Bank *Adjectives*. Do part 1.

2 GRAMMAR adjectives

a What are they? Label the pictures in the USA quiz using an adjective and a noun from each circle.

Adjectives
nice yellow
American New
fast White
blue high

Nouns
food House
school Airlines
taxis jeans
day York

b (1 62) Listen and check. Circle the correct rule.

- Adjectives go *before* / *after* a noun.
- Adjectives *change* / *don't change* before a plural noun.

c ▶ p.126 Grammar Bank 2B. Learn more about adjectives and practise them.

d Cover the the pictures. Can you remember the eight phrases?

1 *American Airlines*
2 _____ 
3 Have a _____! 
4 _____ 
5 The _____ 
6 a _____ 
7 _____ 
8 _____

3 PRONUNCIATION
long and short vowel sounds

> **Long and short vowels**
> Vowel sounds in English are long or short. Long sounds have /ː/ in the phonetic symbol, e.g. /ɑː/.

a Listen and repeat the words and sounds.

 fish	 tree	 cat	 car

 clock	 horse	 bull	 boot

b Match an adjective from circle **A** with an adjective from circle **B** with the same vowel sound. Write them in the chart.

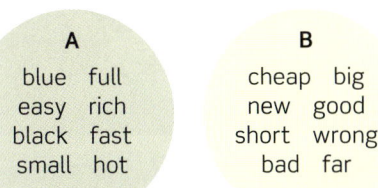

A: blue, full, easy, rich, black, fast, small, hot

B: cheap, big, new, good, short, wrong, bad, far

c 1 65))) Listen and check.

d ▶ p.166 **Sound Bank.** Look at the typical spellings for these sounds.

e **Adjective race** In pairs, in three minutes make phrases with an adjective and a noun with the same vowel sound. Use *a / an* with singular nouns.

Adjectives: old, new, grey, fast, black, good, big, cheap, short

Nouns: book, boots, cars, cat, day, fish, jeans, photo, story

An old photo

f 1 66))) Listen and check. Practise saying the phrases.

4 VOCABULARY adjectives part 2

a ▶ p.152 Vocabulary Bank *Adjectives*. Do part 2.

b Work in pairs. **A** say an adjective. **B** say a famous person.

short ⟩ ⟨ Tom Cruise

5 READING

a Read the descriptions and look at the photos. Who are the two people?

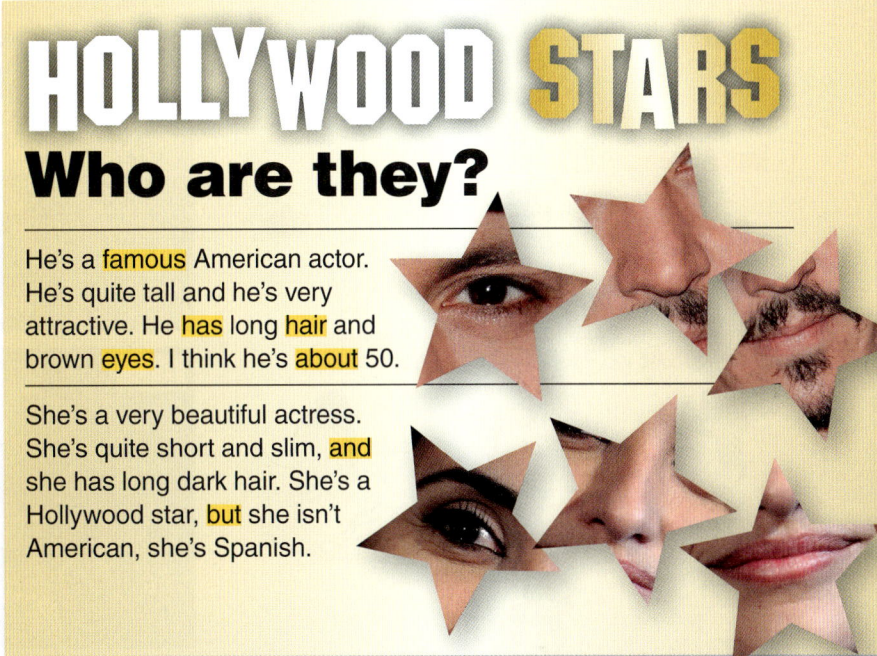

HOLLYWOOD STARS
Who are they?

He's a famous American actor. He's quite tall and he's very attractive. He has long hair and brown eyes. I think he's about 50.

She's a very beautiful actress. She's quite short and slim, and she has long dark hair. She's a Hollywood star, but she isn't American, she's Spanish.

b Read them again. Guess the meaning of the highlighted words.

6 WRITING & SPEAKING

a Think of a famous person from any country in the world. Use the jobs in the box to help you.

actor / actress   musician   politician
singer   sportsman / sportswoman   TV presenter

b Write a short description of the person. Give it to your partner. Can he / she guess who it is?

c Play *Guess the famous person*.

A think of a famous actor / actress.
B ask ten questions using *Is…?* Try to guess the actor / actress.

Is it a man or a woman? ⟩ ⟨ A woman.

Is she American? ⟩ ⟨ Yes, she is.

G imperatives, let's
V feelings
P understanding connected speech

2C After 300 metres, turn right

Please slow down!
Don't worry.

1 VOCABULARY feelings

a Match the words and pictures.

- [ ] hungry
- [ ] sad
- [ ] bored
- [ ] hot
- [ ] thirsty
- [ ] happy
- [ ] angry
- [ ] cold
- [ ] stressed
- [ ] tired
- [1] worried

🔍 **Collocation**
Use be + hungry, thirsty, hot, etc.,
e.g. I'm very hungry.
NOT ~~I have very hungry.~~

b 1 68)) Listen and check. Repeat the phrases.

c Cover the words and look at the pictures. Make ➕ and ➖ sentences about how you feel and tell your partner.

I'm quite hungry.
I'm very tired.
I'm not hot.

2 LISTENING & READING

a 1 69)) The Carter family are on holiday in Ireland. Look at the pictures. Listen and number them 1–5.

A

B

C

D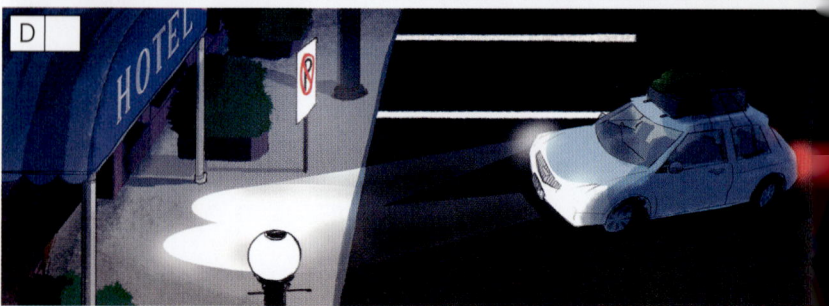

E

16

b Listen again and read. Try to guess what the highlighted phrases mean.

1 **Satnav** After 100 metres turn right.
   Turn right.
   Mum Please slow down! This road is very dangerous.
   Dad Don't worry. You know I'm a good driver.
   Mum Be careful!

2 **Suzy** Dad, this music is terrible. Can you turn it off?
   Dad OK.
   Tim Dad, I'm very hot. Turn the air conditioning on, please.
   Dad Are you hot, Suzy?
   Suzy No, I'm cold.
   Mum Open your window, Tim.

3 **Suzy** I'm thirsty. Where's the water?
   Mum Here you are.
   Tim I'm hungry. Can we stop soon?
   Mum Let's stop at that service station.
   Dad OK.

4 **Tim** Give me my iPod.
   Suzy This is my iPod!
   Dad Be quiet!
   Tim Are we there yet? I'm bored.
   Dad It's not far now. Only 80 kilometres.
   Tim Can you turn the radio on please, Mum?
   Mum OK.
   Dad Oh no!

5 **Suzy** Where are we?
   Dad We're here. At the hotel.
   Tim Great!
   Mum Don't park here. Look at that sign. No parking.
   Dad Don't worry. It's OK. Come on. Let's go.

c 1 70))) Listen to the end of the story. What are the two problems the family have?

3 GRAMMAR imperatives, *let's*

a Look at the highlighted phrases in **2b**. Then complete the chart.

Imperatives		
+	Turn right!	_____ here!
−	_____ _____ right!	Don't park here!
Suggestions		
_____ stop at that service station.		
Come on. Let's _____.		

b ▶ p.126 **Grammar Bank 2C.** Learn more about imperatives and *let's*, and practise them.

c Look at the pictures in **2** and cover the dialogues. Can you remember the imperatives and suggestions with each picture?

d What do the signs mean? Use a verb phrase from the list in a + or − imperative.

be careful	cross the road now	go in here
smoke here	listen to music here	take photos
~~turn left~~	turn off your mobile	eat or drink here

1 Turn left

e Cover the list and look at the pictures. Can you remember the phrases?

4 PRONUNCIATION
understanding connected speech

> 🔍 **Connected speech**
> When people speak they don't usually separate all the words. For example, if a word ends with a consonant and the next word begins with a vowel, they join them together, e.g. Turn‿off the music.

a 1 72))) Listen and write six sentences.

b Practise saying the sentences.

5 SPEAKING

▶ **Communication** *What's the matter?* **A** p.101 **B** p.106. Roleplay dialogues.

6 1 73))) SONG *Please Don't Go* ♫

1 & 2 Revise and Check

GRAMMAR

Circle a, b, or c.

1 Hello. _____ your name?
   a What   b What are   c What's
2 Maria is German. _____ a student.
   a She's   b He's   c It's
3 A Where _____ from?
   B He's from Turkey.
   a he is   b is   c is he
4 They _____ English, they're Scottish.
   a isn't   b aren't   c not are
5 A Are you from Paris?
   B Yes, _____.
   a I am   b I'm   c I are
6 She's Brazilian. _____ name's Daniela.
   a His   b Her   c Your
7 We're from the USA. _____ surname is Mackay.
   a Your   b Their   c Our
8 A What are they?
   B They're _____.
   a watches   b a watch   c watchs
9 A What is it?
   B It's _____.
   a a umbrella
   b an umbrella
   c umbrella
10 Look at those _____.
   a womans   b women   c womens
11 A What are _____ in English?
   B They're keys.
   a that   b this   c these
12 These are very _____.
   a difficult exercises
   b exercises difficult
   c difficults exercises
13 _____ careful! That dog's dangerous.
   a Are   b Be you   c Be
14 Please _____ in the library.
   a not eat   b don't eat   c no eat
15 I'm hungry. _____ stop at the café.
   a Let's   b We   c Don't

VOCABULARY

a Complete with *at*, *from*, *in*, *off*, or *to*.

1 I'm _____ Japan.
2 Nice _____ meet you.
3 What's *bonjour* _____ English?
4 Look _____ the board.
5 Please turn _____ your mobile phone.

b Complete the phrases with these verbs.

Answer Stand Open Read Work

1 _____ the text.   4 _____ the door.
2 _____ in pairs.   5 _____ the questions.
3 _____ up.

c Circle the word that is different.

	one	three	book	five
1	eight	two	seven	file
2	Brazil	Chinese	Hungary	Switzerland
3	Polish	Italian	Japanese	France
4	Africa	Asia	Ireland	Europe
5	sixteen	forty	ninety	eighty
6	Wednesday	Italy	Friday	Monday
7	glasses	purse	headphones	scissors
8	door	window	wall	school
9	wallet	newspaper	book	magazine
10	happy	tired	angry	stressed

d Write the opposite adjective.

1 good   _____   4 tall   _____
2 expensive _____   5 empty   _____
3 dirty   _____

PRONUNCIATION

a Circle the word with a different sound.

	A	B	C	D
1 /iː/	A	B	C	D
2 /aɪ/	Hi	day	my	nice
3 /ɪz/	watches	boxes	files	glasses
4 /dʒ/	Japan	German	good	page
5 /æ/	dangerous	stamps	bad	laptop

b Underline the stressed syllable.

1 a|ddress   2 I|ta|ly   3 ex|pen|sive   4 news|pa|per   5 thir|teen

CAN YOU UNDERSTAND THIS TEXT?

a Read the article once. Do you know any more words which are American English, not British English?

British & American English –
the same, but different

British and American people speak the same language – English, but with some small differences.

VOCABULARY
Some words are different in American English, for example Americans say *zip code*, not *postcode*, *vacation*, not *holiday*, and *cell phone*, not *mobile phone*. Some words have different meanings, for example in British English a *purse* is a thing where women have their money and credit cards. In American English a *purse* is a woman's bag.

SPELLING
Colour, *favour*, and other words that end in *-our* in British English end with *-or* in American English, e.g. *color*, *favor*. *Centre*, *theatre*, and other words that end in *-tre* in British English end with *-ter* in American English, e.g. *center*, *theater*.

GRAMMAR
American grammar is very similar to British grammar, but with some small differences, especially prepositions. For example, Americans say *See you Friday*, but British people say *See you on Friday*.

PRONUNCIATION
The most important difference between American and British English is pronunciation. American accents and British accents are quite different, and when an American starts speaking British people know he or she is American, and vice versa.

b Look at the highlighted words in the text and guess their meaning.

c Read the article again. Mark the sentences **T** (true) or **F** (false).
1 American English and British English are very different.
2 *Holiday* and *postcode* are the same in British and American English.
3 *Purse* has different meanings in American and British English.
4 *Kilometer* is British spelling.
5 British and American grammar are not very different.
6 It's difficult to know from their accent if a person is English or American.

CAN YOU UNDERSTAND THESE PEOPLE?

1 74)) In the street Watch or listen to five people and answer the questions.

1 2 3 4 5

1 Her name is _____.
   a Cecilia   b Cecil   c Cecile
2 Andy's from Newcastle in the _____ of England.
   a North East   b North West   c South East
3 David is _____.
   a Italian   b French   c Spanish
4 Her name is _____.
   a Arya   b Aria   c Arja
5 Karin is _____.
   a Swiss   b Brazilian   c Hungarian

CAN YOU SAY THIS IN ENGLISH?

Do the tasks with a partner. Tick (✓) the box if you can do them.

Can you…?
1 ☐ count from 0–20
2 ☐ count from 20–100 (20, 30, etc.)
3 ☐ say the days of the week
4 ☐ give three instructions: two ➕ and one ➖
5 ☐ introduce yourself and another person
6 ☐ answer the questions below
   • What's your first name / surname?
   • How do you spell it?
   • Where are you from?

Short films Hollywood, Los Angeles
Watch and enjoy a film on iTutor.

G present simple + and −
V verb phrases
P third person -s

They live in a flat.
He doesn't smoke.

3A Things I love about Britain

1 VOCABULARY verb phrases

a Complete the phrases with a verb from the list.

go   read   work   have   listen

1 _____ a newspaper
2 _____ to the radio
3 _____ children
4 _____ to the cinema
5 _____ in an office

b ▶ p.153 Vocabulary Bank *Verb phrases*.

c 2 3))) Listen. Say the phrase.   )))TV   watch TV

2 GRAMMAR present simple + and −

a Look at four things people say about Britain and the British. Do you think they are true or not true? Then read the text and check your answers.

THE BRITISH – IS IT TRUE?

- British people drink tea at 5.00.
- It rains a lot.
- British people like animals.
- The food in Britain isn't very good.

Four foreigners who live in Britain talk about the things people say about the British…

British people drink tea at 5.00. Kati from Hungary
It's true that British people drink a lot of tea (and coffee) but they don't drink tea at a special time. I work for a British company here and my boss drinks tea all the time.

It rains a lot. Nicolai from Russia
It rains a lot, but it doesn't rain every day. Be careful because the weather changes quickly. I always take an umbrella when I go out.

British people like animals. Norma from Mexico
I have a lot of friends here and they all have a dog or a cat. One family that I know has two dogs and five cats. British people love animals!

The food in Britain isn't very good. Hasan from Turkey
The restaurants are quite expensive but they are great, and the food is good in a lot of pubs, too. I share a flat with a Scottish boy, and he cooks every night. He watches all the cooking programmes on TV and he makes great curries!

b Answer the questions with a partner.
1 Look at the highlighted verbs. Why do some verbs end in *-s*?
2 Write the *he / she / it* form of these verbs.

change _____   have _____
cook _____   go _____
make _____   watch _____

3 Find two negative − verbs. How are they different from positive + verbs a) for *he / she / it* b) for all other persons?

c ▶ p.128 Grammar Bank 3A. Learn more about present simple + and −, and practise it.

3 PRONUNCIATION third person -s

a How do you pronounce these plural nouns?

books   keys   watches

b 2 5))) Listen and repeat the third person verb forms.

/s/   She speaks Spanish.
      He drinks coffee.
      She cooks every day.
/z/   It rains a lot.
      He has a cat.
      She does exercise.
      He goes to the cinema on Friday night.
/ɪz/ He watches TV.
      The film finishes in a minute.
      The weather changes a lot.

c 2 6))) Listen. Change the sentence.

))) I live in a flat. She.   She lives in a flat.

d Tell your partner six true things about you: three + and three −. Choose verb phrases from p.153 Vocabulary Bank *Verb phrases*.

I play the guitar. I don't wear glasses.

e Change partners. Tell your new partner the six things about your old partner.

Eva plays the guitar. She doesn't wear glasses.

Starbucks, summer, and other things I ♥ love about Britain

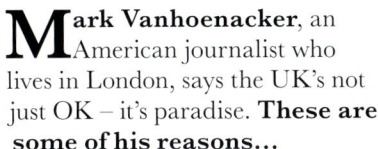

Mark Vanhoenacker, an American journalist who lives in London, says the UK's not just OK – it's paradise. **These are some of his reasons…**

Walking
Britain isn't a good place for cyclists. But for pedestrians it is wonderful. When you walk on a zebra crossing, all the drivers stop.

Banks
British banks are great – you do everything online, and you don't pay when you take money out of an ATM. And if you want to change banks, the banks do all the work, not you.

Drivers
The British are very polite when they drive. They don't hoot, and they are patient with other drivers. They always say thank you when you let them pass.

Boots the Chemist
Chemists in the UK are wonderful, friendly shops and completely different from US pharmacies. Boots sells everything you want, not just medicine, and the shop assistants give you good advice.

No ID Cards
Britain is one of the only places in the world where people don't have ID cards. In the US you need ID when you buy a drink, go to a club, use a credit card, or take an intercity train.

Summers
I love British summers! A good summer day in Britain is dry and warm, but not very hot.

Starbucks
Starbucks isn't British, of course, but I prefer the Starbucks in Britain. They are nice, friendly places where people read the newspaper and drink good coffee. And the waiters don't write your name on the cups – I feel stupid in America when the waiter calls 'Mark, your tall cappuccino with extra chocolate!'

Adapted from an article in The Times

4 READING & SPEAKING

a Look at the photos. In which one can you see…?
- [ ] a cash machine (ATM in American English)
- [ ] a cup of coffee
- [ ] a chemist /ˈkemɪst/
- [ ] a waiter
- [ ] a zebra crossing
- [ ] a cyclist /ˈsaɪklɪst/
- [ ] a pedestrian
- [ ] a driver

b 2 7)) Read and listen to the article. Mark the sentences **T** (true) or **F** (false). Say why the **F** ones are false.

1. Britain is a good country for cyclists and pedestrians.
2. It's expensive to use ATMs in Britain.
3. British drivers are nice to other drivers.
4. Boots the Chemist only has medicine.
5. In Britain people don't have ID cards.
6. Summers in Britain are very hot.
7. In Starbucks in Britain waiters don't use your first name.

c Underline these verbs in the text. What do they mean? Compare your ideas with a partner.

walk	pay	drive	sell	give	need
buy	use	prefer	feel	call	

d Look at each paragraph again. Say if it's the same or different in your country or city.

> Naples isn't a good place for cyclists or pedestrians, because people drive very fast!

> 🔍 **Useful words: Why? and because**
> Use *because* to answer the question *Why?*
> *Why* isn't Naples a good place for cyclists?
> *Because* people drive very fast.

G present simple ?
V jobs
P /ɜː/

3B Work and play

What do you do?
I'm a nurse.

1 VOCABULARY jobs

a Order the letters to make words for jobs.
1 ACTEHRE   T_____
2 ROCAT   A_____
3 TRIEWA   W_____
4 AXTI RREDIV T_____D_____
5 PTIREONICEST R_____

b ▶ p.154 Vocabulary Bank *Jobs*.

c What do you do? Ask five other students in the class.

2 LISTENING

a ⏵ 2 10, 11))) Listen to a game show called *His job, her job*. A team of three people ask Wayne questions about his job and his wife Tanya's job. Write **W** next to the questions they ask Wayne about his job, and **T** next to the questions they ask about Tanya's job.

b Listen again. What are Wayne's answers? Write ✓ (yes), ✗ (no), or **D** (it depends) after each question.

c Look at the answers. What do you think his job is? What do you think her job is?

d ⏵ 2 12))) Listen to the end of the programme. What do Wayne and his wife do?

3 GRAMMAR present simple ?

a ⏵ 2 13))) Complete the questions. Listen and check. Why are questions 3 and 4 different?

1 _____ you work with other people?
  Yes, I _____.
2 _____ you work in an office?
  No, I _____.
3 _____ she work with computers?
  No, she _____.
4 _____ she work at the weekend?
  Yes, she _____.

b ▶ p.128 Grammar Bank 3B. Learn more about present simple ? and practise it.

c In groups of four, play *His job, her job*. Choose jobs from p.154 Vocabulary Bank *Jobs*. Ask questions to guess the jobs.

His job, her job

Where?	work	outside ☐
		in the street ☐
		inside ☐
		in an office ☐
When?	work	in the evening ☐
		at night ☐
		at the weekend ☐
How?	work	with computers ☐
		with other people ☐
		long hours ☐

have special qualifications ☐
speak foreign languages ☐
travel ☐
drive ☐
make things ☐
wear a uniform or special clothes ☐
earn a lot of money ☐

4 PRONUNCIATION /ɜː/

a ♪2 15))) Listen and repeat the words and sounds.

 | bird | nurse | thirty | her | work | journalist

> /ɜː/
> *ur, ir,* and *er* usually = /ɜː/ when they are stressed.
> *or* after *w* usually = /ɜː/ e.g. *work*.

b ♪2 16))) Listen. Which word *doesn't* have the /ɜː/ sound?
1 thirsty   dirty   thirteen   tired
2 earn   here   prefer   service
3 Thursday   sure   turn   Turkey
4 worry   word   worker   world

c Practise saying the sentences.
I prefer Turkish coffee.
Journalists work all over the world.
Shirley is thirty on Thursday.

5 SPEAKING

a Complete the phrases with a verb from the list.

do (x3)   eat   go   listen   read   use   ~~walk~~   watch

In the week
walk to work / school
_____ a computer at work / school
_____ in English
_____ in a café or restaurant
_____ housework

At the weekend
_____ TV in the morning
_____ to music
_____ sport or exercise
_____ homework
_____ to the cinema

b Work in pairs. Ask and answer questions, then change roles.
A Ask **B** the questions.
B Answer the questions. Give more information if you can.
A *Do you walk to school?*
B *No, I don't. I go by bus.*

c Change pairs. Ask your new partner about his / her old partner.
C *Does Akito walk to school?*
A *No, he doesn't. He goes by bus.*

6 READING

a Read the article. Match each text to a photo. What do the three people do?

UNIFORMS – FOR OR AGAINST?

☐ JON

☐ MARIE

☐ SARAH

Three people say what they think…

1 Our uniform is OK. I like the colours, grey and red. The only things I don't like are the **tie**, because it's difficult to put on, and the **skirt**, because I prefer trousers. I think uniforms are a good idea. Everybody looks the same, and it's easy to **get dressed** in the morning – I don't need to think about what to wear.

2 Our uniform is dark **trousers** and a white **nylon top**, a bit like a nurse's uniform. We can't wear anything over the uniform, so it's quite cold in the winter, and it gets dirty very easily because it's white. I'm not against uniforms, but my uniform just isn't practical!

3 Our uniform is very simple – a dark blue **jacket** and trousers and a white **shirt and tie**. I like it, it's nice and **comfortable**, so I'm happy to wear it. And I think it's important that people can see where we are when they need help.

b With a partner, say what the **highlighted** words mean. Check with your teacher or a dictionary.

c Read the article again. Who…?
1 thinks uniforms are a good idea, but doesn't like his / her uniform?
2 likes his / her uniform, but doesn't say anything about uniforms in general?
3 thinks uniforms are a good idea and quite likes his / her uniform?

d Do you wear a uniform at work / school? Do you like it? Why (not)? Do you think uniforms are a good idea?

G word order in questions
V question words
P sentence stress

What kind of films do you like?
I like French films.

3C Love online

1 LISTENING

a Kevin and Samantha want to meet a partner on the internet. Read their profiles and look at their photos. Then cover them and say what you can remember. Do you think they are a good match?

> Kevin is 28. He lives in South London…

Search
I am a: Man
Looking for: Women
Age: 25
to: 35
In: London
[Search]

Log in
Log in to edit your details and access messages.
[Log-in]

Kevin
Age: 28
Lives in: South London
Likes: films, music
Doesn't like: football

Samantha
Age: 26
Lives in: South London
Likes: the cinema, good food
Doesn't like: sport

d 2 18))) Look at the highlighted phrases in the conversation. Listen and repeat them. Practise the conversation with a partner.

> **Showing interest**
> When you have a conversation, react to what your partner says. Use *Me too. Really? How interesting! What about you?* etc.

e 2 19))) Listen to the second part of the conversation. Do you think they want to meet again?

f Listen again and mark the sentences **T** (true) or **F** (false). Say why the **F** ones are false.
1 Samantha likes science fiction films.
2 They like the same kind of music.
3 Their weekends are very different.
4 Samantha pays for their lunch.

g Do you think the internet is a good place to make friends or meet a partner? Why (not)?

b 2 17))) Kevin and Samantha meet in a restaurant for lunch. Cover the conversation and listen. What does Kevin say about…?
1 where he lives   2 his job   3 films he likes

c Listen again. Complete the missing verbs.

S Hi. Are you Kevin?
K Yes. Are you Samantha?
S Yes I am, but call me Sam. Nice to _____ you. Sorry I'm late.
K No problem. You look different from your photo.
S Let's _____ a drink. A beer? Wine?
K No, thanks. Water for me. I don't _____ alcohol at lunchtime.

K I _____ this place.
S Me too. Where do you _____ in South London?
K In Bromley. Near the market. I _____ with my mother.
S Really? What do you _____?
K I'm a teacher. I teach chemistry.
S Chemistry? How interesting.
K Yes, it's a very interesting job. What about you?
S I'm a journalist. You _____ the cinema, Kevin. What kind of films do you _____?
K Science-fiction films. I _____ *Star Wars*.
S Oh.
K Do you _____ *Star Wars*?

2 GRAMMAR word order in questions

a Cover the conversation. Put the words in order to make the questions.

1 want you do drink a
_____ ?

2 in South live London you do where
_____ ?

3 films like kind you of what do
_____ ?

b ▶ **p.128 Grammar Bank 3C.** Learn more about word order in questions and practise it.

3 VOCABULARY & PRONUNCIATION
question words; sentence stress

a (2 21)) Listen and repeat the question words and phrases. How is *Wh-* pronounced in *Who*? How is it pronounced in the other question words?

| How? How many? ~~What?~~ What kind? |
| When? Where? Which? Who? Why? |

b Complete the questions with a question word or phrase from the list in **a**.

1 *What* phone do you have?
I have an iPhone.
2 _____ old are you?
22.
3 _____ brothers and sisters do you have?
I have two sisters.
4 _____ do you prefer, Saturdays or Sundays?
Saturdays.
5 _____ do you have English classes?
On Mondays and Wednesdays.
6 _____ of films do you like?
I like old British films.
7 _____ do you live?
In the city centre.
8 _____'s your favourite actor?
Colin Firth.
9 _____ do you like him?
Because he's very good-looking!

c (2 22)) Listen and check.

d Listen again and repeat the questions. Copy the rhythm.

⌒ **What phone** do you **have**?

e Work in pairs. **A** ask **B** the questions. **B** give your own answers. Then change roles.

4 SPEAKING

a Imagine you meet a new friend online, and you go out for coffee together. Look at the prompts and write eight questions.

Where do you work?
Who is your favourite singer?

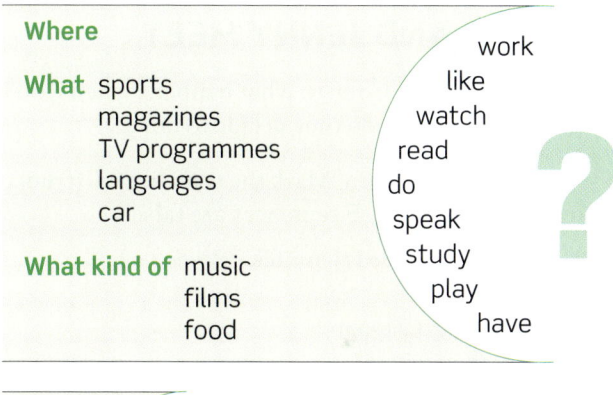

Where		work
What	sports	like
	magazines	watch
	TV programmes	read
	languages	do
	car	speak
What kind of	music	study
	films	play
	food	have

| Who / What | your favourite | TV programme / restaurant / singer / actor |

b Work in pairs with a student you don't know very well.

A Ask **B** your first question.
B Answer the question. Give more information if you can.
A React to **B**'s answer.
B Ask **A** your first question.

A *What kind of music do you like?*
B *I like classical music, especially Mozart.*
A *Really? Me too.*

5 WRITING

▶ **p.111 Writing** *A personal profile.* Write a profile of yourself.

6 (2 23)) SONG *Somethin' Stupid* ♪

Practical English Coffee to take away

1 TELLING THE TIME

a Look at the clock. What time is it?

▶ p. 157 **Vocabulary Bank** *Time.* Do Part 1.

b **Communication** *What's the time?* **A** p.101 **B** p.107.

2 ◼ ROB AND JENNY MEET

a (2 25)) Watch or listen to what happens when Rob and Jenny meet. What do they decide to do?

b Watch or listen again. Mark the sentences **T** (true) or **F** (false). Say why the **F** sentences are false.
  1 Jenny's full name is Jennifer.
  2 Rob is early.
  3 Jenny likes the hotel.
  4 She doesn't like the hotel coffee.
  5 She has a meeting with Daniel at 9.15.
  6 The office isn't very far from the hotel.

3 ◼ BUYING A COFFEE

a Look at the coffee shop menu. Do you know what all the things are?

menu
drinks and cakes

Espresso	single **2.45**	double **2.80**
Americano	regular **3.15**	large **3.95**
Latte	regular **3.45**	large **3.65**
Cappuccino	regular **3.45**	large **3.65**
Tea	regular **2.65**	large **3.10**
Brownie	3.00	
Croissant	3.00	

EPISODE 2

b ⏵2.26 Watch or listen to Rob and Jenny buying coffee. Answer the questions.
1. What kind of coffee do Rob and Jenny have?
2. What do they have to eat?
3. How much is it?

c Watch or listen again. Complete the **You Hear** phrases.

))) You Hear	You Say 💬
Can I _____ you?	What would you like, Jenny? An espresso, please.
_____ or double?	Double. Can I have a latte, please?
_____ or large?	Large.
To have _____ or take away?	To take away.
Anything else?	No, thanks. A brownie for me, please... and a croissant.
OK.	How much is that?
That's £12.45, please.	Sorry, how much?
£12.45. Thank you. And your _____.	Thanks.

> 🔍 **Cultural note**
> barista = a person who works in a coffee shop

d ⏵2.27 Watch or listen and repeat the **You Say** phrases. Copy the rhythm.

e In threes, practise the dialogue.

f 👥 Roleplay the dialogue in groups of three. Then swap roles.
- **A** (book open) You are the barista.
- **B** (book closed) You invite **C** (book closed) to have a drink.
- **A** begins: *Can I help you?*
- **B** asks **C**: *What would you like?*

4 🎬 FIRST DAY IN THE OFFICE

a ⏵2.28 Watch or listen and answer the questions.
1. What's Karen's job?
2. Where in Europe does Jenny have family?
3. Where does she live in New York?
4. Does Karen have family in New York?
5. What does Daniel offer Jenny to drink?
6. What time is his next meeting?

b Look at the **Social English phrases**. Who says them: **R**ob, **K**aren, or **D**aniel?

> **Social English phrases**
> Here we are.
> Is this your first time in [the UK]?
> Would you like something to drink?
> Talk to you later.

c ⏵2.29 Watch or listen and check. Do you know what they are in your language?

d Watch or listen again and repeat the phrases.

> 👤 **Can you...?**
> ☐ tell the time
> ☐ order food and drink in a café
> ☐ meet and introduce people

G Whose...?, possessive 's
V family
P /ʌ/, the letter o

4A Is she his wife or his sister?

Who's that?
He's my nephew – my sister's son.

1 GRAMMAR Whose...?, possessive 's

a How interested are people in your country in the private lives of celebrities? What kind of celebrities? Number the people 1–3 (**3** = very interested, **2** = quite interested, **1** = not very interested).

☐ actors   ☐ royalty
☐ musicians   ☐ TV stars / presenters
☐ sports players   ☐ politicians
☐ others (say what)

b Look at the celebrities in the photos. In pairs, answer the questions for each celebrity.
 1 What does he / she do? Where is he / she from?
 2 Do you know anything about his / her family or private life?
 3 Are you interested in these people? Why (not)?

c With a partner, guess who the other person in each photo is. Choose **a** or **b** in sentences 1–5.

d 🔊 2 30 Listen and check. What does *'s* mean in sentences 1–5?

e ▶ p.130 **Grammar Bank 4A.** Learn more about *Whose...?* and possessive *'s* and practise them.

f Look at some things from the photos. Whose are they?

Whose is the wristband? — *It's George Clooney's.*

1 wristband /ˈrɪstbænd/
2 bow tie /bəʊ ˈtaɪ/
3 T-shirt /ˈtiːʃɜːt/
4 sunglasses
5 tie

2 VOCABULARY family

a ▶ p.155 **Vocabulary Bank** *The family.*

b In pairs, answer the questions.
 Who's...?
 1 your mother's mother   *My grandmother*
 2 your father's brother   _____
 3 your brother's / sister's daughter _____
 4 your aunt's children   _____
 5 your husband's / wife's brother _____
 6 your niece's brother   _____

Who are they with?

You know the celebrity – but who is the other person?

1 She's Justin Bieber's
  a sister   b mother
2 He's Carla Bruni's
  a ex-boyfriend   b ex-husband
3 She's Lionel Messi's
  a wife   b sister
4 She's Jack Nicholson's
  a daughter   b girlfriend
5 He's George Clooney's
  a brother   b father

Justin Bieber

Carla Bruni

Lionel Messi

Jack Nicholson

George Clooney

3 PRONUNCIATION /ʌ/, the letter o

a **2 33**))) Listen and repeat the words and sound.

| /ʌ/ up | mother | brother | son | husband | uncle | cousin |

b ▶ **p.166 Sound Bank.** Look at the different spellings for this sound.

c How is the letter *o* pronounced in these words? Put them in the right column.

| come   do   don't   doctor   go   home   job   London |
| model   money   no   one   Scotland   strong   who |

up	phone	clock	boot
come	don't	doctor	do

d **2 34**))) Listen and check. Practise saying the words.

e Practise the dialogues with a partner.

A Who's that?
B My mother.
A She's very young!
B No, she's sixty-one. She's a doctor.

A Who are they?
B That's my brother and his son.
A Do they live in Scotland?
B No, they don't. They live in London.

4 LISTENING & SPEAKING

a **2 35**))) Listen to Isabel showing a friend photos on her phone. Who are the people in the photos in relation to Isabel?

b Listen again. Write down more information about the people in the photos, e.g. their names, ages, jobs, etc.

c Work with a partner.

A Show B some photos of family or friends on your phone or write their names on a piece of paper.
B Ask three questions about each person.

Who's that?   She's my sister Yolanda.

How old is she?

G prepositions of time (*at, in, on*) and place (*at, in, to*)
V everyday activities
P linking and sentence stress

4B What a life!

> What do you do in the evening?
> I have dinner and watch TV.

1 VOCABULARY
everyday activities

a ⏵ 2 36 Listen to the sounds and number the phrases 1–6.

- [ ] get dressed
- [1] get up
- [ ] have breakfast
- [ ] have a shower
- [ ] go to work / school
- [ ] have a coffee

b What order do *you* do these things in the morning? Tell your partner.

> First I get up, then I...

c ▶ p.156 **Vocabulary Bank** *Everyday activities.*

2 PRONUNCIATION
linking and sentence stress

> 🔍 **Connected speech**
> Remember, when people speak they usually link words together. Sometimes three linked words sound like one word, e.g. *I get up at seven*.

a ⏵ 2 38 Listen and write five sentences.
1. _____.
2. _____.
3. _____.
4. _____.
5. _____.

b ⏵ 2 39 Listen and repeat the sentences. Copy the rhythm.

> I get up at seven.
> I have a shower.
> I go to work.
> I have a sandwich for lunch.
> I get home at six.
> I make the dinner.
> I go to bed at ten.
> What a life!

3 READING & LISTENING

a Read the article. How do you think Nico feels at the end of a typical day? Why? Choose from the adjectives in the list.

> bored   happy   stressed   sad   tired   worried   relaxed

b Read the article again. Guess the meaning of the highlighted words and phrases. Then underline words and phrases connected with restaurants, e.g. *chef*.

c ▶ **Communication** *Nico's day* **A** p.101 **B** p.107.
A Ask **B** questions.
B Find the answers in the text. Then change roles.

> What time does Nico get up? He gets up at...

FATHER & DAUGHTER
– whose day is more **stressful**?

Nico is a chef and has his own restaurant, the Blue Jar. He lives in Chile with his wife and her three children, aged 16, 12, and 9.

0630 I get up and make breakfast for the children. Then I have breakfast – a coffee and cereal – and I read the sports section of the paper.
0715 I go to the market to buy fruit and vegetables for the restaurant.
0845 When I get to the restaurant I check the reservations and my emails, and plan the special menu of the day. I have my second cup of coffee.
1030 I start cooking. The radio is on, and we are busy with breakfast orders, but we also have to prepare the food for lunch.
1200 I check the tables, and have my third coffee.
1330 Suddenly everyone arrives at the same time and the restaurant is full (on a good day). I start to shout instructions at the chefs and waiters. We make lunch for 85 people in about an hour and a half.
1445 I come into the restaurant and talk to the customers, and ask if they are happy with the food. I'm really hungry now.
1530 Finally I have lunch. I don't enjoy it very much because I don't have time to relax.

d 🔊2 40 Listen to Amelia, Nico's 16-year-old stepdaughter, talking about her day. Complete the gaps with a word, a number, or a time.

Morning
6.30 — She gets up.
_____ She starts school.
She has _____ or _____ lessons.

Afternoon
_____ She has lunch. She only has _____ minutes for lunch.
She has _____ or _____ lessons.
_____ She finishes school.
On Mondays and _____ she has extra classes to prepare for the university entrance exam.
On Tuesdays and _____ she has _____ practice.

Evening
She does _____ and studies until dinner.
After dinner she studies until _____.
_____ She goes to bed.

e Look back at the text and the information in **d**. Whose day do you think is more stressful, Nico's or Amelia's? Why?

1600 After lunch I go back to the kitchen and plan the food for the evening menu.
1730 I go home to be with the family for a couple of hours. The children do their homework and I make their dinner.
1930 I go back to the restaurant, which is full again, and I check everything is OK.
2200 I go home and have a shower. Then I collapse on the sofa with a sandwich and a glass of wine.
2300 I go to bed, ready to start again the next day.

4 GRAMMAR prepositions of time (at, in, on) and place (at, in, to)

a Look at some sentences from Amelia's day. Complete them with *in, on, at,* or *to*.
 1 I get up ___ half past six.
 2 ___ the morning we usually have five lessons, sometimes six.
 3 We have lunch ___ school in the cafeteria.
 4 ___ Mondays and Wednesdays I go ___ extra classes.

b 🔊2 41 Listen and check.

c ▶ p.130 **Grammar Bank 4B.** Learn more about prepositions and practise them.

d 🔊2 44 Listen and say the time phrases with the right preposition.

🔊 the weekend ⟶ at the weekend

5 SPEAKING & WRITING

a Work in pairs. Interview your partner about a typical weekday with the questions.

- What time / get up?
- / have breakfast in the morning? What / have?
- How / go to work or school?
- What time / start work or school?
- / have a long lunch break? How long?
- What time / finish work or school?
- What / do after work or school?
- / relax in the evening? What / do?
- When / do English homework?
- What time / go to bed?
- How / feel at the end of the day?

> 🔍 **When you can't be exact**
> What time do you get up? At **about** 7.15.
> What do you have for breakfast? **It depends.**
> If I have time, I have toast or cereal.

b Who do you think has a more stressful day, you or your partner? Why?

c ▶ p.112 **Writing** *A magazine article.* Write about your favourite day.

G position of adverbs and expressions of frequency
V adverbs and expressions of frequency
P the letter *h*

How often do you eat fruit?

Every day.

4C Short life, long life?

1 VOCABULARY
adverbs and expressions of frequency

a **2 45))** Complete the gaps with a 'time' word. Listen and check.

1. sixty seconds = a *minute*
2. thirty minutes = half an _____
3. sixty minutes = an _____
4. twenty-four hours = a _____
5. seven days = a _____
6. four weeks = a _____
7. twelve months = a _____

b ▶ p.157 Vocabulary Bank *Time*. Do parts 2 and 3.

2 GRAMMAR position of adverbs and expressions of frequency

a Read the text about British teenagers. Is it the same in your country?

Today's teenagers may not live as long as their parents

Doctors are worried that today's teenagers have a very unhealthy lifestyle, and may not live as long as their parents' generation. Research shows:

- 30% of teenagers never have breakfast.
- They eat fast food at least two or three times a week and 75% hardly ever eat fruit or green vegetables.
- They don't usually sleep 8 hours a day. (30% sleep only 4–7 hours.) They are often tired in the morning.
- They spend about 31 hours online every week. A lot of teenagers never do sport or exercise.

b Look at the position of the highlighted words and expressions. Circle the correct rule.

1. Adverbs of frequency (e.g. *usually*) go…
   before / after a main verb.
   before / after the verb *be*.
2. Expressions of frequency (e.g. *every week*) go…
   at the beginning / at the end of a phrase or sentence.

c ▶ p.130 Grammar Bank 4C. Learn more about adverbs and expressions of frequency and practise them.

d Make true sentences about you with the verb phrases below and an adverb or expression of frequency. Compare with a partner.

be late for work / school	watch the news on TV
go to the hairdresser	check your email
be tired in the morning	go to the cinema
do housework	chat online

I'm often late for work.
I check my emails five times a day.

3 PRONUNCIATION the letter *h*

a **2 50))** Listen and repeat the words and sound.

| house | how | hardly | healthy | high |
| | have | hungry | happy | |

b **2 51))** Listen. Circle the word where *h* is not pronounced.

Harry's a hairdresser.
He hardly ever has breakfast.
He only has half an hour for lunch.
He often has a hamburger for dinner.
Harry isn't very healthy.

c Practise saying the sentences.

d ▶ p.166 Sound Bank. Look at the typical spellings for this sound.

32

4 READING & SPEAKING

a Work in pairs. Tick (✓) five things which you think help people to live to be a hundred. Then read the article to check.

- [ ] They have a big family.
- [ ] They aren't in a hurry.
- [ ] They sleep eight hours.
- [ ] They have pets.
- [ ] They hardly ever eat meat.
- [ ] They drink a little alcohol.
- [ ] They often go to the doctor.
- [ ] They work outside.
- [ ] They often see friends.

b Read the article again. In which places are these things important?

1 a special kind of water   _____
2 a special kind of food   _____
3 the weather   _____
4 a special kind of drink   _____ ,
                              _____

c <u>Underline</u> new words or phrases in the texts and compare with a partner. Try to guess their meaning. Choose two words to learn from each text.

d Look at the five things in **a** that are in the texts. Are they true for people in your country? Do you think they have a healthy lifestyle?

e ▶ **Communication** *Short life, long life?* p.101 Interview your partner with the questionnaire, then change roles.

5 ② 52)) SONG *Who Wants to Live Forever* 🎵

The secrets of a long life

In three areas of the world a very high number of people live to be 100. Scientists want to know why. What do the three places have in common?

Ecuador

Vilcabamba, a small village in the Andes, is often called 'the Valley of Long Life'. What's its secret? Firstly, Vilcabamba is not very hot or very cold – the temperature is usually between 18 and 27 degrees, and the air is very clean. Secondly, people work hard in the fields, and do a lot of exercise. Thirdly, their diet is very healthy – they eat a lot of fruit and vegetables, and they hardly ever eat meat or fish. The water they drink, from the river in Vilcabamba, is very rich in minerals. They also have a good social life. In Vilcabamba people say, 'The left leg and the right leg help you to be healthy, because they take you to your friends' homes.'

Italy

In Ogliastra, a mountain region of Sardinia, one out of every 200 people lives to be 100, and they are normally very healthy, too. Most of the people in the villages work outside in their fields and with their animals. They have a healthy diet, with a lot of vegetables and not much meat or fish. They hardly ever take any medicine, but they usually drink a little *grappa* before they go to bed. 'Life is hard,' says Fortunato, who is a shepherd, 'but I am never stressed. I never read the newspaper – because I can't read very well.'

Japan

People in Okinawa in Japan do not have big meals. They usually just have vegetables and fish, and often eat soya. Okinawans are very active, and they often work until they are 80 or more. But they also relax every day – they see friends and they meditate. Ushi, from Okinawa, is 107. In the evening she often dances with her daughter and has a glass of *sake*. 'I want to have a boyfriend,' she says. When journalists ask people from Okinawa 'What is your secret?' they answer, 'We are happy, we are always positive, and we are never in a hurry.'

Adapted from a British newspaper

grappa an Italian alcoholic drink
sake a Japanese alcoholic drink
soya a kind of bean typical in Asia

3&4 Revise and Check

GRAMMAR

Circle a, b, or c.

1. I _____ live near here.
   a not   b don't   c doesn't
2. My sister _____ three children.
   a has   b have   c haves
3. _____ English?
   a Are they speak
   b Speak they
   c Do they speak
4. _____ your sister work?
   a Does   b Is   c Do
5. **A** Do you work here?
   B Yes, I _____.
   a work   b do   c am
6. **A** What _____?
   B He's an engineer.
   a he does   b does he   c does he do
7. What languages _____?
   a speak you
   b do you speak
   c you speak
8. Bill is _____.
   a Carla's husband
   b husband's Carla
   c the Carla's husband
9. This is my _____ house.
   a parent's   b parents'   c parent
10. _____ is this book?
    a Who's   b Who   c Whose
11. We usually have lunch _____ two o'clock.
    a in   b on   c at
12. What time do you go _____ bed?
    a in   b to   c at
13. She _____ late for class.
    a never is   b is never   c never does
14. I _____ early.
    a usually get up
    b get usually up
    c get up usually
15. I have an English class _____.
    a one a week
    b one the week
    c once a week

VOCABULARY

a Complete with *at*, *to*, *in*, *on*, or *up*.

1. _____ Saturday night I go to the cinema.
2. I'm a student. I'm _____ university and I live _____ a flat.
3. What time do you usually wake _____?
4. What time do you go _____ work?

b Complete the phrases with these verbs.

do   get   go   have   listen   play   read   take   watch   wear

1. _____ dressed   6. _____ the guitar
2. _____ the dog for a walk 7. _____ to music
3. _____ a shower   8. _____ TV
4. _____ your homework   9. _____ the newspaper
5. _____ shopping   10. _____ glasses

c Circle the word or phrase that is different.

1. brother   uncle   niece   grandfather
2. husband   mother-in-law stepsister   aunt
3. musician   doctor   journalist   factory
4. never   early   always   often
5. hour   minute   once   second

d Complete the questions with *How many*, *Who*, *Why*, *What*, or *Where*.

1. _____ do you live?
2. _____ does your father do?
3. _____ is your favourite family member?
4. _____ hours do you work?
5. _____ do you want to learn English?

PRONUNCIATION

a Circle the word with a different sound.

1. work   here   earn   turn
2. sometimes   cousin   nurse   uncle
3. often   home   coffee   doctor
4. father   that   brother   think
5. /ɪz/ lives watches   finishes relaxes

b Underline the stressed syllable.

1. be|cause   3. un|em|ployed   5. grand|mo|ther
2. den|tist   4. po|lice|man

CAN YOU UNDERSTAND THIS TEXT?

a Read the text and complete the gaps with these verbs in the correct form.

do   drink   drive   earn   eat   have (x2)
know   live   spend   think   travel   work

b Read the text again. Is a typical man from your country similar to the typical British man?

c Look at the highlighted words or phrases in the text and guess their meaning.

Is this the typical British man?

Statistics tell us that the typical British man is 40 years old, ¹_lives_ in a house and is married with two children. He ²_____ more than 40 hours a week and ³_____ about £25,000 a year. He ⁴_____ between fifty minutes and an hour to and from work every day. He ⁵_____ a Ford car and he ⁶_____ he is a good driver.

The typical British man is overweight (he weighs about 82.5 kg) and he ⁷_____ less than 30 minutes exercise a week. He usually sleeps about seven hours a night. He is not a great cook, but he ⁸_____ how to make four dishes, including Spaghetti Bolognese. He ⁹_____ three cups of tea a day and during his life he ¹⁰_____ approximately 35,000 biscuits.

The typical British man ¹¹_____ eight close friends and more than eighty contacts on his mobile phone. He ¹²_____ three TVs, a copy of Queen's *Greatest Hits*, and at least one of the Harry Potter books. He ¹³_____ thirteen hours online every week and forty-five hours a year waiting 'on hold' on the phone.

CAN YOU UNDERSTAND THESE PEOPLE?

2 53))) **In the street** Watch or listen to five people and answer the questions.

Nick   Anya   Alison   Wells   Stacey

1 Nick works between _____ hours a week.
   a 20 and 30   b 30 and 40   c 40 and 50
2 Anya's sister is _____.
   a 20   b 15   c 16
3 Alison usually gets up at about _____ at the weekend.
   a 10.00   b 7.00   c 7.30
4 Wells _____ does sport.
   a hardly ever   b sometimes   c often
5 Stacey _____.
   a has a cat   b has two cats   c doesn't like cats

CAN YOU SAY THIS IN ENGLISH?

Do the tasks with a partner. Tick (✓) the box if you can do them.

Can you…?

1 ☐ say where you live and what you do
2 ☐ say what time you usually get up and go to bed
3 ☐ say what you do on a typical Monday morning
4 ☐ ask your partner questions with the words below
   • What sports…?   • What languages…?
   • What kind of music…? • What TV programmes…?

Short films a British policeman
Watch and enjoy a film on iTutor.

G can / can't
V verb phrases: *buy a newspaper*, etc.
P sentence stress

5A Do you have the X Factor?

Can she dance?

Yes, but she can't sing.

1 VOCABULARY verb phrases

a Can you remember the verbs for things people do in their free time?

d_____ exercise   p_____ the guitar
l_____ to music   g_____ to the gym
w_____ TV   h_____ a coffee

b ▶ p.158 **Vocabulary Bank** *More verb phrases.*

2 GRAMMAR can / can't

a Read about Gary's audition for a British TV programme where people try to become professional singers. Complete it with phrases a–e.

a Can you come with me, please?
b I can't remember the words!
c you can have coffee downstairs.
d we can't hear you.
e ~~Where can I park?~~

b ⏵ 2 55))) Listen and check.

c ⏵ 2 56))) Now listen to Gary and two other people (Justin and Naomi) sing. Vote for the person you want to be in the show.

d ⏵ 2 57))) Listen to the judges. What do they say about each singer? How does Gary feel?

e Look at four sentences with *can / can't*. Match sentences 1–4 with a–d.

1 ☐ You can't sing!
2 ☐ You can't park here.
3 ☐ Can you come with me, please?
4 ☐ You can have coffee downstairs.

a It isn't OK.
b It's possible.
c Please do it.
d You don't know how.

f ▶ p.132 **Grammar Bank 5A.** Learn more about *can / can't* and practise it.

12.30 I arrive in Manchester and drive to the Conference Centre. The traffic is terrible. I'm late!

Guard Hey! You can't park here.
Gary ¹*Where can I park?*
Guard In the car park over there.
Gary OK. Where's the main entrance?
Guard The entrance? It's in the other street.
Gary Thanks!

12.45 I wait for my audition with 350 other singers. I'm very nervous.

6.00 Five hours later! Finally, a woman calls my number.

Organizer You can practise your songs here, and ²_____ Good luck!

Organizer ³_____ It's your turn now.

6.15 I walk onto the stage. I can see a table and three judges.

This is it. Oh no! ⁵_____

Judge What's your song?
Gary *House of the Rising Sun* by The Animals.
Judge Sorry, ⁴_____ Can you speak up?
Gary *House of the Rising Sun.*
Judge You can start when you're ready… Can you start, please?

3 PRONUNCIATION sentence stress

a ⏵ 2 59 Listen and repeat the dialogues. Copy the rhythm.

> A **Can** you **come** to**mor**row?
> B **Yes**. I can **come** in the **morn**ing.
>
> A **Can** you **play** a **mus**ical **ins**trument?
> B **Yes**, I **can**.
> A **What** can you **play**?
> B I can **play** the gui**tar**.
>
> A **Can** we **park here**?
> B **No**, you **can't**. You **can't park** here.

b ⏵ 2 60 Listen. Can you hear the difference?

1. a I can sing.
   b I can't sing.
2. a She can dance very well.
   b She can't dance very well.
3. a He can cook.
   b He can't cook.
4. a I can come to the meeting.
   b I can't come to the meeting.
5. a You can park here.
   b You can't park here.
6. a I can drive.
   b I can't drive.

c ⏵ 2 61 Listen. Circle **a** or **b**.

4 SPEAKING

a ▶ **Communication** *Do you want to be famous?* p.102. Are you musical, artistic, sporty, or good with words? Interview your partner and complete the survey.

b Change partners and tell your new partner what your first partner can and can't do.

5 READING

a *The X Factor* is a British TV programme. Look at the title of the article and the photos. With a partner, guess which two of the singers are 'winners' today. Then read the article and check.

b Look at the highlighted words and phrases related to pop music. With a partner, guess their meaning. Are the words similar in your language?

c Do you have similar programmes to *The X Factor* in your country? Can you remember the names of some of the winners? Where are they now?

6 ⏵ 2 62 SONG *Famous* ♫

X FACTOR winners
WHERE ARE THEY NOW?

'In the future everyone will be famous for fifteen minutes.' Andy Warhol

STEVE BROOKSTEIN
WINNER FIRST SERIES

And then? A recording contract with Sony and a number 1 with his first and only single. Later a job as a singer on a ferry boat between England and Spain.

Today? No recording contract. He gives concerts in pubs in Britain to small audiences.

LEONA LEWIS
WINNER THIRD SERIES

And then? Number 1 hits in the USA and UK and top ten records in many other countries. An appearance at the Olympic closing ceremony and three Grammy awards.

And today? She has a new album coming soon.

LEON JACKSON
WINNER FOURTH SERIES

And then? A recording contract with Sony and a number 1 single, *When you believe*.

And today? He gives concerts in small nightclubs and pubs in the UK. He now plays the guitar and piano, too, but he doesn't have a recording contract.

ALEXANDRA BURKE
WINNER FIFTH SERIES

And then? 1 million copies sold of her version of Leonard Cohen's *Hallelujah*. Three number 1 singles.

And today? She has a recording contract with Epic Records and she is also the face of *Sure Women*, a deodorant.

Adapted from a British newspaper

G present continuous
V verb phrases
P /ŋ/

What are they doing?
They're having a party.

5B Love your neighbours

1 VOCABULARY & SPEAKING
verb phrases

a ◯3 2))) Read the article about neighbours. Then listen to eight sounds, and write a–h in the boxes.

Noisy neighbours
the top problems!

Sometimes it is difficult to love your neighbours, especially when they make a lot of noise. These are some things people do that cause problems in the UK (not in order).

- [ ] Their babies cry.
- [ ] Their dogs bark.
- [ ] They talk loudly or argue a lot.
- [ ] They have noisy parties.
- [ ] Their children shout all the time.
- [ ] They have the TV on very loud.
- [ ] They play loud music.
- [ ] They play musical instruments.

b Which do you think are the top three in the UK? Which do you think are the top three in *your* country?

c Do the questionnaire with a partner.

Are your neighbours noisy?
Are you a noisy neighbour?

1 Do you live in a house or a flat?
2 Do you have neighbours…?
   a upstairs
   b downstairs
   c next door
3 Are your neighbours…?
   a very noisy
   b quite noisy
   c not very noisy
4 Which of the things in **a** do they do? Do they make any other noises?
5 Are you a noisy neighbour? Which of the things in **a** do you or your family do?

2 GRAMMAR present continuous

a **3 3))** Look at the picture of the flats. Why do you think the couple in flat 5 can't sleep? Listen and check.

b Listen again and complete the dialogues with verbs from the list.

arguing   crying   doing   getting   going
happening   having   saying   shouting (x2)

1
Man Are you awake?
Woman Yes. What's that noise?
M They're _____ a party downstairs.
W Again! What time is it?
M 12.00.

2
W Who's _____?
M People in the street. From the party.
W What's _____? Why are they _____?
M I can't hear.
W Are they _____?
M No, they aren't. They're _____ goodbye. Excuse me! We're trying to sleep. It's 1.00 in the morning!

3
M Oh no. Now the baby next door is _____!
W What's the time?
M It's 5.00.
W What are you _____? Where are you _____?
M I'm _____ up. I can't sleep with that noise.

c Complete the sentences.
   [+] They _____ having a party in number 8.
   [?] _____ they arguing?
   [−] No, they _____ arguing. They're saying goodbye.

d Read the rule and (circle) the right word.
   We use the present continuous (*be* + verb+ *-ing*) to talk about *now* / *every day*.

e ▶ **p.132 Grammar Bank 5B.** Learn more about the present continuous and practise it.

f **3 5))** Listen to the sounds. What's happening? Write six sentences.

3 PRONUNCIATION & SPEAKING /ŋ/

a **3 6))** Listen and repeat the words and sound.

ŋ singer	singing dancing going doing
	studying language wrong young
	think bank pink thanks

b In pairs, point and ask and answer about the people in the flats.

What's he doing?   He's playing the guitar. What are they doing?

c ▶ **Communication** *Spot the differences* **A** *p.102* **B** *p.107*. Describe the pictures and find eight differences.

4 LISTENING

a **3 7))** Look at the photo and read about Rebecca Flint. Then listen to her talking about noise rules where she lives. Does she think they are a good thing or a bad thing?

Switzerland
The sound of silence

Switzerland has very strict anti-noise rules, especially for people who live in flats. **Rebecca Flint**, a British woman who lives and works in the Swiss town of Chur, tells us about a life without noise.

b Listen again and complete the sentences.

During the week
1 She can't _____ between 12.30 and 2.00 p.m.
2 She can't _____ without headphones or _____ after 10 p.m.
3 She can't have a _____ or a _____ after 10 p.m.

On Saturdays
4 She can _____, but it can't be loud after 10 p.m.

On Sundays
5 She can't _____ furniture or put a _____ on the wall.
6 She can't _____ the washing machine.

c Do you think these are good or bad rules? Why (not)? Do you have any similar rules in your country? What happens if you make a lot of noise late at night?

G present simple or present continuous?
V the weather and seasons
P places in London

Look! It's raining!
It always rains here.

5C Sun and the City

1 VOCABULARY & LISTENING
the weather and seasons

a Look at the photo and answer the questions.
1. What city is it?
2. What monument can you see?
3. What's the weather like? Do you think it's typical weather there?

b ▶ p.159 **Vocabulary Bank** *The weather and dates.* Do part 1.

c 3 10))) Listen to a travel guide talking about the weather in London. Mark the sentences **T** (true) or **F** (false).
1. It's often very hot or very cold.
2. The normal temperature in the summer is 32°C.
3. It often snows in the winter.
4. In spring and autumn the weather changes a lot.
5. It's often grey and foggy in London.

d What's the weather like where you live in the different seasons?

2 READING & SPEAKING

a Read the guidebook extract about things to do in London, and find the answers to the 'Where can you…?' questions. Answer with **SH** (Somerset House), **SK** (South Kensington), or **HH** (Hampstead Heath).

b Read the text again. Underline three new words in each paragraph. Compare with a partner.

c Talk to a partner.
- Which of the three places would you prefer to go to? Why?
- Where is a good place to go in *your* town…?
  – when it's very cold
  – when it's raining
  – when the sun is shining
- What can you do in these places?

WHAT TO DO IN LONDON…

1 WHEN IT'S VERY COLD

Go ice skating at Somerset House. Somerset House is a beautiful 18th century building on the river Thames. In the winter, the area in front of the house is made into an ice-skating rink. There is a skating school, where you can have lessons, and there are also late-night sessions and DJ nights. In November and December there is an enormous Christmas tree, and the café serves special Christmas food.

2 WHEN IT'S RAINING

Go to South Kensington, and visit three wonderful museums. You can walk from one to the other because they are all very near. The Science Museum is very popular with adults and children, and also the Natural History Museum, which has life-size robotic dinosaurs and other fascinating exhibits. The third museum, the Victoria and Albert Museum, is full of art and design from all over the world. It has an amazing collection of fashion from the 17th century to the present day. And if the sun comes out, cross the road into Kensington Gardens, one of London's many parks, and visit the famous statue of Peter Pan.

3 WHEN THE SUN IS SHINING

Go to Hampstead Heath, London's biggest park. From the top of Parliament Hill, in the south part of the Heath, you can see many of London's famous monuments, including St Paul's Cathedral and the London Eye. Have a picnic, and then, if it's hot, walk to the open-air swimming pool, where you can swim with plants and trees all round you. It is a magical place, and you can't believe that you are in the middle of a capital city.

WHERE CAN YOU…?

1			learn to do something new
2			eat outside
3			have a fantastic view
4			see beautiful old clothes
5			do some exercise
6			have fun after 9 p.m.
7			see some animals that don't exist today
8			see a famous character from a book

3 GRAMMAR present simple or present continuous?

a 🔊 3 11 Jack and his Swedish girlfriend Ingrid are on the London Eye. Cover the conversation and listen. Tick (✓) the places they see.

☐ Trafalgar Square ☐ St Paul's Cathedral
☐ Buckingham Palace ☐ Westminster Abbey
☐ The Houses of Parliament ☐ Big Ben

b Listen to the conversation again, and put the verbs in brackets into the present continuous or the present simple.

> I Come on, let's stand over there.
> J It_'s moving_. (move). We _____ (go) up. Look, that's St Paul's Cathedral.
> I Where? Oh yes, I can see it. Is that Buckingham Palace?
> J Yes, and the Queen's at home.
> I How do you know?
> J Because the flag _____ (fly). It only _____ (fly) when she's at home.

> I I think it _____ (start) to rain. Oh, yes look, it _____ (rain).
> J It always _____ (rain) when we're sightseeing!
> I We _____ (go) down now. I _____ (love) the view of the river with Big Ben and the Houses of Parliament.
> J Me too. Go and stand there. I _____ (want) to take a photo.

> I Quick, the door _____ (open). Let's go.

c Read the conversation again, and focus on the verbs *fly* and *rain*. When do we use the present simple? When do we use the present continuous?

d ▶ p.132 Grammar Bank 5C. Learn more about the present simple and present continuous and practise them.

e ▶ Communication *What do you do? What are you doing now?*
A *p.103* B *p.108*.

4 PRONUNCIATION places in London

a 🔊 3 13 Place names in London are sometimes difficult for visitors to pronounce and understand. Listen. Under<u>line</u> the stressed syllable in the **bold** words.

Tra|fal|gar Square   the Lon|don Eye   Ox|ford Street   St Paul's Ca|the|dral
Leices|ter Square   Bu|cking|ham Pa|lace   The Hou|ses of Par|lia|ment
West|min|ster A|bbey   the Ri|ver Thames   Co|vent Gar|den

b Listen again and repeat the names.

c Practise with a partner. Imagine you are in a taxi.

Where do you want to go?   To Trafalgar Square, please.

5 WRITING

a Are social networking sites, e.g. Twitter or Facebook, popular in your country? What kind of people use them? Do you or your friends use them?

b ▶ p.113 Writing *Social networking.* Write Facebook posts to say what you are doing on holiday.

Practical English In a clothes shop

1 VOCABULARY clothes

a Match the words and pictures.

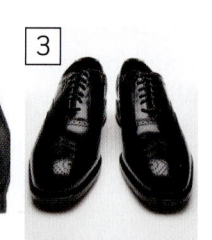

☐ a jacket /ˈdʒækɪt/
☐ jeans /dʒiːnz/
☐ a shirt /ʃɜːt/
☐ a T-shirt /ˈtiːʃɜːt/
☐ a skirt /skɜːt/
☐ shoes /ʃuːz/
☐ a sweater /ˈswetə/
☐ trousers /ˈtraʊzəz/

b 3 14)) Listen and check. Practise saying the words.

2 MEETING IN THE STREET

a 3 15)) Watch or listen to Jenny and Rob. What problem does Rob have?

b Watch or listen again. Complete the sentences.
1 Rob has a _____ for Jenny.
2 Jenny has another meeting with _____.
3 Rob has an interview in _____ minutes.
4 Jenny's meeting is at _____ past nine.
5 Rob needs to buy a new _____.
6 They go to a clothes _____.
7 Jenny needs to answer her _____.

c 3 16)) Look at the information box. Listen and repeat the phrases.

> 🔍 **Apologizing**
> I'm sorry.   That's OK.
> I'm so sorry.   Don't worry.
> I'm really sorry.   No problem.

d Cover the box. In pairs, practise apologizing and responding.

3 BUYING CLOTHES

a 3 17)) Watch or listen to Rob buying a shirt. Answer the questions.
1 What size does Rob want?
2 Does he try it on?
3 How much is the shirt?

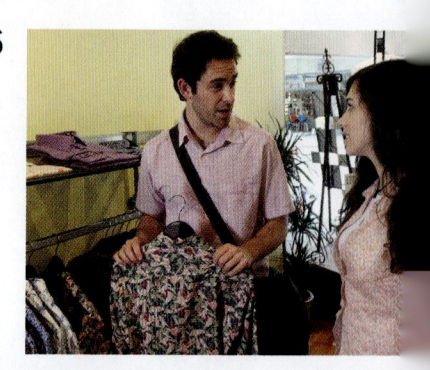

42

EPISODE 3

b Watch or listen again. Complete the **You Hear** phrases.

🔊 You Hear	You Say 💬
Can I _____ you?	Yes, what size is this shirt?
Let's see. It's a small. What _____ do you need?	A medium.
This is a _____.	Thanks. Where can I try it on?
The changing _____ are over there.	Thank you.
_____ is it?	It's fine. How much is it?
	It's £44.99.

c ③ 18 🔊 Watch or listen and repeat the **You Say** phrases. Copy the rhythm.

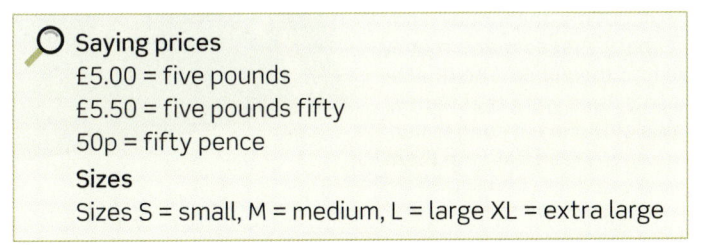

> 🔍 **Saying prices**
> £5.00 = five pounds
> £5.50 = five pounds fifty
> 50p = fifty pence
>
> **Sizes**
> Sizes S = small, M = medium, L = large XL = extra large

d Practise the dialogue with a partner.

e 👥 In pairs, roleplay buying clothes.

  A (book open) You are the shop assistant. Start with *Can I help you?*
  B (book closed) You are the customer. Buy a T-shirt, a jacket, or jeans.

f Swap roles.

£75   £24.50   £82.99

4 📺 JENNY'S ON THE PHONE

a ③ 19 🔊 Watch or listen and mark the sentences **T** (true) or **F** (false).

1 Jenny is talking to Eddie.
2 She says she doesn't like London.
3 She says she likes the people in the office.
4 Jenny is standing outside the shop.
5 Eddie thinks that Rob is her boss.
6 Jenny loves Rob's new shirt.

b Watch or listen again. Say why the **F** sentences are false.

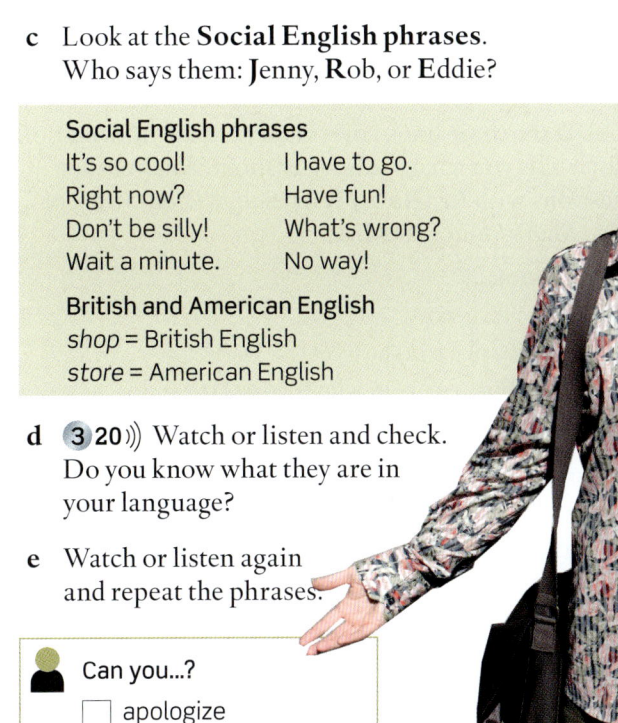

c Look at the **Social English phrases**. Who says them: **J**enny, **R**ob, or **E**ddie?

> **Social English phrases**
> It's so cool!   I have to go.
> Right now?   Have fun!
> Don't be silly!   What's wrong?
> Wait a minute.   No way!
>
> **British and American English**
> *shop* = British English
> *store* = American English

d ③ 20 🔊 Watch or listen and check. Do you know what they are in your language?

e Watch or listen again and repeat the phrases.

> 👤 **Can you…?**
> ☐ apologize
> ☐ buy clothes
> ☐ say prices

iTutor   43

G object pronouns: *me, you, him,* etc.
V phone language
P /aɪ/, /ɪ/, and /iː/

Do you like her?
Yes, I want to meet her.

6A Reading in English

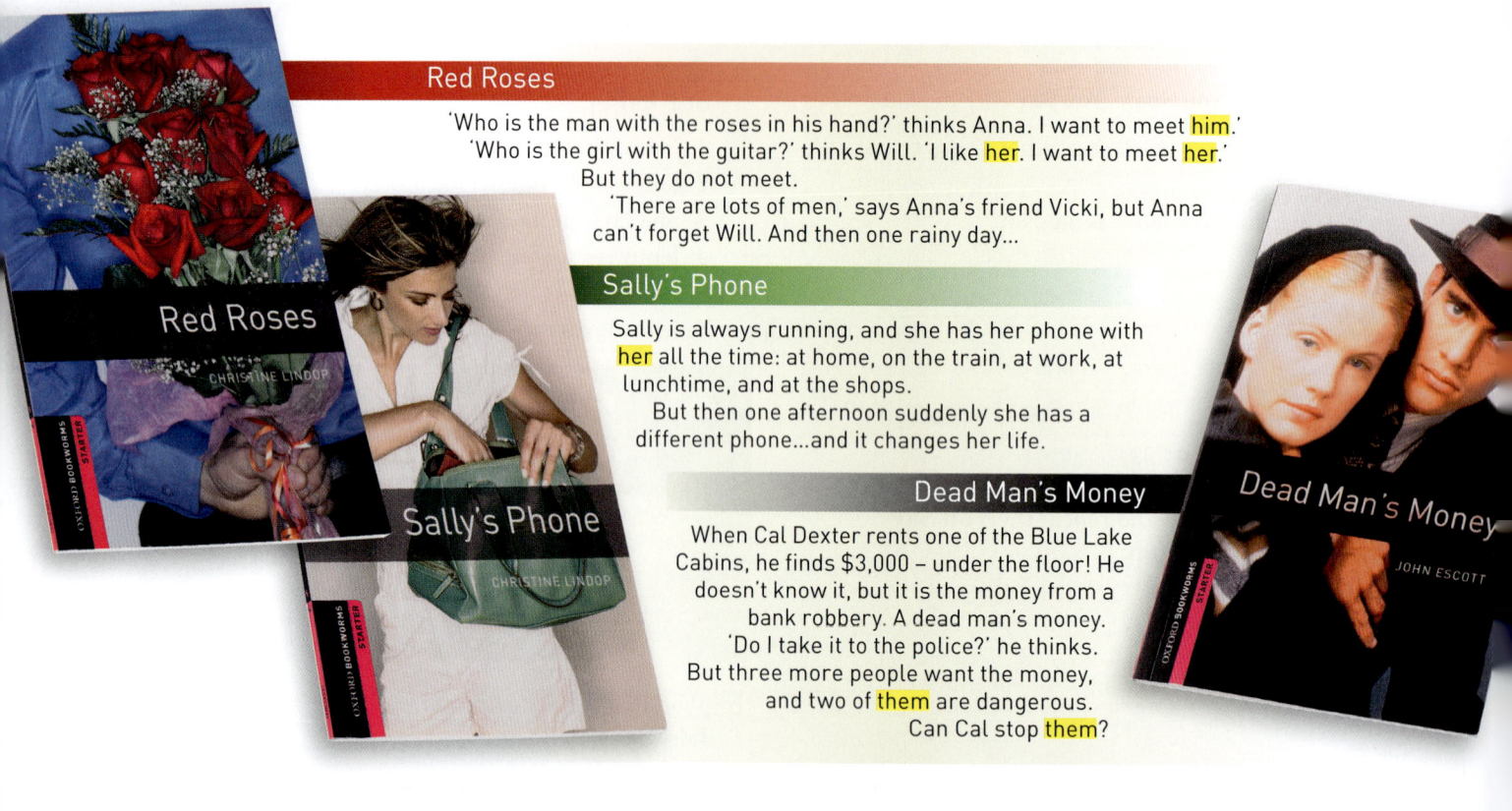

Red Roses
'Who is the man with the roses in his hand?' thinks Anna. 'I want to meet him.'
'Who is the girl with the guitar?' thinks Will. 'I like her. I want to meet her.'
But they do not meet.
'There are lots of men,' says Anna's friend Vicki, but Anna can't forget Will. And then one rainy day…

Sally's Phone
Sally is always running, and she has her phone with her all the time: at home, on the train, at work, at lunchtime, and at the shops.
But then one afternoon suddenly she has a different phone…and it changes her life.

Dead Man's Money
When Cal Dexter rents one of the Blue Lake Cabins, he finds $3,000 – under the floor! He doesn't know it, but it is the money from a bank robbery. A dead man's money.
'Do I take it to the police?' he thinks.
But three more people want the money, and two of them are dangerous.
Can Cal stop them?

1 GRAMMAR object pronouns

a Look at the three book covers and read the information which tells you what the book is about. Answer the questions with *Red Roses* (**RR**), *Sally's Phone* (**SP**), or *Dead Man's Money* (**DMM**).

Which book…?
1 ____ is a love story
2 ____ takes place in the USA
3 ____ is about a person who is quite stressed
4 ____ is about a man in a difficult situation
5 ____ is about a person who is romantic
6 ____ has a gadget which is important

b Look at the highlighted words in the texts. Who do they refer to?

him = the man with the roses

c ▶ p.134 Grammar Bank 6A. Learn more about object pronouns and practise them.

d 3 22))) Listen and say the sentences with a pronoun instead of the name(s).

))) I like Anna.   I like her.

2 PRONUNCIATION /aɪ/, /ɪ/, and /iː/

a 3 23))) Say the three groups of words and match them to a sound picture. Listen and check.

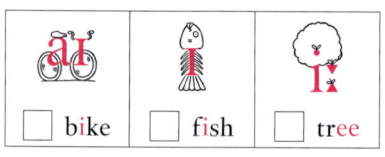

☐ bike   ☐ fish   ☐ tree

1 him it his ring finish pick
2 he she me meet read leave
3 I my buy smile nice tonight

b 3 24))) Listen. Can you hear the difference?

1 a he's   b his   4 a leave b live
2 a me   b my   5 a this   b these
3 a it   b eat   6 a we   b why

c 3 25))) Listen and tick (✓) the word you hear.

d 3 26))) Listen to this love story. Practise telling it.

They live in a big city.
He works in an office, she's a writer.
She meets him in the gym. She likes his smile.
He thinks she loves him. He buys her a ring.
But finally she says goodbye.

3 READING & LISTENING

a **3 27** Read and listen to an extract from *Sally's Phone*. Answer the questions.

> **CHARACTERS:**
> - **Sally**, a young woman
> - **Claire**, Sally's friend from work
> - **Andrew**, Sally's boyfriend
> - **Paul**, a young man
> - **Katharine**, Paul's sister

1. Where are Claire and Sally?
2. Why doesn't Sally buy the skirt immediately?
3. What do they do when they finish shopping?
4. Why does she phone her mother?
5. What is Paul doing when Sally is talking to her mother?
6. What happens when he stands up?
7. Do they go out of the café together?

b Read the extract again. With a partner guess the meaning of the highlighted verbs.

c **3 28** Read and listen to the next part of the story. Why are Paul and Sally having problems?

> **Pronouns and possessive adjectives**
> When you read, be careful with different kinds of pronouns and possessive adjectives, e.g. *he*, *his*, *him*, etc. Make sure you know who (or what) they refer to.

d Read the extract again. With a partner, say who the highlighted pronouns and possessive adjectives refer to.

*Paul wants to phone **his** mother.* **his** = Paul's

e Underline words or phrases in the extract about phones or phoning, e.g. *rings*, *answers the phone*, etc.

f What do you think happens in the end?

> **Reading in English**
> Reading Graded Readers, e.g. the Oxford Bookworms series, helps you to learn and remember vocabulary and grammar. Buy or borrow a Starter level book (with a CD if possible).

4 SPEAKING

▶ **Communication** *Reading in English* p.103. Interview your partner.

Sally's Phone

Lunchtime

It is one o'clock. Sally and Claire are looking at skirts.
  'Do you like this one, Sally?' Claire says.
  'Yes, it's beautiful, but I never wear red.'
  'Do you like red?' Claire asks.
  'Yes, I do – but Andrew doesn't.'
  'Well,' Claire says, 'it's a beautiful skirt. You like red. What do you want to do?'
  Sally buys the skirt.
Claire goes back to work, but Sally wants a coffee. She goes into a café. She buys a coffee and sits down. Then she phones her mother.
  'Hi, Mum. I have a new skirt – it's beautiful. I want to wear it tonight.'
  'What colour is it?'
  'It's red.'
  'That's nice. Red is a good colour for you,' says her mother.
Next to Sally, Paul is finishing his coffee. He phones his friend and talks to him. Then he stands up. The bag with the red skirt falls on the floor.
  'Oh! I'm sorry,' Paul says. 'That's OK,' Sally says. He puts down his phone and picks up the bag. 'Here's your bag.'
  'Thank you.' She smiles.
  'What a nice smile!' Paul thinks.
Paul picks up his phone and goes out of the café. Sally finishes her coffee. She picks up her bag and her phone, and goes back to work.

Sally's Phone

Afternoon

Paul is in his office.
  A phone rings.
  'What's that noise?' Paul thinks.
He answers the phone. It is Andrew.
  'Hello, Sally?'
  'It isn't Sally, it's Paul.'
  'Paul? Paul who? Where's Sally?'
  'Who's Sally? There's no Sally here.'
  'Huh!'
Andrew finishes the call.
Paul wants to phone his mother. He finds 'Mum' on the phone, and presses the button.
  'Hello Mum. It's Paul.'
  'Paul? Who's Paul? I'm not Paul's mum. I'm Sally's mum.'
  'What's happening?' Paul thinks.
  'What number is that?' he asks.
  'It's 0783 491839.'
  'I'm very sorry,' Paul says. 'It's the wrong number.'
  'That's OK,' Sally's mum says. 'What a nice voice!' she thinks.
Sally is at work.
  Ring ring!
She answers the phone.
  'Hello, is Paul there?'
  'No, I'm sorry, this is…'
  'Can you give a message to him? This is his sister Katharine. There's a party at my house tonight. It's my birthday.'
  'But I…'
  '8 o'clock – OK. Bye.'

G like + (verb + -ing)
V the date; ordinal numbers
P consonant clusters; saying the date

6B Times we love

> I love reading. What kind of books do you like?

1 VOCABULARY & PRONUNCIATION the date

a Number the months 1–6.

☐ April   ☐ June
☐ February ☐ March
☐ January ☐ May

b ▶ p.159 **Vocabulary Bank** *The weather and dates.* Do part 2.

> 🔍 **Ordinal numbers** *first, fourth,* etc.
> Some ordinal numbers can be difficult to say because they end in two or more consonant sounds, e.g. si**xth** /sɪksθ/.

c 🔊 3 31 Listen and repeat the ordinal numbers. Then practise saying them.

fifth   sixth   eighth   twelfth

d 🔊 3 32 How do you say these dates? Listen and check.

1/3   2/11   3/5   4/6
5/1   6/7   12/9   17/10
20/8   23/2   28/4   31/12

e Listen again and repeat the dates. Copy the rhythm.

⌒
the **first** of **March**

f What days are public holidays in your country?

g Ask the other students in your class *When's your birthday?* Does anyone have the same (or nearly the same) birthday as you?

2 READING

a Read the first part of the text. What's special about the third Monday in January and the third Friday in June?

Favourite Times

In the UK the third Monday in January is the most depressing day of the year, says psychologist Dr Cliff Arnall, who calls it Blue Monday. Why? Because it's winter, the weather is usually grey and cold, the days are dark, and Monday is the first day of the working week. People are also often short of money after Christmas, and some people feel bad after breaking their New Year resolutions. And the happiest day of the year? 'The third Friday in June,' says Dr Arnall. And it's easy to see why – it's summer, it's warm outside, the evenings are light, and the weekend starts now!

We asked our readers about the days and times during the year that make them feel good.

1 What's your favourite time of day? Why?
2 What's your favourite day of the week? Why?
3 What's your favourite month? Why?
4 What's your favourite season? Why?
5 What's your favourite public holiday? Why?

b Read the questions and Joe's and Rose's answers and complete them with phrases a–f.

a every week is different   d I love cooking
b I like making plans   e the days are long
c I hate getting up early   f I like being awake

c Look at the highlighted words and phrases and guess their meaning.

Joe 24

1 Ten thirty at night. Because it's the time of day when I can really relax.
2 Saturday. Because ¹_____ during the week, and Saturday is the first day when I can stay in bed until 12 if I want!
3 August. Because my birthday is in August and I'm usually on holiday.
4 The summer. Because the weather's good, ²_____, and people are in a good mood.
5 January 1st. Because it's the start of a new year, and ³_____.

Rose 35

1 Early morning. Because ⁴_____ when other people are asleep, and the light is beautiful.
2 It depends. Because ⁵_____!
3 May. Because the world is pale green, and asparagus is in season!
4 Autumn. Because the leaves are red and yellow, and it's a time for lots of wonderful fruit and vegetables. ⁶_____!
5 Easter Sunday. Because I love chocolate, and I always have a lot of Easter eggs!

asparagus 
Easter egg 
New Year resolutions promises we make on December 31st, e.g. to eat or drink less in the new year
Easter Sunday an important Christian holiday in March or April

3 LISTENING

a 3 33)) Listen to Martin answering the questions in *Favourite Times*. Complete column 1.

1 What's your favourite…?	2 Why?
time of day:	
during the week _____	_____
at the weekend _____	_____
day of the week _____	_____
month _____	_____
season _____	_____
public holiday _____	_____

b Listen again and complete column 2.

4 GRAMMAR *like + (verb + -ing)*

a Complete the chart with a verb from the list.

don't like   hate   don't mind   like   love

😊😊	I _____
😊	I _____
😐	I _____
☹	I _____
☹☹	I _____

b What form of the verb follows *like*, *love*, *don't mind*, and *hate*?

c ▶ p.134 **Grammar Bank 6B.** Learn more about *like + (verb + -ing)* and practise it.

5 SPEAKING & WRITING

a Write a verb or verb phrase for each picture. Use the *-ing* form of the verb.

b In pairs, ask and answer about each activity.

A *Do you like reading?*
B *Yes, I love it.*

A *What writers do you like?*
B *I like Terry Pratchett. What about you?*

c Interview your partner with the five questions from *Favourite Times* in **2**.

d Write an article called *My favourite times*. Add photos or drawings if you can. Use the texts in **2** as a model.

G revision: *be* or *do*?
V music
P /j/

What kind of music do you like?
R&B and hip hop.

6C Music is changing their lives

1 VOCABULARY music

a ▶3 35 Listen and number the kinds of music 1–9. Can you name any other kinds of music in English?

☐ hip hop   ☐ rock   ☐ classical   ☐ Latin   ☐ jazz   ☐ reggae /ˈreɡeɪ/   ☐ blues   ☐ heavy metal   ☐ R&B

b What kind of music do / don't you like?   *I like rock, but I don't like R&B.*

c Do the music quiz in small groups.

MUSIC QUIZ

1 What kind of music are these people famous for?
a Beyoncé
b Louis Armstrong
c Jay-Z
d Yehudi Menuhin
e Queen
f Bob Marley

2 Where are they from? Match the singers and bands to their countries.
a ☐ Coldplay   1 Germany
b ☐ Rihanna   2 Ireland
c ☐ Placido Domingo 3 Britain
d ☐ Black Eyed Peas 4 Barbados
e ☐ U2   5 Spain
f ☐ Fools Garden   6 the USA

3 Whose music do you hear in the soundtrack of these films / shows?
a We Will Rock You
b This Is It
c Yellow Submarine
d Amadeus
e Mamma Mia!

2 GRAMMAR revision: *be* or *do*?

a Circle the right words.
1 What kind of music *are you* / *do you* listen to?
2 *I'm not* / *I don't* like hip hop.
3 *Are you* / *Do you* play in a band?
4 She *isn't* / *doesn't* listening to you.
5 Where *are* / *do* Coldplay from?

b ▶ p.134 Grammar Bank 6C. Learn more about *be* and *do* and practise them.

c ▶3 38 Listen and make the questions.

 ))) They're German.   *Are they German?*
 ))) He plays the guitar.   *Does he play the guitar?*

3 PRONUNCIATION /j/

a ▶3 39 Listen and repeat the words and sound.

| yacht | yes   you   yellow |
| | young   your   yoga   year |

🔍 **Hidden /j/ sound**
Some words with the /uː/ sound (spelled with *u* or *ew*) also have a /j/ sound before the /uː/, e.g. music /ˈmjuːzɪk/, NOT /ˈmuːzɪk/.

b ▶3 40 Listen and repeat the sentences. Then practise saying them.
1 That young musician plays beautiful music.
2 He usually uses a yellow pencil.
3 The new students start in January this year.

4 SPEAKING

a Read the music questionnaire. Complete the questions with *are* or *do*. Complete question 6 with the names of six musicians / bands you either love or hate.

Music questionnaire

1. _____ you a big fan of a singer or band?
   _____ you a member of a fan club or forum?
2. How often _____ you...?
   - go to concerts or gigs
   - go dancing
   - watch MTV (or other music channels)
   - download music
   - look for song lyrics on the internet
   - sing karaoke
3. How _____ you usually listen to music?
   - on the radio
   - online
   - on your iPod/MP3 player
   - on CDs
4. What kind of music _____ you like listening to when you are...?
   - sad
   - happy
   - stressed
5. _____ you listening to a particular song or piece of music a lot at the moment?
6. What _____ you think of...?

   Male musicians
   _____

   Female musicians
   _____

   Bands
   _____

> **Giving opinions**
> I like him.
> I don't like her.
> I think they're   great / fantastic.
>   OK / not bad.
>   awful / terrible.

b Take turns to interview a partner with the music questionnaire. Ask for more information. Do you have similar musical tastes?

5 READING

a Do you play a musical instrument? What? Do you enjoy playing it?

b Read the article. How is music changing the lives of young people in Venezuela?

Music is changing their lives

Inside the **concert hall** a top **orchestra** is playing brilliantly. Their young **conductor**, Gustavo Dudamel, is one of the best in the world. But we are not in New York, London, or Vienna. We are in Caracas, the capital of Venezuela. The orchestra is the Simón Bolívar Youth orchestra, and its conductor and young musicians come from the poorest families in the country. They are a product of *El Sistema* ('the system' in Spanish), a project started in 1975 to save poor children from crime and drug addiction through classical music.

Today more than 270,000 young Venezuelans from the *barrios* (poor areas in Caracas) are learning to play instruments. They **practise** Beethoven and Brahms instead of learning to steal and shoot. Gisella, aged 11, says 'I am learning the **viola** because I want to escape from the *barrio*. In Venezuela now it's cooler to like Strauss than salsa.' Edgar, 22, who plays in the orchestra, says 'sometimes when we finish late I stay in town – it's dangerous to go home at that time. But now most of my friends are here. We are a family as well as an orchestra.'

Dudamel is now also the Musical Director of the Los Angeles Philharmonic, one of the USA's top orchestras. But he returns frequently to Caracas to conduct. 'I miss my orchestra, but I will never leave them. They're family,' he says.

Adapted from an article in The Guardian

c Look at the highlighted words. With a partner, guess their meaning.

d Do you know of any other projects to help poor children?

6 WRITING

▶ p.113 Writing *An informal email.* You are going to write a similar email to a penfriend.

7 ③ 41))) SONG *Lemon Tree* ♫

5 & 6 Revise and Check

GRAMMAR

Circle a, b, or c.

1 She _____ the piano.
   a can play   b can to play   c cans play
2 _____ come tonight?
   a Do you can   b You can   c Can you
3 **A** What's that noise?
   B _____ a party upstairs.
   a They having
   b They're having
   c They're have
4 The weather is cold, but _____ raining.
   a it doesn't   b it isn't   c it not
5 **A** What _____ doing?
   B I'm studying for an exam.
   a are you   b do you   c you are
6 Look! The Queen's flag _____.
   a fly   b flies   c is flying
7 The museum _____ at 2.00 on Mondays.
   a closes   b is closing   c close
8 **A** What _____?
   B I'm a nurse.
   a are you doing   b do you do   c do you
9 Our son always phones _____ every day.
   a we   b us   c our
10 Is your sister at home? I need to speak to _____.
   a him   b she   c her
11 Do you like _____ housework?
   a doing   b do   making
12 I don't mind _____ early.
   a get up   b getting up   c to get up
13 **A** _____ hungry?
   B Yes. What's for dinner?
   a Do you   b Have you   c Are you
14 What song _____ listening to?
   a are you   b do you   c you are
15 What time _____ she usually go to bed?
   a do   b is   c does

VOCABULARY

a Complete the phrases with these verbs.

buy call dance forget have hear play run take tell

1 _____ a noise   6 _____ a party
2 _____ a musical instrument   7 _____ photos
3 _____ somebody's birthday   8 _____ a marathon
4 _____ a present for your mother 9 _____ a taxi
5 _____ somebody a secret   10 _____ a tango

b Complete the sentences with *for*, *in*, *on*, *to*, or *at*.

1 She goes to bed _____ about eleven o'clock.
2 They have their TV _____ very loud.
3 I can't find the keys. Can you look _____ them?
4 I need to talk _____ the doctor.
5 I'm coming! Wait _____ me!
6 My birthday's _____ July.
7 Their wedding is _____ 2nd March.

c **Circle** the word that is different.

1 cloudy   wet   snowy   shine
2 shine   rain   blow   fog
3 autumn   season   spring   winter
4 first   third   seven   twelfth
5 twenty-second twenty-five twenty-one   twenty-three
6 May   Sunday   December   June
7 call   phone   ring   message
8 band   rock   reggae   jazz

PRONUNCIATION

a **Circle** the word with a different sound.

1 driving   wrong   change   long
2 ice   windy   spring   winter
3 snow   go   now   cold
4 third   the   tenth   Thursday
5 /juː/   music   student   beautiful   blues

b Underline the stressed syllable.

1 neigh|bour   2 re|mem|ber   3 Ju|ly   4 Fe|bru|a|ry   5 cla|ssi|cal

CAN YOU UNDERSTAND THIS TEXT?

a Read the text and answer the questions.

Where is a good place to go in Dublin if you want to...?
1 have lunch or dinner
2 see animals
3 buy a present
4 hear stories about famous places
5 have a drink without paying

b Look at the highlighted words or phrases in the text and guess their meaning.

c Read the text again and underline the thing you would like to do most.

Dublin – *the friendly city*

People don't usually think of capital cities as friendly, but people told me that Dublin is the exception, so I went there to see if it was true – and it was! Local people greet you like an old friend, they want to know everything about you, and about your day. The tourist guides are really friendly; for example, at the Guinness factory (somewhere you must go) they offer you a free glass of Guinness. The bus drivers on the tour buses (an excellent way to get around Dublin) tell very interesting and amusing stories about all the buildings and monuments they go past. They stop at all the main tourist attractions, for example Phoenix Park, the home to Dublin's zoo, St Patrick's Cathedral, and the main shopping areas (Grafton Street and O'Connell Street). When you want something to eat, the Temple Bar area is the place to go. Even in the restaurants Irish people want you to be happy. They often sit you at tables with other people, and the waiters tell jokes when they serve the food to make you laugh. In general, the food is great and very good value for money, there are lots of things to see, and hotels are cheap – how can you not be happy and friendly with all that?

Nick McCarthy *Coventry Telegraph* October 26 2010

CAN YOU UNDERSTAND THESE PEOPLE?

3 42))) **In the street** Watch or listen to five people and answer the questions.

Alison and Ben   Tiffany   Joel   Anya

1 Which sentence is true?
   a Ben can't play a musical instrument.
   b Alison can play the guitar well.
   c Ben can play the guitar, but not very well.
2 Tiffany _____.
   a has noisy neighbours
   b doesn't have noisy neighbours
   c is the noisy neighbour
3 Joel's favourite month is May because the weather is _____.
   a hot   b nice   c sunny
4 Ben doesn't like _____.
   a classical music   b heavy metal   c rock music
5 At the moment Anya is reading _____.
   a a romantic novel   b a biography   c a trilogy

CAN YOU SAY THIS IN ENGLISH?

Do the tasks with a partner. Tick (✓) the box if you can do them.

Can you...?
1 ☐ say two things you can do well, and two things you can't do (e.g. cook)
2 ☐ say three things you can or can't do in class (e.g. use your mobile)
3 ☐ say what kind of books you usually read, and what you are reading at the moment
4 ☐ ask your partner questions with the words below
... tired? Why?
... like watching sport on TV? Which sports?
... enjoying your English classes?
... play a musical instrument? Which one?

Short films Williamsburg, New York
Watch and enjoy a film on iTutor.

G past simple of *be*: was / were
V word formation: *paint* > *painter*
P sentence stress

> Who was she?
> She was a famous writer.

7A At the National Portrait Gallery

1 GRAMMAR was / were

a Read about the National Portrait Gallery in London and answer the questions.
1. Where is it?
2. What can you see there?
3. When is it open?
4. How much does it cost?

b 3 43))) Look at a photo which is in the National Portrait gallery. Cover the dialogue and listen. Who are the two people in the photo?

> **A** I love that photo. Who are they?
> **B** I think it's King Edward VIII and Wallis Simpson. Let's see. Yes, that's right.
> **A** When was he king? I don't remember a King Edward.
> **B** Well, he was only king for 11 months, in 1936, I think. He was Queen Elizabeth II's uncle.
> **A** Why was he only king for a short time?
> **B** Because he was in love with Wallis Simpson, the woman in the photo. She was American. The government was against the marriage because she was divorced. It was a terrible scandal. In the end he abdicated* and they got married.
> **A** Who was the next king?
> **B** His brother, George VI.
> **A** Were Edward and Wallis happy?
> **B** I think they were happy. They were together for the rest of their lives.

* abdicate stop being king or queen

c Listen again and read the dialogue. Then complete the gaps.

Present simple	Past simple
He is the king.	He _____ the king.
She is divorced.	She _____ divorced.
They are happy.	They _____ happy.

d ▶ p.136 **Grammar Bank 7A.** Learn more about *was / were* and practise it.

National Portrait Gallery

The National Portrait Gallery has a collection of portraits of famous British men and women, from the 16th century to the present day. The portraits are both paintings and photographs. The National Portrait Gallery is near Trafalgar Square, five minutes from the National Gallery, London's most important art gallery. It is open daily and entrance is free.

2 PRONUNCIATION & SPEAKING
sentence stress

a 3 45))) Listen and repeat. Copy the rhythm.

+ I **was** at a **party**.   She was **born** in **Mexico**.
  My **parents** were **angry**.
− He **wasn't** at **home**.   They **weren't** very **happy**.
? **When** were you **born**?   **Where** was the **hotel**?
  Was it **expensive**? **No**, it **wasn't**.
  Were they at the **concert**? **Yes**, they **were**.

b 3 46))) Say the sentences in the past simple.

))) I'm at home.   I was at home.

c ▶ **Communication** *Where were you?* **A** p.103 **B** p.108.

3 READING

a Look at three more pictures from the National Portrait Gallery. Do you know who the people are or anything about them?

b (3 47)) Read and listen to three audio guide extracts. Check your answers to **a**.

1. Henry VIII was born in 1491. He was King of England from 1509 to 1547 and is famous for separating the Church of England from the Roman Catholic Church, and for his six wives. When he was young, as in this picture, he was very strong and good-looking. He was an excellent sportsman, and was also a good musician and poet. However, in his old age he was very fat and always in pain.

2. The Brontë sisters, Charlotte, Emily, and Anne, were born between 1816 and 1820 in a small village in the north of England. They were all writers, but only Charlotte, with her novel *Jane Eyre*, was famous in her lifetime. Their brother Branwell, the painter of this portrait, was originally in the picture between Emily and Charlotte. He wasn't happy with his self-portrait and now the painting shows only the three sisters.

3. Helena Bonham Carter, the actress, was born in London in 1966. Her mother is half Spanish and her father, who died in 2004, was the grandson of Herbert Asquith, the British Prime Minister from 1908 to 1916. Her first big role was as Lucy Honeychurch in *A Room with a View*, and her other roles include The Red Queen in *Alice in Wonderland*, Bellatrix Lestrange in the Harry Potter films, and Queen Elizabeth in *The King's Speech*. She has two children with her partner Tim Burton, a film director.

c Read the texts again and answer the questions.
1. How long was Henry VIII King of England?
2. What was he good at when he was a young man?
3. Were the Brontë sisters famous when they were alive?
4. Why isn't their brother in the picture?
5. Who was Helena Bonham Carter's great-grandfather?
6. What was her first famous film?

d Cover the texts. What can you remember?

4 VOCABULARY word formation

a Find words in the texts for people made from these words:
1. sport _____
2. music _____
3. poetry _____
4. write _____
5. paint _____
6. act _____ (OR actor)
7. direct film _____

> **Word building: professions**
> We often add -*er* or -*or* to a verb, e.g. *writer, actor*.
> We often add -*ian*, -*ist*, or -*man*/*woman* to a noun, e.g. *musician*.

b Are the words below verbs or nouns? Do you know the words for the people?
1. sing _____
2. compose _____
3. politics _____
4. science _____
5. police _____
6. novel _____
7. business _____
8. sail _____
9. art _____
10. invent _____

c (3 48)) Listen and check. Underline the stressed syllable. Practise saying the words.

d Write the names of four famous people in each circle. Ask a partner.

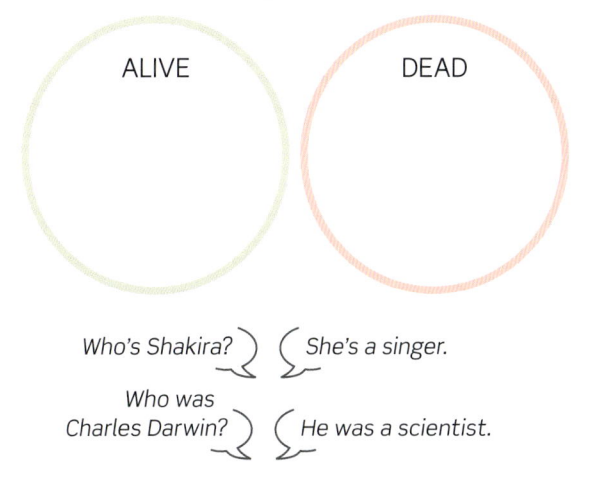

ALIVE   DEAD

Who's Shakira? — *She's a singer.*
Who was Charles Darwin? — *He was a scientist.*

5 LISTENING & WRITING

a (3 49)) Listen to five clues about two famous people. Do you know who they are?

b With a partner write clues about a famous man and a woman (both dead).

c Read your clues to another pair. Do they know the people?

G past simple: regular verbs
V past time expressions
P -ed endings

What did they want to do?
They wanted to go to the match.

7B Chelsea girls

1 READING & LISTENING

a 🔊 3 50 Read and listen to the true story about a journey. Number the sentences 1–7.
- ☐ The taxi arrived at the girls' house.
- ☐ They looked out of the window.
- ☐ They chatted and listened to music.
- ☒ 1 The girls wanted to go to a match.
- ☐ The taxi stopped in a street with pretty houses.
- ☐ They called a taxi.
- ☐ The taxi driver typed their destination into his satnav.

b 🔊 3 51 Listen and check. Do you think they were in London?

c 🔊 3 52 Listen to the news story on the radio. Where were they?

d ▶ **Communication** *Stamford Bridge* p.103. Read some tourist information about the place they were in and look at the map.

e Do you think it is easy to make a mistake like this? Whose fault was it?

2 GRAMMAR
past simple: regular verbs

a Read the text again and highlight ten more past simple regular verbs +, one past simple negative sentence –, and one past simple question ?.

b In pairs, complete the chart and answer questions 1–3.

Present simple	Past simple
They want to go to the match.	They _____ to go to the match.
They don't talk to the taxi driver.	They _____ to the taxi driver.
Where do you want to go?	Where _____ to go?

1 What letters do you add to a regular verb in the past simple, e.g. *call*?
2 What do you do if the verb ends in *e*, e.g. *type*?
3 What happens to verbs which end with one vowel and one consonant, e.g. *chat*, *stop*?

c ▶ p.136 Grammar Bank 7B. Learn more about past simple regular verbs and practise them.

The *taxi* journey

Althorp House

Charles Spencer, Princess Diana's brother, has three daughters, 18-year-old Kitty, and 15-year-old twins Eliza and Amelia. They live in Althorp, a large country house near Northampton, about 85 miles (136 kilometres) north of London.

The Spencer sisters

One of the sisters and her friend wanted to go to a football match in London. It was a Premier League match between Chelsea and Arsenal at Stamford Bridge. They called a taxi to take them to London and back. The taxi arrived and the driver typed Stamford Bridge into his satnav. The girls relaxed in the back of the car. They probably chatted, listened to music on their iPods, and texted their friends. They didn't talk to the taxi driver.

Two hours later the taxi stopped. They looked out of the window. It was a street with pretty houses.

The girls were a bit surprised, and they asked the taxi driver where they were. 'In Stamford Bridge,' he said. 'Where did you want to go?'

Adapted from a news website

Stamford Bridge Stadium

d Stand up and move around the class. Ask *Did you… yesterday?* questions with the verb phrases below. When somebody answers *Yes, I did*, write their name.

YESTERDAY

Find a person who…

- used satnav _____
- watched a football match _____
- chatted online _____
- studied for an exam _____
- cooked dinner _____
- arrived at work / school late _____
- listened to the radio _____
- started a new book _____
- worked / studied until late _____
- played a computer game _____

Did you use satnav yesterday? *No, I didn't. Did you…?*

3 PRONUNCIATION -ed endings

> **Past simple regular verbs**
> The *e* in *-ed* is not usually pronounced, and *-ed* is pronounced /d/ or /t/, e.g. *closed* /kləʊzd/, *stopped* /stɒpt/. The *-ed* is pronounced /ɪd/ **only** in verbs which end with the sound /t/ or /d/, e.g. *waited* /ˈweɪtɪd/ *ended* /ˈendɪd/.

a 3 54))) Listen and repeat the verbs.

1 -ed = /d/	2 -ed = /t/	3 -ed = /ɪd/
called	looked	wanted
arrived	relaxed	chatted
listened	stopped	texted

b 3 55))) Look at the verbs in the list. Circle the ones that belong to group 3. Listen and check.

played finished started travelled asked missed
cooked needed watched lived liked typed

c 3 56))) Listen to some verb phrases. Make true + or – sentences about yesterday.

))) *play tennis* (*I played tennis yesterday. / I didn't play tennis yesterday.*

4 VOCABULARY & SPEAKING
past time expressions

a Number the past time expressions 1–10.

- [ ] yesterday morning
- [ ] last night
- [ ] last month
- [ ] three days ago
- [1] five minutes ago
- [ ] last week
- [ ] last summer
- [ ] the day before yesterday
- [ ] a year ago
- [ ] in 2009

> **Past time expressions**
> We say *last week, last month* NOT ~~the last week, the last month~~.

b 3 57))) Listen and check. Then listen and repeat.

c Look at the questionnaire below. Tell your partner true sentences with past time expressions. Ask for more information.

I cried at the end of a film last week. *Oh really? What was it?*

When was the last time you…?

* cried at the end of a film
* travelled by plane
* started a new hobby
* walked more than 10 km
* booked tickets online 
* downloaded a song
* played sport
* missed an English class
* watched a really good film 
* called a friend
* danced

7C A night to remember

G past simple: irregular verbs
V go, have, get
P sentence stress

What did you do?
We went to a restaurant.

1 READING

a Look at the photos and read the introduction to the article. For each photo, say why you think the night was memorable.

b Read about two people's nights, and match them to a photo.

c Read the texts again and match the questions to their answers in the texts.

- [ ] What time did you get back?
- [ ] What was the weather like?
- [ ] Why was it a memorable night?
- [ ] When was it? Where were you?
- [ ] What did you wear?
- [ ] Who were you with?
- [ ] What did you do?

Why do we remember some nights in our lives?

Is it because we went to a beautiful place, met interesting people, heard wonderful music, or saw a fantastic film? We asked people all over the world to tell us about a night that they can never forget…

Maria Julia from Argentina

1 It was in August two years ago when I was on holiday in Athens.

2 I wanted to see a man that I knew a little when I was at university. He was Greek and he lived in Athens. I called him many times, but he didn't answer. Suddenly, on my last night, he came to my hotel.

3 I felt embarrassed, because my clothes weren't very special – a green skirt and a white T-shirt and Greek sandals – and my hair was a mess.

4 We went out and walked around the centre of Athens. We spoke English, but he taught me some Greek words and I taught him some Spanish.

5 It was a warm night with a beautiful full moon.

6 I got back to the hotel at 3 a.m.

7 It was a magical evening – an Argentinian woman with a Greek man on the other side of the world in those dark streets, with the lights from the Parthenon up on the hill!

Mehmet from Turkey

1 It was last year. I was in Istanbul, where I live.

2 I was with my friends. It was my best friend's birthday.

3 I wore a black T-shirt and blue jeans.

4 We went to a great place called Cezayir. It's an old building with a great restaurant. We had dinner, and after dinner we had a coffee in the bar. Then we went to the beach at Florya and we had a swim. It was fantastic. The water wasn't very clean, but we didn't mind!

5 It was a hot night and the sea was really warm.

6 After our swim, we were tired and decided to go back, but I couldn't find my car keys! We went back to the beach and we looked everywhere, but it was too dark. In the end I left the car at the beach and I went home in my friend's car! I got home really late, at 5.00 in the morning.

7 It was a memorable night because we had a fantastic dinner and swim, but also because I lost the car keys – it was my father's car and he was really angry!

2 GRAMMAR past simple: irregular verbs

a Look at the article again and find the past tense of these irregular verbs.

can	could	/kʊd/
come		/keɪm/
feel		/felt/
get		/gɒt/
go		/went/
have		/hæd/
hear		/hɜːd/
know		/njuː/
leave		/left/
lose		/lɒst/
meet		/met/
see		/sɔː/
speak		/spəʊk/
teach		/tɔːt/
wear		/wɔː/

b (3 58)) Listen and check. Practise saying the verbs.

c ▶ p.136 Grammar Bank 7C. Learn more about past simple irregular verbs and practise them.

d Work in pairs. A re-read the text about Maria Julia, B re-read the text about Mehmet.

e ▶ Communication A night to remember
A p.103 B p.108. Test your partner's memory. Whose night do you think was more fun?

3 LISTENING

a You are going to listen to David from Spain talking about his memorable night. Look at photo C from 1. Where was he? Why was it a memorable night?

b (3 60)) Listen and check.

c Listen again. Correct the information.
1 It was on 11th August. *No, it was on 11th July.*
2 He was in Buenos Aires.
3 He watched the match in a restaurant.
4 He wore a Spanish football shirt and a yellow scarf.
5 The match was in the evening.
6 There were a lot of English tourists there.
7 After the match they went to a bar in the city centre.
8 It was quite cold that night.
9 He got to the hotel at 4.00 in the morning.

4 VOCABULARY go, have, get

a Can you remember these phrases about Mehmet? Write *went*, *had*, or *got*.
1 We ___ to a great place called Cezayir.
2 We ___ dinner, and after dinner we ___ a coffee in the bar.
3 Then we ___ to the beach at Florya and we ___ a swim.
4 I ___ home really late, at 5.00 in the morning.

b ▶ p.160 Vocabulary Bank *go, have, get.*

5 PRONUNCIATION sentence stress

a Look at the questions in 'A memorable night' below. What words are missing?

b (3 62)) Listen and repeat the questions. Copy the rhythm.

A memorable night...
- When / it?
- Where / you?
- Who / with?
- What / wear?
- Where / go?
- What / do?
- What / the weather like?
- What time / get home?
- Why / it a memorable night?

6 SPEAKING & WRITING

a Think about a time you had a memorable night. Look at the questions in 5b and plan your answers.

b Interview your partner about their night.

c Write about your night. Answer the questions in 5b, and use the article in 1 to help you.

7 (3 63)) SONG Summer Nights ♫

Practical English Getting lost

1 A FREE MORNING

a (3 64)) Rob and Jenny are planning what to do on their free morning. Watch or listen once. What is the problem?

b Watch or listen again. Complete the sentences with a word, a name, or a number.

1. Rob suggests that they go _____.
2. He says that they can _____ bikes.
3. _____ phones _____.
4. Rob needs to interview an _____.
5. Rob asks if he can do the interview on _____.
6. Rob and Jenny arrange to meet at _____ o'clock outside the Tate Modern*.

> 🔍 **Cultural note**
> * The Tate Modern is a famous art gallery in London.

2 VOCABULARY directions

a Match the words and pictures.

- [ ] on the <u>corner</u> /ˈkɔːnə/
- [ ] at the <u>traffic lights</u> /ˈtræfɪk laɪts/
- [ ] a <u>bridge</u> /brɪdʒ/
- [ ] <u>o</u>pposite /ˈɒpəzɪt/
- [ ] turn left /tɜːn left/
- [ ] turn right /tɜːn raɪt/
- [ ] go straight on /streɪt/
- [ ] go past (the church) /pɑːst/

b (3 65)) Listen and check.

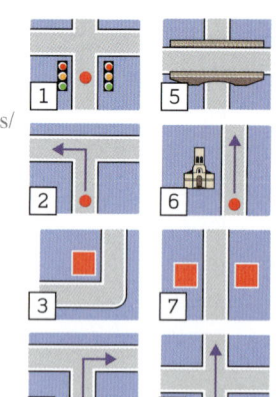

3 ASKING THE WAY

a (3 66)) Jenny is trying to find the Tate Modern. Watch or listen. Is it A, B, C, or D?

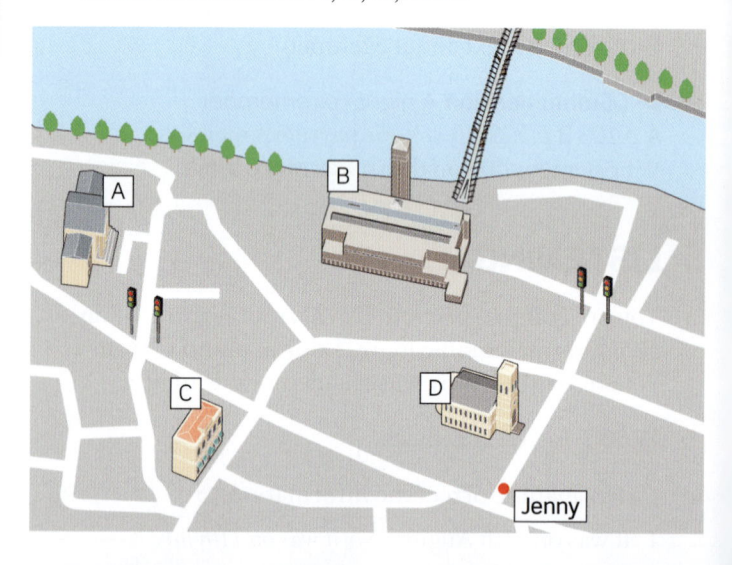

EPISODE 4

b Watch or listen again. Complete the **You Hear** phrases.

You Say	You Hear
Excuse me, please. Where's the Tate Modern?	_____, I don't live here.
Excuse me. Is the Tate Modern near here?	The Tate Modern? It's near here, but I don't know exactly _____. Sorry.
Thank you.	
Excuse me. Can you tell me the way to the Tate Modern, please?	Yes, of course. Go straight on. Go _____ the church, then turn _____ at the traffic lights. And it's at the end of the street.
Sorry, could you say that again, please?	Yes, go straight on. Go _____ the church, then turn _____ at the traffic lights. And it's at the end of the street. You can't _____ it!
Thank you.	

c 3 67))) Watch or listen and repeat the **You Say** phrases. Copy the rhythm.

d Practise the dialogue with a partner.

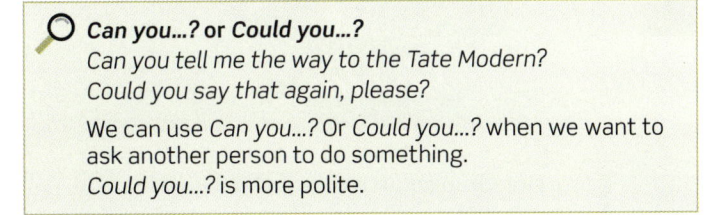

> **Can you...? or Could you...?**
> Can you tell me the way to the Tate Modern?
> Could you say that again, please?
>
> We can use *Can you...?* Or *Could you...?* when we want to ask another person to do something.
> *Could you...?* is more polite.

e In pairs, roleplay the dialogue. **A** ask for directions to building A (the library). Start with *Excuse me, where's...?* **B** give directions. Then swap roles. Ask for directions to building C (the post office).

4 JENNY AND ROB GO SIGHTSEEING

a 3 68))) Watch or listen to Jenny and Rob. Mark the sentences **T** (true) or **F** (false).

1. The Millennium Bridge is for cars and people.
2. It was the first new bridge over the Thames for 100 years.
3. Rob interviewed the engineer last year.
4. Jenny doesn't like Shakespeare.
5. Daniel phones and invites Jenny to dinner.
6. Jenny accepts the invitation.
7. There's a gift shop on the top floor of the Tate Modern.
8. The Tate Modern was a power station until 1981.

b Watch or listen again. Say why the **F** sentences are false.

c Look at the **Social English phrases**. Who says them: **J**enny, **R**ob, or **D**aniel?

> **Social English phrases**
> What a view!
> What would you like to visit?
> What is there to see?
> We could go to the Globe Theatre.
> Would you like to meet for lunch?
> That's really nice of you.
> Maybe another time?
> Yes, of course.

d 3 69))) Watch or listen and check. Do you know what they are in your language?

e Watch or listen again and repeat the phrases.

> **Can you...?**
> ☐ ask for and understand directions
> ☐ give simple directions
> ☐ ask someone to do something in a polite way

G past simple: regular and irregular
V irregular verbs
P past simple verbs

Did you hear anything during the night?
No, I didn't. I was very tired.

8A A murder story

1 READING

a Read the back cover of a murder story. Then cover it and look at the photographs. Can you remember who the people are?

Who's Amanda? — She's Jeremy's wife.

b 4 2)) Read and listen to the story. Mark the sentences **T** (true) or **F** (false). Correct the **F** sentences.

1 Somebody killed Jeremy between 12.00 a.m. and 2.00.
2 The inspector questioned Amanda in the living room.
3 Jeremy went to bed before Amanda.
4 Amanda and Jeremy slept in the same room.
5 Somebody opened and closed Amanda's door.
6 Amanda got up at 7.00.
7 Amanda didn't love Jeremy.

c Look at the highlighted irregular verbs in the story. What are the infinitives?

1 was = be

2 PRONUNCIATION
past simple verbs

a 4 3)) Listen to the pronunciation of these verbs in the past simple.

| thought | could | found | heard | read |
| said | saw | took | taught | wore |

b 4 4)) Now match the verbs in **a** with a word below which rhymes. Listen and check. Practise saying the words.

book _____   bed _____ _____
round _____   four _____ _____
bird _____   port _____ _____
good _____

c 4 5)) Find and underline nine past simple **regular** verbs in the story. How do you pronounce them? Listen and check.

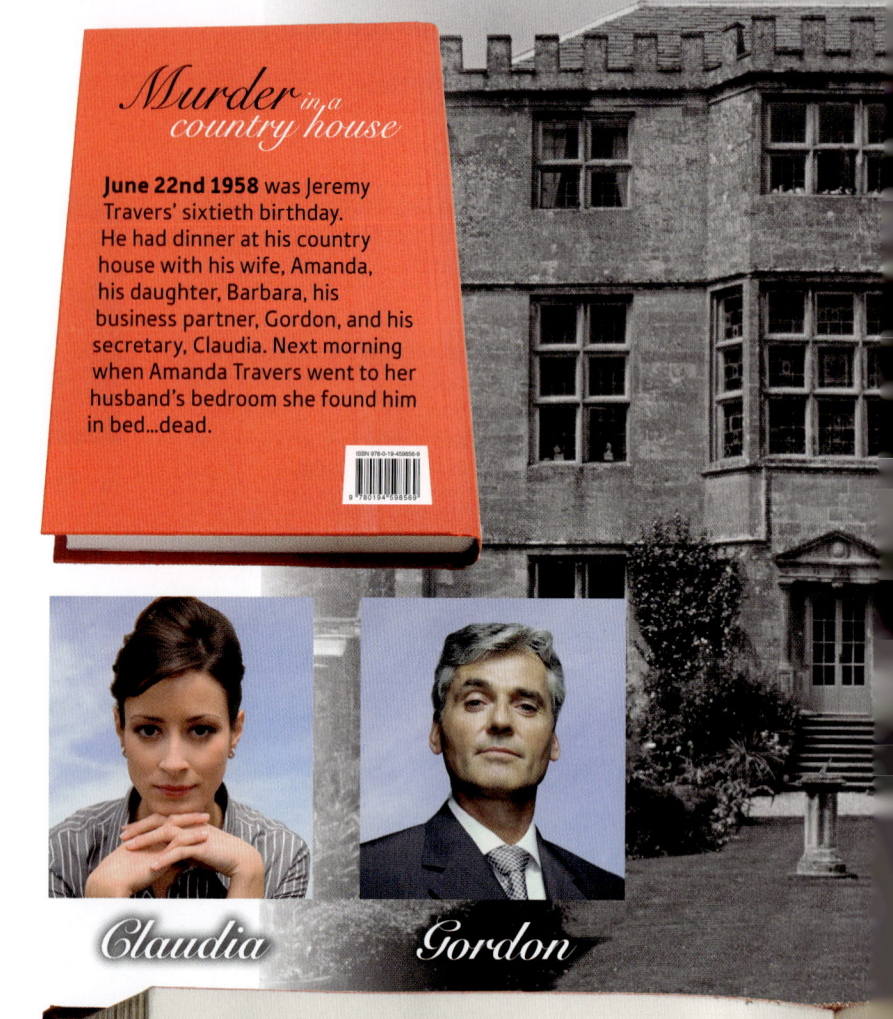

Murder in a country house

June 22nd 1958 was Jeremy Travers' sixtieth birthday. He had dinner at his country house with his wife, Amanda, his daughter, Barbara, his business partner, Gordon, and his secretary, Claudia. Next morning when Amanda Travers went to her husband's bedroom she found him in bed…dead.

Claudia   *Gordon*

Inspector Granger arrived at about 9.00. He ¹was a tall man with a big black moustache. Amanda, Barbara, Claudia, and Gordon ²were in the living room. The inspector ³came in.
  'Mr Travers died between midnight last night and seven o'clock this morning,' he ⁴said. 'Somebody in this room killed him.' He looked at them one by one, but nobody ⁵spoke.
  'Mrs Travers, I want to talk to you first. Come into the library with me, please.'
  Amanda Travers followed the inspector into the library and they ⁶sat down.
  'What did your husband do after dinner last night?'
  'When we finished dinner Jeremy said he was tired and he ⁷went to bed.'
  'Did you go to bed then?'
  'No, I didn't. I went for a walk in the garden.'
  'What time did you go to bed?'
  'About quarter to twelve.'
  'Was your husband asleep?'

3 LISTENING

a ◀4 6, 7, 8))) Listen to the inspector question Barbara. Write the information in the chart. Listen again and check. Then do the same for Gordon and Claudia.

	Amanda	*Barbara*	*Gordon*	*Claudia*
What did they do after dinner?	She went for a walk.			
What time did they go to bed?	11.45.			
Did they hear anything?	Jeremy's door opened and closed.			
Possible motive?	She hated him.			

b Compare your chart with a partner. Who do you think was the murderer: Amanda, Barbara, Gordon, or Claudia? Why?

c ◀4 9))) Now listen to what happened. Who was the murderer? Why did he / she kill Mr Travers? Were you right?

4 GRAMMAR past simple: regular and irregular

a Cover the story and look at these verbs. Are they regular or irregular in the past simple? Write the past simple form + and – for each verb.

come kill close speak sleep sit hate walk

+ *came*   – *didn't come*

b ◀4 10))) Listen and check.

c ▶ p.138 Grammar Bank 8A. Learn more about past simple regular and irregular verbs and practise them.

d ▶ p.165 Irregular verbs Tick (✓) the irregular verbs you know. Choose three new ones and learn them.

5 SPEAKING

▶ **Communication** *Police interview* **A** *p.104* **B** *p.108*. Interview robbery suspects. Are they telling the truth?

'I don't know, inspector. We…we [8]slept in separate rooms. But I [9]saw that his door was closed.'
'Did you hear anything when you were in your room?'
'Yes, I [10]heard Jeremy's bedroom door. It opened. I [11]thought it was Jeremy. Then it closed again. I [12]read in bed for half an hour and then I went to sleep.'
'What time did you get up this morning?'
'I [13]got up at about 7.15. I [14]had breakfast and at 8.00 I [15]took my husband a cup of tea. I [16]found him in bed. He was…dead.'
'Tell me, Mrs Travers, did you love your husband?'
'Jeremy is…was a difficult man.'
'But did you love him, Mrs Travers?'
'No, inspector. I hated him.'

G *there is / there are, some / any* + plural nouns
V the house
P /eə/ and /ɪə/, sentence stress

Is there a garage?
Yes, there is.

8B A house with a history

1 VOCABULARY the house

a Read the advertisement for a house to rent. Would you like to rent it? Why (not)?

b Cover the advertisement. What can you remember about the house?

c With a partner, think of three things you can usually find in a bedroom, a bathroom, and a living room.

d ▶ p.161 **Vocabulary Bank** *The house.*

TO RENT
Beautiful country house.
Very quiet. Six bedrooms, four bathrooms, large garden. Five miles from Witney. Perfect family house.
LOW PRICE.

2 LISTENING

a (4 13))) Kim and Leo are a young couple from the USA. They want to rent the house in **1**. Cover the dialogue and listen to their conversation with Barbara. Which three rooms in the house do they go into?

b Listen again and complete the dialogue.

K The garden is wonderful, I love it.
L Is there a ¹ *garage*?
B Oh yes, there's a big garage over there. Let's go inside the house.

   This is the ² _____. There are five rooms on this floor, the kitchen, the ³ _____, the living room, the ⁴ _____, the library...
L Wow! There's a library, Kim!
B This is the living room.
L I love the furniture, the old sofa, the armchairs, the ⁵ _____...
B And this is the ⁶ _____. It's very big, as you can see.
K Is there a dishwasher?
B No, there isn't. It's an old house, you see.
L Never mind. I think it's lovely. Is there a ⁷ _____ downstairs?
B Yes, there's one ⁸ _____ and there are three upstairs.
K Are there any ⁹ _____ with children?
B No, there aren't any neighbours near here. But there are some families with children in the village.
K That's great. You lived in this house, is that right, Mrs...?
B Call me Barbara, dear. Yes, I lived here. A long time ago. Now I live in the village. Let's go ¹⁰ _____...

c (4 14))) Listen. What does Kim say about one of the bedrooms? Whose bedroom was it?

62

d **4 15**)) Kim and Leo go to the local pub. Listen and answer the questions.

1 What do they have to drink? Why?
2 What does the barman tell them…?
   a about what happened in the house
   b about Barbara
   c about what happened to the house later
3 What do Kim and Leo decide to do?

3 GRAMMAR there is / there are

a In groups of three, practise the dialogue in **2b**. Then complete the chart.

	singular	plural
+	There's a garden.	There ___ some families in the village.
−	There ___ a dishwasher.	There aren't any neighbours.
?	___ ___ a garage?	___ ___ any neighbours?

b What's the difference between…?
1 There are **three** families in the village.
2 There are **some** families in the village.

c ▶ **p.138 Grammar Bank 8B.** Learn more about *there is / there are* etc. and practise it.

4 PRONUNCIATION

/eə/ and /ɪə/, sentence stress

a **4 17**)) Listen and repeat the words and sounds.

ch**air**	
ear	

b Put the words in the right place.

beer	careful	dear	wear	here	they're
near	stairs	there	we're	hear	where

c **4 18**)) Listen and repeat the words.

d **4 19**)) Listen and repeat. Copy the rhythm.

A **Are** there any **stairs**?
B **Yes**, they're **over there**.

A **Is** there a **bank near here**?
B **Yes**.
A **Where**?
B There's **one** in the **square**.

e Practise the dialogues with a partner.

f Ask your partner questions with *Is there a…in your…? Are there any…in your…?* Give more information in your answers if you can.

| TV   books   plants   pictures |
| mirror   fireplace   lamps |
| kitchen   bedroom   bathroom |
| dining room   living room |

Is there a TV in your kitchen?
No, there isn't, but there's one in the living room.

5 SPEAKING

a Look at the questionnaire **Your home**. Interview a partner. Ask for and give more information if you can.

Your home
- Do you live in a house or a flat?
- How old is it?
- How big is it?
- How many bedrooms are there? bathrooms?
- Is there a study? a garden or a balcony? a garage? central heating or air conditioning?
- Do you like it? Why (not)?

b Draw a simple plan of your living room. Show the plan to your partner and describe the room.

This is the living room. It's quite big and it's very light. There are two sofas and an armchair.

6 WRITING

▶ **p.114 Writing** Describing your home.
Write a description of your house or flat.

7 **4 20**)) SONG *House of the Rising Sun* ♫

G there was / there were
V prepositions: place and movement
P silent letters

8C A night in a haunted hotel

Were there any pictures on the wall?
Yes, there was a picture of a lady.

1 READING

a Do you believe in ghosts? Are there buildings in your town / city that people think are haunted?

b Read the text once and find out:
 1 Who are the ghosts in the two hotels?
 2 Tick (✓) the things that happen in the hotels:
  a ☐ people hear strange noises   d ☐ lights go on and off
  b ☐ people see somebody   e ☐ things fall on the floor
  c ☐ doors open and close   f ☐ people feel that somebody is watching them

c Look at the highlighted words in the text related to hotels and guess their meaning.

d Would you like to stay in one of these hotels? Why (not)?

WOULD YOU LIKE TO STAY IN A HAUNTED HOTEL?

THERE ARE MANY HOTELS IN BRITAIN THAT PEOPLE SAY ARE HAUNTED. IF YOU ARE FEELING BRAVE, YOU CAN STAY THE NIGHT IN ONE OF THESE HOTELS.

ENGLAND GOSFORTH HALL INN

Gosforth Hall is a small hotel in Cumbria in the north of England, built in 1658. People say the hotel has the ghost of a Catholic priest. He usually appears in Room 11. There is a secret tunnel that goes from behind the fireplace in the hotel lounge to Room 11. In 17th-century England, Catholic priests used the tunnel to hide from Protestants.

The owner of the hotel, Rod Davies, says: 'I didn't believe in ghosts before I came here, but strange things happen in the hotel. One guest woke up in the middle of the night and saw a tall man standing next to his bed. He checked out the next morning.' Rod's wife says: 'One night a lot of books fell off a shelf in the lounge. And sometimes when I am working I feel that someone is watching me, but when I turn round nobody is there.'

GHOST HUNTERS: Ask for Room 11   www.gosforthhallhotel.co.uk

SCOTLAND COMLONGON CASTLE

Comlongon is a 15th-century castle in a small village near Dumfries in south-west Scotland. The castle is haunted by the Green Lady, the ghost of Lady Marion Carruthers. Lady Marion was unhappy because she was married to a man she did not love, and in 1570 she jumped from the castle walls and killed herself. Many strange things happen in the hotel – doors open and close, and lights go on and off in empty rooms. An American couple once opened the door of their room and saw a young woman sitting on the bed. They left because they thought they were in the wrong room. In fact it was their room, but when they came back the room was empty.

GHOST HUNTERS: Ask for The Carruthers suite.   www.comlongon.com

2 VOCABULARY prepositions: place and movement

a Look at the pictures of the ghosts from the hotel. Where is the woman sitting? Where is the man standing?

b ▶ p.162 **Vocabulary Bank** *Prepositions: place and movement.*

3 PRONUNCIATION silent letters

> 🔍 **Silent letters**
> Some English words have a 'silent' letter,
> e.g. in *cupboard* /ˈkʌbəd/ you don't pronounce the *p*.

a ◀4 23)) Listen and cross out the 'silent' letter in these words.

| building | castle | could | friend | ghost | guest |
| half | hour | know | listen | talk | what | write |

b Practise saying the words.

4 LISTENING

A British newspaper, the *Sunday Times*, sent one of its journalists, Stephen Bleach, to Gosforth Hall Inn. They asked him to spend the night in Room 11.

a ◀4 24)) Listen to **part 1** of Stephen's night. Correct the information in these sentences.

1 He arrived at Gosforth Hall early in the evening.
2 There were four other guests in the hotel.
3 He talked to one of the guests.
4 He had dinner in the bar.
5 He went to his room at 11.00.
6 Room 11 was on the first floor.
7 The room was quite small.
8 There was a TV and a remote control.
9 There was a horror film on TV.
10 He went to sleep at the end of the film.

b ◀4 25)) Do you think Stephen saw the ghost? Listen to **part 2** and find out. Listen again and answer the questions.

1 Did he wake up during the night?
   If yes, what time?
2 Did anything strange happen?
   If yes, what?
3 Did he 'feel' the ghost?
4 Was he frightened?
   ☐ very ☐ a little ☐ not at all
5 Would he like to go back?
   Why (not)?

5 GRAMMAR
there was / there were

a ◀4 26)) Complete the sentences from the listening with *was*, *wasn't*, *were*, or *weren't*. Then listen and check.

1 There _____ many other guests in the hotel.
2 There _____ only three.
3 There _____ an old TV on a table.
4 There _____ a remote control.

b ▶ p.138 **Grammar Bank 8C.** Learn more about *there was / there were* and practise it.

6 SPEAKING

▶ **Communication** *The Ghost Room*
A *p104* **B** *p.109*. Look at the picture of another haunted hotel room for one minute. Try to remember what there was in the room.

Gosforth Hall Inn - Room 11

7&8 Revise and Check

GRAMMAR

Circle a, b, or c.

1. The Brontë sisters _____ all writers.
   a was b were c is
2. Where _____ Shakespeare born?
   a was b were c is
3. _____ the tickets expensive?
   a Was b Were c Did
4. I _____ a good film on TV last night.
   a watched b watch c watches
5. They _____ at Stamford Bridge stadium.
   a didn't arrived
   b don't arrived
   c didn't arrive
6. _____ you see the football match last night?
   a Did b Do c Was
7. We _____ to Istanbul three years ago.
   a go b were c went
8. When _____ in Los Angeles?
   a you live
   b did you lived
   c did you live
9. I _____ you at the party last night.
   a didn't saw b didn't see c don't saw
10. What time _____ home?
    a did you get b you did get c you got
11. _____ a big table in the living room.
    a There are b There is c It is
12. How many bedrooms _____?
    a there are b are there c are they
13. There aren't _____ pictures on the walls.
    a any b some c a
14. _____ only three guests in the dining room.
    a There was b There were c There is
15. How many people _____ in the hotel?
    a there were
    b was there
    c were there

VOCABULARY

a Complete the professions with -er, -or, -ist, or -ian.
   1 act____   3 paint____   5 scient____
   2 art____   4 music____

b Complete the phrases with have, go, or get.
   1 _____ a good time   4 _____ a taxi
   2 _____ an email   5 _____ a holiday
   3 _____ away for the weekend

c Complete the sentences with back, by, in, out, or to.
   1 I went _____ with my friends on Saturday night.
   2 They went home _____ car.
   3 What time did you get _____ the restaurant?
   4 I was born _____ 1982.
   5 After lunch I went _____ to work.

d Label the pictures.
   1 _____ 2 _____ 3 _____ 4 _____ 5 _____

e Write the prepositions.
   1 _____ 2 _____ 3 _____ 4 _____ 5 _____

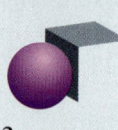

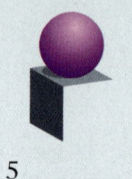

PRONUNCIATION

a Circle the word with a different sound.
   1 /ɪd/   wanted   waited   lived   ended
   2 /ɔː/   saw   wore   thought could
   3 /e/   heard   met   said   left
   4 /eə/   near   there   wear   stairs
   5 /h/   hall   heating hour   behind

b Underline the stressed syllable.
   1 mu|si|cian 2 a|go 3 ye|ster|day 4 be|tween 5 fire|place

CAN YOU UNDERSTAND THIS TEXT?

a Read the text and mark the sentences **T** (true) or **F** (false).

1 Arthur Conan Doyle was Scottish, but he worked in England.
2 He started writing stories about Sherlock Holmes at university.
3 Conan Doyle lived at 221b Baker Street in London.
4 In 1893 he didn't want to write more Sherlock Holmes stories.
5 Sherlock Homes didn't die in Austria.
6 Sherlock Holmes is very popular today.

b Look at the highlighted words or phrases in the text and guess their meaning.

The man who wrote
SHERLOCK HOLMES

Arthur Conan Doyle was born in Edinburgh on 22nd May 1859. He studied medicine at Edinburgh University and as a student he began writing short stories. He became a doctor in the south of England, but at first he didn't have many patients. So in his free time he began writing stories about a brilliant detective, Sherlock Holmes. Conan Doyle based Holmes' personality on his professor at university. Holmes, who lives at 221b Baker Street in London, is famous for solving difficult crimes and mysteries using his great intelligence. The Sherlock Holmes stories soon became very popular, but in 1893 Conan Doyle became tired of his detective, and decided to 'kill' him. In *The Final Problem* Sherlock Holmes and his enemy, Professor Moriarty, die when they fall off the Reichenbach Falls in Switzerland. But people were very unhappy to lose Sherlock Holmes, and there were letters in many newspapers asking for him to come back. Finally, in 1901 Conan Doyle brought him back in a new story, *The Hound of the Baskervilles*. He explained that Holmes did not die in the Reichenbach Falls, but miraculously survived. Conan Doyle died on 7th July 1930, but Sherlock Holmes continues to live both in the stories and in many film versions. Recently he was the inspiration for the character Dr Gregory House in the TV series *House*.

CAN YOU UNDERSTAND THESE PEOPLE?

4 28)) In the street Watch or listen to five people and answer the questions.

Heba   Polly   Alison   Sarah Jane   Ben

1 Heba _____.
  a has family in New York
  b lives in Egypt
  c was born in Cairo
2 Polly went out for dinner on _____.
  a Friday   b Saturday   c Sunday
3 Alison likes her kitchen because _____.
  a it's really big
  b she can eat there
  c it's practical for cooking
4 Sarah Jane can see _____ from her study.
  a a tree in her garden
  b the sea
  c her mother's house
5 Yesterday evening Ben _____.
  a went out to the pub
  b worked at home
  c went to bed early

CAN YOU SAY THIS IN ENGLISH?

Do the tasks with a partner. Tick (✓) the box if you can do them.

Can you…?

1 ☐ say three things about a famous (dead) person from your country
2 ☐ say five things you did last week, using past time expressions, e.g. *last night*, *yesterday*, (*three*) *days ago*, etc.
3 ☐ say where and when you were born
4 ☐ ask your partner five questions about yesterday

Short films Edinburgh Castle
Watch and enjoy a film on iTutor.

G countable / uncountable nouns; *a / an*, *some / any*
V food
P the letters *ea*

What did you have for lunch?

A pizza and some salad.

9A What I ate yesterday

1 VOCABULARY food

a What food words do you know in English? With a partner, try to think of five words.

b ▶ p.163 Vocabulary Bank *Food*.

2 READING

a Look at the photos which show meals that three people – a model, a boxer, and a writer – ate yesterday. Guess which person ate which meal.

b Read three articles from a series *What I ate yesterday* in *The Times* newspaper. Check your answers to **a**.

c Read the articles again. Answer the questions with **M** (the model), **B** (the boxer), or **W** (the writer). Who…?

1 doesn't like eating during the day
2 doesn't eat anything between meals
3 didn't have any home-cooked food for lunch or dinner
4 had fruit for dessert at lunchtime
5 never eats meat
6 didn't drink any alcohol yesterday
7 had a drink and a snack before dinner
8 doesn't eat anything for breakfast
9 has a strange breakfast habit

d With a partner, look at the highlighted words related to food and guess their meaning. Use the photos to help you.

e Whose food do you prefer? Why?

sushi a typical Japanese dish made with rice
porridge hot cooked cereal which British people often have for breakfast
chorizo a kind of Spanish sausage

What I ate yesterday

Laura Bailey *model*

Breakfast I never miss breakfast! I had some cereal and fruit, and a piece of toast. I'm a bit unusual because I have tea and coffee in the morning. I don't mind in which order, but I need to have both.

Lunch I was at my studio all day, so I got takeaway vegetarian sushi from a restaurant called *Itsu*. I became a vegetarian 20 years ago and now I can't imagine living any other way.

Dinner I picked up my children from school and we had a snack – cheese and biscuits. In the evening I went to my favourite pizzeria, and I had a vegetarian pasta dish, and two glasses of white wine.

James deGale *boxer*

Breakfast I woke up and went running for an hour and a half, then I came home and had a cup of tea and some porridge. Then I went to the gym and trained.

Lunch I had a bowl of pasta with chorizo and bacon in tomato sauce with cheese on top, and an apple and an orange. I have an important fight soon, so my diet has to be very strict now. Three meals a day, and no snacks.

Dinner I had a grilled chicken breast and vegetables – mushrooms, sweetcorn and tomatoes. My mum made it – she's a fantastic cook.

Lionel Shriver *writer*

Breakfast I had an enormous cup of espresso coffee with some milk and a little cream. It's all that I need and gives me energy for the whole day.

Lunch I don't eat lunch. I don't understand people who can eat three meals a day. How do they find the time to do anything else?

Dinner First I had a glass of sherry and a bowl of popcorn. Then I had grilled fish with some brown rice and vegetables – peppers and onions. For dessert I had a piece of chocolate cake. I drank red wine.

3 GRAMMAR countable / uncountable nouns; a / an, some / any

a Look at the photos. Complete the gaps with *a*, *an*, or *some*.

1 _____ strawberry
2 _____ tomato
3 _____ rice
4 _____ biscuits
5 _____ onion

b ▶ p.140 Grammar Bank 9A. Learn more about countable / uncountable nouns, etc. and practise them.

c Make sentences with *there's a / an / some…* and *there are some…* Choose food and drink from p.163 Vocabulary Bank *Food*.

4 PRONUNCIATION the letters *ea*

a How is *ea* pronounced in these words? Put them in the correct column.

| bread | breakfast | eat | healthy | ice cream |
| meat | peas | steak | tea | |

tree	egg	train

b (4 31)) Listen and check. Practise saying them. Which is the most common pronunciation of *ea*?

5 SPEAKING

a Make a food diary for yesterday. Write down what food and drink you had. Use **Vocabulary Bank** *Food p.163* to help you.

Breakfast *a cup of coffee, some cereal*

b Work in pairs. Tell each other what you had yesterday. Was it very similar or very different?

For breakfast I had a cup of coffee and some cereal.

6 LISTENING

a What cookery programmes do you have on TV in your country? What do you think of them? Do you sometimes cook their recipes?

b (4 32)) Listen to part 1 of a TV cooking competition called *Get ready! Cook!* where contestants have to cook a starter, a main course, and a dessert. Answer the questions.

1 How many ingredients are there in the bag?
2 How long do the contestants have to cook their dishes?
3 Name *three* of the basic ingredients they can use.

c (4 33)) Listen to part 2. Complete the dishes that Jack and Liz make.

Jack	Judge's comments
1 _____ and _____ soup	
2 _____ breasts filled with cream _____	
3 pancakes with _____ sauce	

Liz	Judge's comments
1 carrot and _____ salad with _____ dressing	
2 _____ with creamy _____ sauce	
3 _____ and _____ mousse	

d ▶ **Communication** *Get ready! Cook! p.109* Look at the photos of their dishes. Whose dishes do you prefer?

e (4 34)) Listen to part 3. What does the judge say about Jack and Liz's dishes? Who wins?

f In pairs, think of one of your favourite dishes. Write the ingredients you need. Tell your partner.

G quantifiers: *how much / how many*, *a lot of*, etc.
V food containers
P /ʃ/ and /s/

How much salt does it have?
Not much.

9B White gold

1 VOCABULARY food containers

a ◀4 35❙)) Match the words and pictures. Listen and check.

☐ a **b**ottle   ☐ a **b**ox   ☐ a **c**an   ☐ a **c**arton   ☐ a jar   ☐ a **p**acket   ☐ a tin

b ◀4 36❙)) Listen and write five phrases.

c Make phrases with the containers and the words below.

a packet of biscuits

biscuits   chocolates   Coke   crisps   juice   jam   milk   salt   sugar   tuna

2 GRAMMAR

quantifiers: *how much / how many*, *a lot of*, etc.

a Look at the pictures at the bottom of the page. Then ask and answer questions about the food.

a lot   quite a lot   a little   none

How much sugar is there in dark chocolate?
I'm not sure. I think there's a lot.

b ▶ **Communication** *Sugar and salt* p.109. Check your answers to **a**.

c Complete the sentences with a food or drink from **a**.
1 There **isn't any** salt in _____.
2 There's **a little** sugar in _____.
3 There's **quite a lot of** salt in _____.
4 There's **a lot of** sugar in _____.

d ▶ **p.140 Grammar Bank 9B.** Learn more about quantifiers and practise them.

3 PRONUNCIATION /ʃ/ and /s/

a ◀4 38❙)) Listen and repeat the words and sounds.

ʃ shower	sugar fish	s snake	salt sweets

b ◀4 39❙)) Put the words in the right column. Listen and check.

cereal   cinema   delicious   fresh
information   centre   rice   crisps   reception
salad   science   shopping   special   sure

c ◀4 40❙)) Listen and repeat the dialogue. Then practise it with a partner.

A Are you **s**ure thi**s** is salt? I think it'**s s**ugar.
B No, I'm **s**ure it'**s** salt. I put **s**ome in the ri**c**e salad.
A Let'**s** taste the salad... Aargh. It wa**s s**ugar. I told you.
B Sorry!

How much sugar?   *How much salt?*

4 SPEAKING

a Read the questionnaire and complete the questions with *How much* or *How many*.

> **How much sugar and salt do YOU have a day?**
>
> **Sugar**
> 1 _____ spoonfuls of sugar do you have in your tea or coffee?
>   a three or more   b two   c one   d none
> 2 _____ cans of cola (or other fizzy drinks) do you drink a day?
>   a three or more   b two   c one   d none
> 3 _____ fruit or fruit juice do you have a day?
>   a a lot   b quite a lot   c not much   d none
> 4 _____ sweets or biscuits do you eat a week?
>   a a lot   b not many   c very few   d none
>
> **Salt**
> 5 How often do you add salt to your food at the table?
>   a always   b often   c sometimes   d never
> 6 _____ takeaway food do you eat?
>   a a lot   b quite a lot   c not much   d none
> 7 _____ bread do you eat a day?
>   a a lot   b quite a lot   c a little   d none
> 8 _____ cheese do you eat a week?
>   a a lot   b quite a lot   c a little   d none

b In pairs, interview your partner. Do you think he / she needs to eat less sugar and salt?

c Work in pairs. **A** say how much you eat / drink of the things below. **B** respond and ask for more information. Then say if you think **A** has a healthy diet or not. Swap roles.

> fish   meat   potatoes   vegetables   chocolate
> fast food   eggs   pasta   olive oil   butter

I eat a lot of fish.   *How often do you eat fish?*

5 READING

a Read the magazine article *White Gold*. With a partner, complete the facts with *sugar* or *salt*.

b Read the article again, and highlight five new words or phrases. Compare with a partner.

c Did any of the facts surprise you?

6 🔊 4 41 SONG *Sugar Sugar* 🎵

WHITE GOLD
FASCINATING FACTS ABOUT SUGAR AND SALT

At different times in history, both sugar and salt were called 'white gold', because they were so expensive and difficult to get. But there are many more interesting facts about sugar and salt…

- Christopher Columbus introduced ^{1}_____ to the New World in 1493 on his second voyage.
- If you eat too much ^{2}_____ (about 1 gram per kilogram of weight), you can die. This was a method of ritual suicide in ancient China.
- Salzburg in Austria was called 'the city of ^{3}_____' because of its mines.
- If you want to check if an egg is fresh, put it in a cup with water and ^{4}_____. If the egg floats, it isn't very fresh.
- In Brazil fuel made from ^{5}_____ is used in cars instead of petrol.
- Americans eat or drink about 2.25 kilos of ^{6}_____ a month.
- ^{7}_____ is used to make glass, washing powder, and paper.
- ^{8}_____ kills some bacteria, and so helps food to last longer, which is why bacon and cheese contain a lot.
- If you put ^{9}_____ into a vase of flowers, the flowers last longer.
- ^{10}_____ only contains energy. It doesn't contain any vitamins or minerals.
- *Sure* and ^{11}_____ are the only two words in the English language that begin with 'su' and are pronounced 'sh'.
- We need to have a little ^{12}_____ in our diet, but not more than 6g a day, which is about one teaspoon.

9C Quiz night

G comparative adjectives
V high numbers
P /ə/, sentence stress

"Is Scotland bigger than Wales?"
"Yes, it's three times bigger."

1 VOCABULARY high numbers

a Read three questions from a radio quiz show. Choose the right answer for each question.

1 What is the approximate population of the UK?
 a 42,000,000
 b 52,000,000
 c 62,000,000

2 How many calories are there in a Big Mac?
 a 670
 b 485
 c 305

3 How far is it from New York City to Los Angeles?
 a about 4,000 km
 b about 2,500 km
 c about 5,000 km

b 4 42)) Listen and check. How do you say the three answers?

c ▶ p.148 **Vocabulary Bank** *Days and numbers.* Do part 4.

d Look at the numbers below. Correct the mistakes.

175	a hundred seventy-five
2,150	two thousand and one hundred and fifty
3,009	three thousand nine
20,000	twenty thousands
3,000,000	three millions

e 4 44)) Listen and write the ten numbers you hear.

f Answer the questions with a partner.
1 What's the population of your town / city?
2 What's the population of your country?
3 How far is it from your town / city to…?
 a London
 b New York

2 LISTENING

a 4 45)) What quiz shows are popular in your country? Listen to the introduction to a quiz show called *Quiz Night*. Answer the questions.
1 How long do the contestants have to say if the sentences are true or false?
2 How much do they win if they get…?
 a the first answer right _____
 b the second answer right _____
 c the third answer right _____
 d all eight answers right _____
3 If they get an answer wrong, how much do they lose?
4 What can a contestant do if they are not sure of the answer?

b In pairs, look at the sentences from *Quiz Night*. Write **T** (true) or **F** (false).

c 4 46)) Listen to a contestant on *Quiz Night*. Check your answers to **b**. How much does she win?

d Listen again for why the answers are true or false. Write down any numbers you hear.

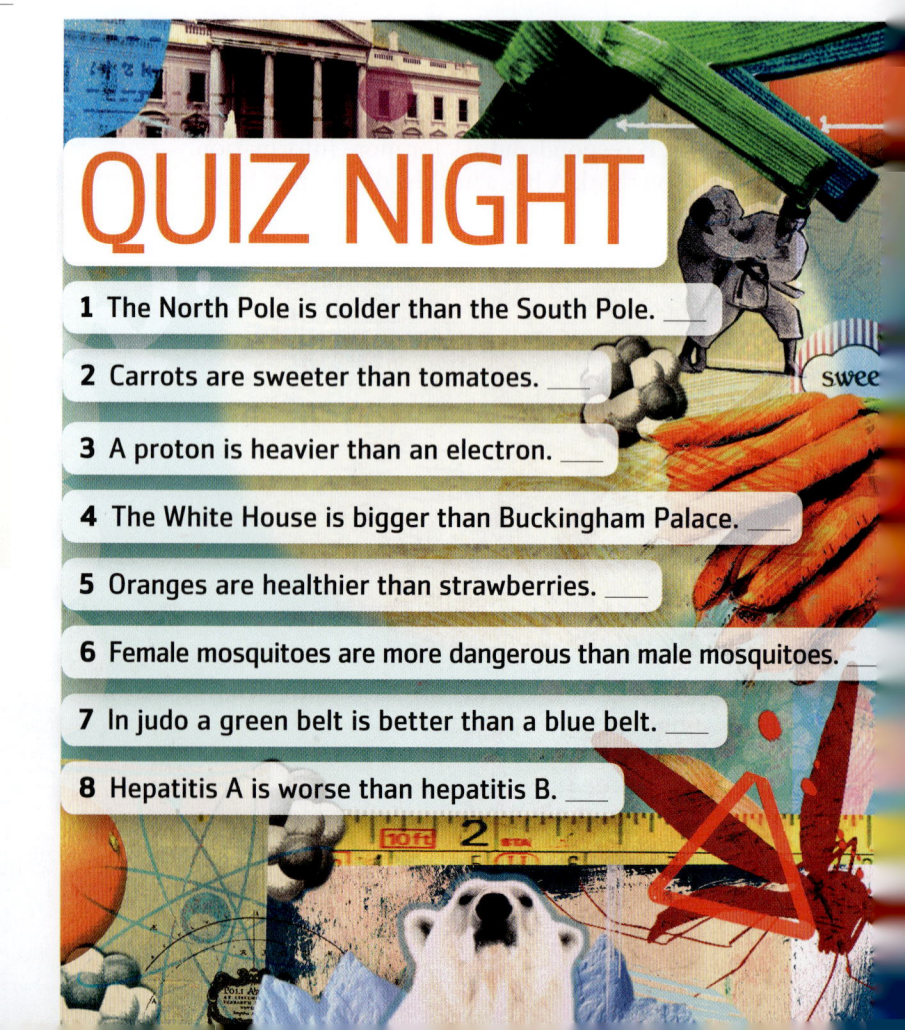

QUIZ NIGHT

1 The North Pole is colder than the South Pole. ___
2 Carrots are sweeter than tomatoes. ___
3 A proton is heavier than an electron. ___
4 The White House is bigger than Buckingham Palace. ___
5 Oranges are healthier than strawberries. ___
6 Female mosquitoes are more dangerous than male mosquitoes. ___
7 In judo a green belt is better than a blue belt. ___
8 Hepatitis A is worse than hepatitis B. ___

3 GRAMMAR comparative adjectives

a Look at the adjectives in the quiz sentences. In pairs, answer the questions.

Using adjectives to compare two things:
1 What two letters do you put at the end of one-syllable adjectives (e.g. *cold*)?
2 Why is *big* different?
3 What happens when an adjective ends in *-y*?
4 What word do you put in front of long adjectives (e.g. *dangerous*)?
5 What's the comparative form of *good* and *bad*?
6 What's the missing word?
   China is bigger ___ Japan.

b ▶ p.140 Grammar Bank 9C. Learn more about comparative adjectives and practise them.

4 PRONUNCIATION
/ə/, sentence stress

a (4 48)) Listen to the eight quiz sentences from **2**. How is *than* pronounced? How is *-er* pronounced at the end of a word?

b Listen again and repeat the sentences. Copy the rhythm.

5 SPEAKING
▶ **Communication** *Quiz Night* **A** p.105 **B** p.110. Play *Quiz Night*.

6 READING

a Read about two quiz shows. Do you have the same or similar shows in your country? Do you enjoy them?

b Now read about Pat Gibson. Why is he 'the best quiz contestant in the country'?

c Read the article again and complete it with a verb from the list in the past simple.

| answer | be | become | get | ~~have~~ |
| help | know | phone | win | |

d With a partner, look at the highlighted words in the texts related to quiz shows and guess their meaning.

e Would you like to be a contestant on a quiz show? Which one?

Who Wants to Be a Millionaire?
A quiz show where contestants can win a maximum prize of one million pounds if they can answer multiple choice questions which become more and more difficult. Contestants have three possibilities of getting help: they can ask the audience, reduce the four choices to two, or they can phone a friend.

Mastermind
A quiz programme where contestants answer questions on a specialist subject which they choose, and then answer general knowledge questions.

Q Who is the best quiz contestant in the country?
A Pat Gibson

Last night Pat Gibson [1] *had* a big party after winning *Mastermind* on BBC TV. But it [2]_____ not his first celebration party. Last April Mr Gibson [3]_____ £1 million in *Who Wants to Be a Millionaire?* and [4]_____ the first person in Britain to win both quizzes.

In the *Mastermind* final Pat, a 43-year-old computer programmer who is obsessed with trivia, beat five other contestants, including a university lecturer. During the competition he [5]_____ questions on several specialist subjects, for example film director Quentin Tarantino and science fiction author Iain M Banks.

In *Who Wants to Be a Millionaire?* he [6]_____ to the final question and still had the possibility of phoning a friend for help. He was sure that he [7]_____ the answer, but he [8]_____ Mark Kerr, a friend, to double-check it. Mark was happy to help him – six weeks before, Pat [9]_____ Mark to win £250,000 on the same show as **his** phone-a-friend!

Adapted from a news website

Practical English At a restaurant

1 🎬 AN INVITATION TO DINNER

a ◉ 4 49))) Watch or listen and mark the sentences **T** (true) or **F** (false).
1 Jenny and Rob worked last night.
2 Jenny wants to read Rob's article.
3 It's Eddie's birthday today.
4 Rob and Daniel invite Jenny to dinner.
5 Jenny says yes to Rob.

b Watch or listen again. Say why the **F** sentences are false.

c ◉ 4 50))) Read the information box. Listen and repeat **B**'s phrases.

> 🔍 **Responding to what somebody says**
> 1 **A** It's my birthday today.   **B** Happy birthday!
> 2 **A** We won the cup!   **B** Congratulations!
> 3 **A** I have my driving test tomorrow. **B** Good luck!
> 4 **A** I got all my English homework right. **B** Well done!
> 5 **A** I didn't get the job.   **B** Oh dear! Never mind.

d ◉ 4 51))) Listen and respond with phrases from the box.
))) *I got two goals this afternoon.*   (*Well done!*

2 VOCABULARY
understanding a menu

a Complete the menu with **Main courses**, **Desserts**, or **Starters**.

b ◉ 4 52))) What do the highlighted words mean? How do you pronounce them? Listen and check.

c Cover the menu. In pairs, try to remember what's on the menu.

Luigi's

2 courses **£15.00**
3 courses **£22.50**

1 _____

Onion soup
Mozzarella and tomato salad

2 _____

Grilled chicken breast with vegetables
Mushroom ravioli
Seafood risotto

3 _____

Home-made vanilla ice cream with hot chocolate sauce
Fresh fruit salad
Tiramisu

EPISODE 5

3 ORDERING A MEAL

a (4 53)) Watch or listen to Jenny and Daniel having dinner. What food do they order?

b Watch or listen again. Complete the **You Hear** phrases.

))) You Hear	You Say
Good evening. Do you have a _____?	Yes, a table for two. My name's Daniel O'Connor.
Come this _____, please.	
Are you ready to _____?	Yes. The soup and the mushroom ravioli, please. I'd like the mozzarella salad and then the chicken, please.
What would you _____ to drink?	Just water for me. A bottle of mineral water, please.
_____ or sparkling?	Is sparkling OK? Yes, sparkling.
Thank you, sir.	Thank you.

c (4 54)) Watch or listen and repeat the **You Say** phrases. Copy the rhythm.

d Practise the dialogue in groups of three.

e In groups of three, roleplay the dialogue. **A** is the waiter. Start with *Good evening. Do you have a reservation?* **B** and **C** go to *Luigi's*. Then swap roles.

4 THE END OF THE MEAL

a (4 55)) Watch or listen and answer the questions.
1. How does Jenny normally celebrate her birthday?
2. Do they order dessert or coffee?
3. What does Daniel say to Jenny after the meal?
4. How does Jenny answer?
5. Does Barbara give Jenny good news or bad news?
6. Where does Jenny want to go after the meal?

b Look at the **Social English phrases**. Who says them: **J**enny, **D**aniel, the **w**aiter, or **B**arbara?

Social English phrases	
Nothing special.	The same for me, please.
Would you like a dessert?	Go ahead.
Not for me, thanks.	Good news?
A decaf espresso.	Could I have the bill, please?

c (4 56)) Watch or listen and check. Do you know what they are in your language?

d Watch or listen again and repeat the phrases.

> **Can you...?**
> ☐ use common phrases, e.g. *Good luck, Congratulations*, etc.
> ☐ understand a menu
> ☐ order a meal

iTutor

G superlative adjectives
V places and buildings
P consonant groups

> What's the oldest building in your town?
> I'm not sure. Probably the cathedral.

10A The most dangerous road...

1 VOCABULARY places and buildings

a Complete these famous tourist sights with a word from the list. Do you know what countries / cities they are in?

Bridge   Castle   Mountains   Square   Street

1 Trafalgar _____
2 The Golden Gate _____
3 Wall _____
4 Edinburgh _____
5 The Rocky _____

b 5 2)) Listen and check.

c ▶ p.164 Vocabulary Bank *Places and buildings*.

2 GRAMMAR superlative adjectives

a Look at the photos. Do you know what countries they are in?

b 5 4)) With a partner, complete the captions with a phrase from the list. Listen and check.

the biggest   the busiest   the most dangerous
the longest   the most popular   the widest

c Complete the chart with superlatives from **b**.

Adjective	Comparative	Superlative
big	bigger	the biggest
long	longer	
wide	wider	
busy	busier	
dangerous	more dangerous	
popular	more popular	

d What letters do you add to a one-syllable adjective to make a superlative? What words do you put before longer adjectives?

e ▶ p.142 Grammar Bank 10A. Learn more about superlative adjectives and practise them.

1 The Louvre is _____ art gallery in the world.

2 Vasco da Gama Bridge is _____ bridge in Europe.

3 The Yungas Road is _____ road in the world.

4 Tiananmen Square is _____ square in the world.

5 Avenida 9 de Julio in Buenos Aires is _____ street in the world.

6 Shinjuku Station in Tokyo is _____ railway station in the world.

3 PRONUNCIATION consonant groups

a **5 6))** Listen and repeat the adjectives in **2c**.

> **Consonant groups**
> Words which have two or three consonants together, e.g. *fastest*, can be difficult to pronounce.

b **5 7))** Listen and repeat these superlatives.

the mo**st** expensive   the mo**st** exciting   the **o**l**d**e**st**
the mo**st** beautiful   the **sm**alle**st**

c ▶ **Communication** *Cities quiz* **A** p.105 **B** p.110. Complete the questions with superlative adjectives. Then ask and answer the questions with a partner.

4 READING

a Read the article below and look at the photo. Would you like to go cycling there? Why (not)?

b Read the article again. Then cover the text and answer the questions in pairs.
1 Where is the North Yungas Road?
2 Why is it called 'Death Road'?
3 How wide is the road?
4 Why is it popular with cyclists?
5 When is the most dangerous time of year to go?
6 Why is the road similar to London Bridge and the Sydney Opera House?
7 Why didn't Marte enjoy cycling on the Yungas Road?

c In pairs, guess the meaning of the highlighted words.

d Is cycling popular in your country / region? Is there an area that is very popular for cyclists? Why?

5 SPEAKING & WRITING

a Work in pairs.

A Imagine you are a tourist in your town (or nearest big town) who only speaks English. Ask **B**, who lives in the town, questions 1–5. Get as much information as you can.

B You live in your town. **A** is a tourist who doesn't speak your language. Answer his / her questions (1–5). Explain everything very clearly and give as much information as you can!

Then swap roles for questions 6–10.

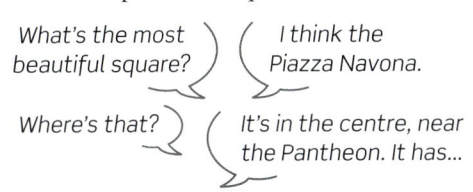

What's the most beautiful square?   *I think the Piazza Navona.*

Where's that?   *It's in the centre, near the Pantheon. It has…*

A
1 What's _____ square? (beautiful)
2 What's _____ way to get around? (easy)
3 What's _____ museum? (interesting)
4 What's _____ time of year to visit? (good)
5 What's _____ place to eat typical food? (nice)

B
6 What's _____ building? (old)
7 What's _____ place to go for a day trip? (nice)
8 What's _____ area to walk at night? (dangerous)
9 Where's _____ place to buy a souvenir? (good)
10 What's _____ area to go at night? (popular)

b Imagine you want to advertise your town / city for tourists. Write an advert using superlative adjectives. Add photos if you can.

Come to Kielce. It isn't the biggest or the most beautiful town in Poland, but it has the cleanest air and the most delicious cheesecake…

Cycling on the most dangerous road in the world

High in the Andes, the North Yungas Road goes from La Paz, the highest capital city in the world, to Coroico in the Yungas region of Bolivia. The road is only about three metres wide and the Coroico river lies 200 metres below. Bolivians call it 'El Camino de la Muerte' (Death Road) because of the number of accidents, and in 1995 it was officially declared 'the most dangerous road in the world.'

'One mistake and you are dead.'

Since a new road opened in 2006, there are fewer buses and lorries on the old road. But now thousands of mountain bikers come from all over the world to have the most exciting ride of their lives. They start at La Cumbre, 4,700 metres above sea level, and go down to 1,525 metres, travelling at nearly 80 km an hour down the narrow road. During the rainy season, from December to March, only experienced cyclists can take part, but some die every year on the road. So, why do people do it?

Andrew Jagoo, 26, from Melbourne, said after finishing the ride, 'If you go to London, you have to see London Bridge and if you go to Sydney, you have to see the Opera House and if you go to Bolivia, you have to do the most dangerous road.'

Marte Solberg, 22, from Norway said, 'A lot of people said it was fun, but I was scared of falling over and dying. I was worried because I had no experience of mountain biking. One mistake and you are dead. I asked myself a thousand times, "Why am I doing this?"'

Adapted from a news website

G be going to (plans), future time expressions
V holidays
P sentence stress

> What are you going to do?
> I'm going to travel round Europe.

10B CouchSurf round the world!

1 LISTENING

a Read the dictionary definition for *couch*, and look at the CouchSurfing website. What do you think CouchSurfing is?

> **couch** /kaʊtʃ/ *noun* **1** a long comfortable seat for two or more people to sit on (= a sofa) **2** the bed in a doctor's room for a patient to lie on

[CouchSurfing website screenshots]

Basic information: Male, 22. DJ. Has couch.
Languages: French, English
Description: I love travelling.

Host: **Artur Dorner**
Location: Vienna, Austria
Basic information: Male, 27. PhD student. Has couch.
Languages: German, English
Description: I love meeting people and showing them my wonderful city. Better to come at weekends when I have more time!

Host: **Judit Hetzke**
Location: Budapest, Hungary

b 5 8))) Listen to part of a radio travel programme. Were you right? How does CouchSurfing work?

c 5 9))) Now listen to the speaker give more details about CouchSurfing. Mark the sentences **T** (true) or **F** (false).

1 ☐ CouchSurfers usually pay their host a little money.
2 ☐ You need to create a profile on the website.
3 ☐ When you find a person with a bed, you call them to agree the days you want to stay.
4 ☐ You have to offer other people a bed in your house or flat.
5 ☐ CouchSurfing is safe because you can read what other travellers say about the host.
6 ☐ The host always shows their guests their city.
7 ☐ You can CouchSurf all over the world.

d Would you like to go CouchSurfing? Why (not)? Would you like to have a stranger to stay in *your* house? Why (not)?

2 GRAMMAR *be going to* (plans)

a 5 10))) A British newspaper asked their travel journalist to try CouchSurfing. Cover the dialogue and listen to the interview. What are his plans?

b Listen again and complete the gaps with a verb.

> **Presenter** Tell me about your plans, Philip.
> **Journalist** I'm going to ¹_____ round Europe – to Paris, Vienna, and Budapest.
> **P** How long are you going to ²_____ in each city?
> **J** Just one night in each place.
> **P** Who are you going to ³_____ with?
> **J** In Paris I'm going to stay with a guy called Théo, in Vienna with a guy called Artur, and in Budapest with a woman called Judit.
> **P** Are you going to ⁴_____ on a couch?
> **J** Only in Vienna, luckily. In the other places I have a bed.
> **P** How are you going to ⁵_____?
> **J** I'm going to ⁶_____ by train.
> **P** What are you going to ⁷_____ in each place?
> **J** I don't just want to see the typical tourist sights. I hope I'm going to ⁸_____ things that aren't in a guide book.
> **P** Well, have a good trip and good luck!

c Look at the highlighted sentences in the dialogue. Then answer the questions.
1 What form is the verb after *going to*?
2 Do we use *going to* to talk about the past, the present, or the future?

d ▶ p.142 **Grammar Bank 10B.** Learn more about *be going to* (plans) and practise it.

e Number the future time expressions 1–8.

☐ tonight   ☐ tomorrow night
☐ next year ☐ today (1)
☐ tomorrow morning ☐ next week
☐ next month ☐ tomorrow afternoon

f 5 12))) Listen and check. Then listen again and repeat. Make four true sentences about your plans.

78

3 PRONUNCIATION & SPEAKING
sentence stress

a ◯13))) Listen and repeat the highlighted phrases in **2b**. Copy the rhythm.

I'm **go**ing to **tra**vel round **Eu**rope.

b ▶ **Communication** *What are you going to do?* **A** *p.105* **B** *p.110*. Interview a partner about his / her plans.

4 READING

a Read the journalist's blog for his trip. Did he have a good time?

b Read the blog again and tick (✓) the things that were a problem.
1 He didn't arrive at the right time at one of the houses.
2 He couldn't understand the host's friends very well.
3 One host didn't have much time to show him the city.
4 One of the hosts didn't speak very good English.
5 He did something wrong in one of the flats.
6 He didn't like the food that one of the hosts cooked.

c Read the blog again and look at the highlighted verb phrases. With a partner, say what you think they mean.

Paris: Théo
I met Théo at the Place D'Italie metro station. He's 24 and his English is good. At his apartment I met his flatmate, Roger. They were very friendly. They made me a delicious dinner of crêpes and ham and eggs. Then they took me to Footsie, a great bar near the Opéra. Some friends came and in the end the conversation changed to French. That was difficult for me and I got tired. Finally, we went to a party near Montmartre. It was great! Lots of friendly people. I went back to Théo's flat on the back of his bicycle.

Vienna: Artur
I stayed with Artur, a biochemistry student. He was friendly, but when I arrived I wanted to have a bath and I forgot to turn off the tap. The bathroom was full of water. Oops!

Budapest: Judit
I got off the train at the wrong station so I arrived late at Judit's flat. She wasn't very happy. She's a journalist for the Hungarian channels MTV and TV2 and she's an incredibly busy woman. In the afternoon she took me with her to a shopping centre to help her choose a dress for a party. That was a bit surreal! In the evening we had dinner together in the Castro bar in the city centre. Next day I flew home to London, tired but happy. I'm definitely going to do it again!

Adapted from a news website

5 VOCABULARY & SPEAKING
holidays

a Complete the holiday phrases using a verb from the list.

go   have   see   stay   show

1 _____ in a hotel / with a friend / for a week
2 _____ somebody round your town / city
3 _____ the sights
4 _____ by train (bus, plane) / back home
5 _____ a good time / nice meals

b In pairs, plan a holiday. You are going to visit **three** cities in the same continent. Your holiday can be a maximum of **ten** days.

Answer the questions:
- What cities are you going to visit?
- Where are you going to stay?
- How are you going to get there?
- How long are you going to stay in each city?
- What are you going to do in each place?

> 🔍 **Making suggestions**
> Let's (go to...)   I prefer to (go to...)
> Why don't we (go to...)? That's a good idea.

c Change partners. Tell each other about your holiday plans.

> *We're going to go to South America – to Buenos Aires, Rio, and Montevideo. We're going to CouchSurf because we don't have much money...*

d Do you prefer your new partner's plans? Would you like to change partners and go with him / her?

6 WRITING

▶ **p.115 Writing** *A formal email*. Make a reservation in a Bed and Breakfast.

79

G *be going to* (predictions)
V verb phrases
P the letters *oo*

Am I going to fall in love?
Yes, and you're going to be very happy.

10C What's going to happen?

1 VOCABULARY verb phrases

a Do people in your country go to fortune-tellers, or use fortune-telling sites on the internet? Do *you* believe in fortune-telling?

b Match the fortune-teller's cards and verb phrases.

- [ ] become famous
- [ ] get a new job
- [ ] get married
- [ ] meet somebody new
- [ ] fall in love
- [ ] get a lot of money
- [ ] have a surprise
- [A] be lucky
- [ ] travel
- [ ] move house

2 READING & LISTENING

a 5 14))) Read and listen to **PART 1** of a story. In pairs, answer the questions.
1 Who does Jane want to see?
2 Who is going to tell her about her future? Why?
3 Why couldn't she see the man very well?

b 5 15))) Listen to part 2. Then, with a partner, complete the information.
1 Jane has a problem with her _____.
2 She chooses _____ cards.
3 Her first card means she's going to be _____.
4 Jane asks the fortune-teller if she's going to _____ with her boyfriend.

c 5 16))) Read and listen to **PART 3**. In pairs, answer the questions.
1 What's the second card? What does it mean?
2 Why is this a problem for Jane?
3 What's her third card? What does it mean?
4 Who's Jim? Where did Jane meet him?
5 What do you think the fourth card is going to be?

d 5 17))) Listen to part 4. Then, with a partner, complete the information.
1 Her fourth card means she is going to _____ her boyfriend and go away with Jim to _____.
2 Very soon they are going to _____.
3 Jane asks if she is going to be _____ and the fortune-teller says _____.
4 She pays the fortune-teller £_____.

e 5 18))) Read and listen to **PART 5**. In pairs, answer the questions.
1 Who was the fortune-teller?
2 Why did he pay Madame Yolanda £100?
3 What's the fifth card? What do you think is going to happen?

It's written in the cards

PART 1

'Come in,' said a voice. Jane Ross opened the door and went into a small room. There was a man sitting behind a table.
  'Good afternoon,' said Jane.
  'I want to see Madame Yolanda, the fortune-teller.'
  'Madame Yolanda isn't here today,' said the man. 'But don't worry. I'm going to tell you about your future. What questions do you want to ask?' Jane looked at the fortune-teller. She couldn't see him very well because the room was very dark.

PART 3

He turned over the second card.
  'Mm, a house. A new house. You're going to move, very soon, to another country.'
  'But my boyfriend works here. He can't move to another country.'
  'Let's look at the next card,' said the fortune-teller. He turned over the third card.
  'A heart. You're going to fall in love.'
  'Who with?' asked Jane.
  'Let me concentrate. I can see a tall dark man. He's very attractive.'
  'Oh, that's Jim,' said Jane.
  'Who's Jim? Your boyfriend?'
  'No. Jim's a man I met at a party last month. He's an actor, from New York. He says he's in love with me. It was his idea for me to come to Madame Yolanda.'
  'Well, the card says that you're going to fall in love with him.'
  'Are you sure?' asked Jane. 'But what about my boyfriend?'
  'Let's look at the fourth card,' said the fortune-teller.

PART 5

The fortune-teller stood up. He turned on the light. At that moment an old woman came in. 'So, what happened?' she asked.
  'It was perfect! She believed everything,' said Jim. 'I told you, I'm a very good actor. She was sure I was a fortune-teller!'
  He gave the woman £100.
  'That's Jane's £50 and another £50 from me. Thanks very much, Madame Yolanda. Bye.'
  Madame Yolanda took the money. The fifth card was still on the table, face down. She turned it over. It was the plane. She looked at it for a minute and then she shouted:
  ' Wait, young man! Don't travel with that girl – her plane is going to...'
  But the room was empty.

3 GRAMMAR be going to (predictions)

a Look at these two sentences. Which one is a <u>plan</u>? Which one is a <u>prediction</u>?
  1 She's going to be very lucky.
  2 She's going to go on holiday next week.

b ▶ p.142 Grammar Bank 10C. Learn more about *be going to* (predictions) and practise it.

c Write four predictions, about the **weather**, **sport**, **your town** / **country**, and **you**. Use *I think…going to…*
  I think it's going to snow tonight.

d Compare your predictions with a partner. Do you agree?

4 PRONUNCIATION the letters *oo*

> **The pronunciation of *oo***
> *oo* can be pronounced /ʊ/ (e.g. *book* /bʊk/) or /uː/ (e.g. *spoon* /spuːn/). Use your dictionary to check the pronunciation of new *oo* words.
> Be careful, *room* can be pronounced /rʊm/ or /ruːm/.

a **5 20**))) Listen to the two sound words. Can you hear the difference in the vowel sound?

ʊ bull	uː boot

b **5 21**))) Listen and write the words in the right column.

afternoon   book   choose   cook   food   good
look   moon   school   soon   spoon   too   took

c **5 22**))) Listen and check.

d Practise saying the sentences.

  Good afternoon.   *It's too soon!*
  Look at the moon!   *Is the food good?*
  He's a good-looking cook.

5 SPEAKING

Roleplay fortune-telling.

A Look at the ten cards in **1**. Secretly, number the cards 1–10 in a different order.
B Choose five numbers 1–10.
A Predict **B**'s future using those cards.
B Ask for more information. Then change roles.

A *I'm going to tell you about your future. Your first card is a star. You're going to become famous. You're going to be on TV...*

B *Great! What programme?*

6 **5 23**))) SONG *Fortune Teller* ♪

9 & 10 Revise and Check

GRAMMAR

Circle a, b, or c.

1 There's _____ milk in the fridge.
  a some b any c a
2 We don't need _____ bread.
  a no b any c a
3 How _____ fruit do you eat a day?
  a much b many c a lot
4 I drink _____ coffee.
  a much b a lot c a lot of
5 A How much salt do you eat?
  B _____.
  a A little b A few c Much
6 A Is there any sugar?
  B No, sorry, _____.
  a there isn't none
  b there isn't any
  c there isn't some
7 Tea is _____ coffee in this café.
  a cheaper that
  b more cheap than
  c cheaper than
8 Oranges are _____ than bananas.
  a more healthy b healthier c healthyer
9 My English is _____ than my brother's.
  a gooder b better c more good
10 This is _____ size that we have.
  a the biggest b the most big c the bigger
11 It's _____ restaurant in the city.
  a the baddest b the worst c the worse
12 What's _____ park in your town?
  a the most beautiful
  b most beautiful
  c the more beautiful
13 _____ to buy my ticket this afternoon.
  a I go b I going c I'm going
14 _____ to get married?
  a Do they going
  b They are going
  c Are they going
15 I think _____ tomorrow.
  a it snows
  b it's snowing
  c it's going to snow

VOCABULARY

a Circle the word that is different.

1 breakfast   lunch   dessert   dinner
2 strawberries mushrooms   onions   peas
3 orange juice sugar   milk   mineral water
4 crisps   chips   tomatoes   potatoes
5 fruit salad ice cream   cake   chicken

b Match the food and the containers.

| beer fruit juice rice tomatoes honey |

1 a can of _____   3 a jar of _____   5 a carton of _____
2 a tin of _____   4 a packet of _____

c Circle the right word or phrase.

1 It's *a hundred twenty* / *a hundred and twenty* miles from here.
2 The population is about three *million* / *millions*.
3 That new *department shop* / *department store* is great.
4 Let's have a drink at one of those cafés in the *square* / *bridge*.
5 Where is the main railway *centre* / *station*?

d Complete the phrases with these verbs.

| become fall get go have meet move see show stay |

1 _____ in a hotel   6 _____ the sights in a city
2 _____ by bus   7 _____ somebody new
3 _____ famous   8 _____ somebody round your city
4 _____ married   9 _____ a great meal
5 _____ in love   10 _____ house

PRONUNCIATION

a Circle the word with a different sound.

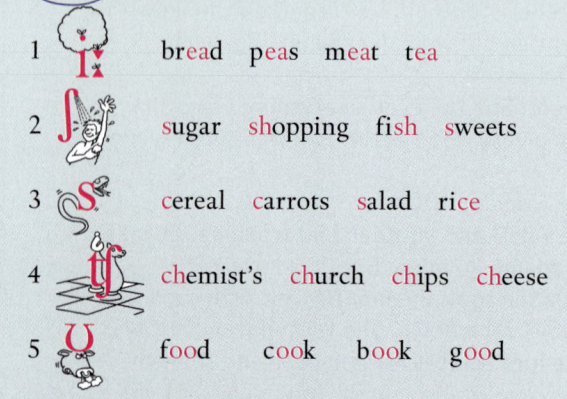

1 br**ea**d   p**ea**s   m**ea**t   t**ea**
2 **s**ugar   **sh**opping   fi**sh**   **s**weets
3 **c**ereal   **c**arrots   sa**l**ad   **r**ice
4 **ch**emist's   **ch**urch   **ch**ips   **ch**eese
5 f**oo**d   c**oo**k   b**oo**k   g**oo**d

b Underline the stressed syllable.

1 cho|colate   3 su|per|mar|ket   5 dan|ge|rous
2 de|ssert   4 in|teres|ting

CAN YOU UNDERSTAND THIS TEXT?

a Read the article once. Then read it again and choose a, b, or c.

1 In British supermarkets people now _____.
   a buy more healthy food than before
   b buy less healthy food than before
   c buy the same kind of food they bought before
2 When people have a problem or big change in their lives they often _____.
   a eat unhealthy food   b eat a lot   c eat healthy food
3 If you want to eat healthily, you need to _____.
   a spend a lot of money
   b learn to cook
   c stop worrying about what you eat

b Look at the highlighted words or phrases in the text and guess their meaning.

The British diet – STILL UNHEALTHY

Britain has a problem with obesity (more than 50% of the population are fat or overweight) and the government says we need to have a healthier diet. However, British shoppers are continuing to fill their supermarket baskets with unhealthy food.

A survey of 12 million consumers showed that 44 per cent of people have the same unhealthy eating habits that they had four years ago. The survey also found that shoppers who normally have a very healthy diet start buying junk food, e.g. frozen pizzas, crisps, and cakes, if there is a crisis in their lives, for example divorce, moving house, or losing a job.

Another thing the survey showed is that there is not much difference in price between a healthy shopping basket and an unhealthy one. A typical healthy basket costs, on average, £71.78 compared with £71.18 for an unhealthy one. Martin Hayward, the director of the study said 'Many people don't eat healthily because they worry that healthy food is more expensive, but the survey shows that this is not true. We believe the reason why some people eat unhealthily is because they don't know how to cook so they buy ready-made meals.'

CAN YOU UNDERSTAND THESE PEOPLE?

5 24)) **In the street** Watch or listen to five people and answer the questions.

Yvonne   Alison   Joel   Andy   Arja

1 Yvonne doesn't eat much _____.
   a fruit   b sugar   c salt
2 Alison is good at cooking _____ food.
   a Italian   b Indian   c Indonesian
3 Joel likes Barcelona because there are a lot of _____.
   a great shops   b great buildings   c great beaches
4 Andy is going to travel for _____.
   a a month   b three months   c three weeks
5 When Arja compares the US to her country she doesn't mention _____.
   a the food   b the buildings   c the weather

CAN YOU SAY THIS IN ENGLISH?

Do the tasks with a partner. Tick (✓) the box if you can do them.

Can you…?

1 ☐ say what you usually have for breakfast
2 ☐ compare your country with the UK in three ways
3 ☐ ask your partner four questions with the superlative of the **bold** adjective
   • What's _____ present you've ever bought? **expensive**
   • What's _____ film you've seen this year? **good**
   • What's _____ holiday you've ever had? **bad**
   • What's _____ place you've ever been to? **cold**
4 ☐ ask your partner what he / she is going to do
   • tonight   • tomorrow   • next weekend

Short films the history of the sandwich
Watch and enjoy a film on iTutor.

G adverbs (manner and modifiers)
V common adverbs
P word stress

How do they dress? They dress very fashionably, but casually.

11A First impressions

1 READING

a Look at the photos of three cities. Do you know what countries they are in?

Atlanta

Malmö

Valencia

b Read two blogs on a UK travel website, about people's first impressions of two of these cities. Which two are they?

c Read the blogs again. Answer with the names of the cities.

Where…?
1 do people eat a lot of salt and sugar
2 do TV programmes have subtitles
3 are the days very short in winter
4 do a lot of people have bad habits when they drive
5 is the city safer than the writer thought
6 are the houses colourfully painted
7 do you see men looking after young children
8 do people speak very slowly

Travel blogs

16 September **Moira in _____**

The driving
I think people drive quite dangerously, which surprised me because I thought they were careful drivers here. They don't drive fast, but people are always on the phone in the car, which you don't often see in the UK nowadays.

The food
The food can be delicious, but I think people eat very unhealthily. In restaurants they often add salt to their food. And they drink litres of Coke! The headquarters of the Coca-Cola company is based here, and they even have a Coca-Cola museum. Once I went to a coffee shop and asked for a double espresso, no milk no sugar. I had to repeat my order three times, because the waitress couldn't understand me. She said people here only ask for lattes and cappuccinos with lots of sugar!

The people
In general, people are very friendly. The people I'm staying with, who live just outside the city, know all their neighbours really well. They often don't lock their doors, which surprised me because people say it's a dangerous city. They speak incredibly slowly, with a strong accent and sometimes I have a problem understanding them.

14 December **Mark in _____**

The weather
It's December – and it gets dark at about 3 p.m., which is depressing! There's a lot of snow at the moment, but all the buses and trains are running perfectly, not like in Britain where everything stops when it snows!

The houses
All the houses are painted in pretty colours, like red, green and blue, and many houses have a yellow and blue flag. Inside the houses are decorated beautifully with lots of flowers and modern wooden furniture.

The people
People are friendly and polite, but quite formal. They dress fashionably but casually, and of course you see a lot of very blonde women here. You also see a lot of men who are looking after very young babies. Everybody speaks English really well, maybe because a lot of the TV is in English with subtitles.

d Find words in the blogs which mean:

Moira
Para 1	_____ adv	at this time
Para 2	_____ noun	the office where the leaders of an organization work
Para 3	_____ verb	close with a key

Mark
Para 4	_____ adj	sth making you feel sad
Para 5	_____ adj	made from a tree
Para 6	_____ adv	not in a formal way

e Which of the two cities would you prefer to live in? Why?

2 GRAMMAR adverbs

a Look at the highlighted adverbs in the blogs. Answer the questions.
1 What two letters are added to an adjective to make an adverb?
2 Which adverb is the same word as the adjective?
3 Which is the adverb from *good*?
4 Which four adverbs are describing other adverbs?

b Now look at the highlighted adverbs again in Moira's first paragraph. Complete the rules with *before* or *after*.
1 Some adverbs describe how people do things.
   They go _____ the verb or verb phrase.
2 Some adverbs describe another adverb (or adjective).
   They go _____ the adverb (or adjective).

c ▶ p.144 Grammar Bank 11A. Learn more about adverbs and practise them.

d (5 27)) Listen and say what is happening. Use an adverb.

They're speaking quietly.

3 PRONUNCIATION word stress

a Underline the stressed syllable in the adjectives.

Adjectives	Adverbs
dan|ge|rous	dangerously
po|lite	politely
beau|ti|ful	beautifully
in|cre|di|ble	incredibly
care|ful	carefully
fa|shio|na|ble	fashionably
ca|su|al	casually
per|fect	perfectly
un|heal|thy	unhealthily

b (5 28)) Listen and check. Repeat the adjectives.

c (5 29)) Now listen and repeat the adverbs. Does the stress change?

4 LISTENING & SPEAKING

a (5 30)) Listen to Jemma talking about the third city. In general, is she positive, negative, or neutral about it?

b Listen again. Then, with a partner, complete Jemma's sentences.

Eating out
People spend a lot of time in [1]_____ and [2]_____.
People who [3]_____ go out to a bar to have [4]_____. They don't have it in their [5]_____.
When people go out in big groups, [6]_____ _____ all sit at one end of the table and [7]_____ _____ at the other.

The women
Women here talk very [8]_____ and very [9]_____.
Women dress [10]_____ _____.

Work
There's a myth that the Spanish don't [11]_____ _____, but I don't think it's [12]_____.
People have a [13]_____ lunch break, but they finish work very [14]_____.

c Answer the questions in small groups.

1 In your country or city how do people...?
- dress for special occasions
- treat tourists
- drive
- eat at lunchtime during the week
- speak foreign languages
- behave at sports matches
- decorate their houses

2 Think of a time when you went to another country or another city / region in your country for the first time. What did you notice about...?
- the people
- the food
- the driving
- the houses
- the weather

5 WRITING

Choose two headings from the blogs in **1** or the listening in **4**. Write two paragraphs, either about your country or a country you have visited.

11B What do you want to do?

G verbs + *to* + infinitive
V verbs that take the infinitive
P sentence stress

> Would you like to get a new job?
> No, I want to stay where I am.

1 READING & SPEAKING

a Read about the website 43things.com. How does it work?

> **43Things** is a website where people write things that they want to do. There are always 43 different ambitions. Some are trivial, some are more serious. Other people respond and write about their experiences and sometimes give advice.

b Read today's 43 things and responses A–E. Match the responses with five things people want to do. Do you think their advice is good?

c Complete the phrases from the text with a verb from the list.

| be<u>co</u>me | bite | choose | climb /klaɪm/ |
| down<u>load</u> | go | learn | spend | <u>vi</u>sit |

1 _____ a mountain
2 _____ on a safari
3 _____ to cook
4 _____ less time on the internet
5 _____ the lyrics
6 _____ five things you really like eating
7 _____ a Goth
8 _____ all the continents
9 _____ my nails

d Cover the verbs and try to remember them.

2 GRAMMAR verbs + *to* + infinitive

a Look at the highlighted verbs in the text. What's the form of the next verb? Which one is different?

b ▶ p.144 **Grammar Bank 11B.** Learn more about verbs + *to* + infinitive and practise them.

What do you want to do with your life?

On 43Things today, people want to…

climb Mount Kilimanjaro   get up earlier   go on a safari
get a new job   have very long hair   have more time for myself
learn to cook   learn to dance like Shakira   make a short film
visit all the continents   spend less time on the internet   write a novel
read 12 books a month   run a half marathon   see Radiohead live
learn to speak Italian   stop biting my nails   get married
go to Iceland   write a song   become a Goth   paint my kitchen
spend less money on clothes   stop eating meat   stay awake for 24 hours

A Spend less time on Facebook, for example only two hours at the weekend. Stop using Second Life if you use it. (I uninstalled it).

B Get a Laura Pausini CD. Download the lyrics to a song and translate them – you can use Google Translate for this. Listen carefully to the pronunciation, and then sing along with her (I sang "Incancellabile").

C You just need to stop cutting it! Don't worry about the latest fashions. Go for it!

D Choose five things you really like eating (e.g. roast chicken and chocolate cake) and then look at recipes on the internet. Choose the recipes that you'd like to try, preferably ones that aren't too difficult. Make the five things again and again until they're perfect. It isn't difficult, you just need to practise.

E Wear black clothes. Be yourself, and listen to bands like The Cult and The Mission.

> **Second Life®** a website which is a free 3D virtual world where users can socialize, create new personalities, and interact with other users
> **Laura Pausini** an Italian pop singer, popular in several European and Latin American countries

86

3 PRONUNCIATION sentence stress

a 5 32))) Listen and repeat the dialogue. <u>C</u>opy the <u>rhy</u>thm. How do you pronounce *to*?

> A **Would** you **like** to **go** to **Iceland**?
> B **No**, I **wouldn't**.
> A **Why not**?
> B **Because** I **don't like** the **cold**.

b 5 33))) Listen to another dialogue. Complete the missing stressed words.

> A _____ you _____ to _____ a _____ _____?
> B _____, I'd _____ to.
> A _____?
> B Because I _____ my _____. It's _____ _____.

c Practise the dialogues with a partner.

d In pairs, choose ten ambitions from **What do you want to do with your life**? Ask your partner questions using *Would you like to...?*

> Would you like to climb Mount Kilimanjaro?
>
> Yes, I would. / No, I wouldn't.

4 SPEAKING

Work in pairs. Take turns.
A Tell your partner about the things below.
B Respond to what A says. Ask questions.
A Ask *What about you?*

- a country you **want to go** to
- something you **would like to learn to do**
- something you **need to do** tomorrow
- a holiday you **are planning to have** soon
- a famous person **you hope to meet** one day
- a film you **want to see** soon
- a dangerous sport **you would like to try**
- something you **need to buy** soon
- a singer or group you **hope to see** one day

> I really want to go to Australia.
>
> Oh, yes? Why Australia?

5 WRITING

a Create a class page for **43Things**. Write three things you really want to do. Your teacher will write some of them on the board.

b Read other students' ambitions and choose one that you know something about. Write a response (like the ones in **43Things**) to give advice or talk about your experience.

6 5 34))) SONG *Don't Tell Me that it's Over* ♫

G articles
V the internet
P word stress

11C Men, women, and the internet

Do men and women use the internet in the same way?
No, they don't. They're very different.

1 VOCABULARY & PRONUNCIATION
the internet

a Do you ever visit any of the websites on this page, or websites like them? How much time do you spend a day on the internet? Do you use it mainly for your work / studies or for pleasure?

b Look at some words and phrases related to the internet. Match them with their definitions.

a|ttach|ment   down|load   goo|gle   log in   on|line
search for   skype   so|cial net|work   up|load   wi|fi

1	_____	*adj, adv* on the internet
2	_____	*noun* sth you send with an email, e.g. a document or a photo
3	_____	*verb* to move sth from your computer to an internet site, e.g. photos
4	_____	*verb* to move sth from an internet site to your computer, e.g. music, films
5	_____	*verb* to type words into the search engine *Google®* to find information about sb / sth
6	_____	*verb* to make a telephone call over the internet
7	_____	*verb* to type your username (usually your name or email address) and a password to begin using a computer or a website
8	_____	*noun* a way of connecting a computer to the internet without wires
9	_____	*noun* a website that people use to communicate, e.g. *Facebook*, *Twitter*, etc.
10	_____	*verb* to try to find sb or sth, e.g. on the internet

Dictionary abbreviations
sth = something   **sb** = somebody

c 5 35)) Listen and check. Repeat the words. Underline the stressed syllable in the multisyllable words.

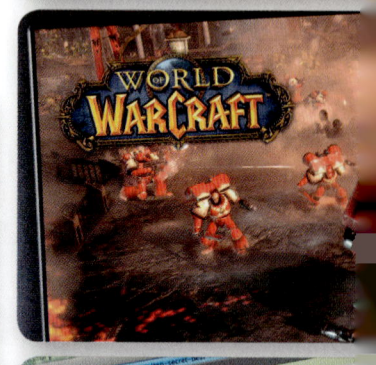

88

2 SPEAKING & LISTENING

a With a partner, look at some things which people do on the internet. For each one say if you do it often, sometimes, hardly ever, or never.

I often send emails for work. What about you?

- [ ] send personal emails
- [ ] send emails for work
- [ ] read the news
- [ ] buy things on shopping websites
- [ ] buy things on *eBay* (or a similar site)
- [ ] get sports information
- [ ] visit websites about health and medicine
- [ ] use social networks
- [ ] play games
- [ ] download music
- [ ] visit forums about diet or looking after children
- [ ] use online banking
- [ ] use online maps for directions
- [ ] book tickets and hotels online

b Now go through the list again and write **M** if you think men do them more than women, **W** if you think women do them more than men, and **ND** if you think there is no difference.

c 5 36)) Listen to an interview with a UK marketing expert about how men and women use the internet. Check your answers.

d Do you think the situation is the same in your country?

3 GRAMMAR articles

a Complete the email with *a*, *an*, *the*, or – (= no article).

Sent: Friday, 8 July 16:13
To: Carola Whitney
Subject: **Re: Hello!**

Hi Carola

Thanks for your email. I would really like to write to you and practise my English.

I'm ¹_____ student at Buenos Aires University – it's ²_____ biggest university in Argentina. I'm studying ³_____ medicine. I live in Buenos Aires with my grandmother, ⁴_____ my mother's mother, because my family live in ⁵_____ small town quite far away, but I go ⁶____ home at ⁷_____ weekend.

I love listening to ⁸_____ classical music, and ⁹_____ last week I went to ¹⁰_____ amazing concert at ¹¹_____ Opera House here.

b ▶ **p.144 Grammar Bank 11C.** Learn more about articles and practise them.

c Work in pairs. **A** choose a circle, think of three things, three places, etc. and tell **B**. **B** respond and ask for more information. Then change roles.

I love fish, strawberries, and chocolate cake. I don't like tomatoes.

Tomatoes? Why not?

- 3 kinds of food you love (and one you don't like)
- 3 things you always have in your bag or pocket
- 3 things you sometimes do on Saturday evening
- 3 things you do first thing in the morning
- 3 things women usually like doing (but men don't)
- 3 things you did last night
- 3 jobs you would like to do (and one you wouldn't)
- 3 things men usually like doing (but women don't)

Practical English Going home

1 JENNY'S LAST MORNING

a **5 38))** Watch or listen and mark the sentences **T** (true) or **F** (false).

1 Rob arrives late.
2 He has a coffee with Jenny.
3 Jenny has good news for him.
4 The job offer is for a year.
5 Rob thinks *A writer in New York* is a good name for the column.
6 Rob needs time to think.

b Watch or listen again. Say why the **F** sentences are false.

2 VOCABULARY public transport

a Match the words and pictures.

- [ ] bus
- [ ] plane
- [ ] taxi
- [ ] train
- [ ] coach
- [ ] tram

b **5 39))** Listen and check.

c Complete the headings with a word from **a**.

1 _____
You get one at a ~ rank.
They are also called cabs.
People usually give the driver a tip (= some extra money, about 5-10%).
In London they are black.

2 _____
You get one at an airport.
First you have to check in.
Then you go through security to the Departure lounge.
Finally you go to your Gate.

3 _____
You get one at a station.
You normally need to get a ticket first.
Then you need to find the right platform.
Some go underground in big cities. In London, this is called *The Tube*.

4 _____
You get one at a ~ station or a ~ stop.
Intercity ones are also called coaches.
You can buy a ticket in advance or sometimes you can pay the driver.
In London they are red.

d Cover the columns and look at the headings. Try to remember the four facts about each type of public transport.

EPISODE 6

3 GETTING TO THE AIRPORT

a 5 40))) Watch or listen to Jenny's three conversations. How does she get to the airport?

b Watch or listen again. Complete the **You Hear** phrases.

You Say	))) You Hear
Could you call me a taxi, please?	Yes, of course. _____ to?
To Paddington station.	And when would you like it _____?
Now, please.	
How much is it?	That's £_____, please.
Make it £15. And could I have a receipt?	Thank you very much, _____.
Could I have a ticket to Heathrow Airport, please?	Single or _____?
Single, please.	Standard or _____ class?
Standard, please.	That's £18.
Can I pay by credit card?	Yes, of _____.

c 5 41))) Watch or listen and repeat the **You Say** phrases. Copy the rhythm.

d Practise the dialogue with a partner.

e In pairs, roleplay the dialogue. Then swap roles.

A (book open) You are the receptionist, the taxi driver, and the ticket clerk. The taxi costs £11.60. The ticket costs £18.90.

B (book closed) You want to get a taxi to Victoria Station, and then a train to Gatwick Airport. Begin with *Could you call me a taxi, please?*

4 SAYING GOODBYE

a 5 42))) Watch or listen and answer the questions.

1 What does Jenny leave in the hotel?
2 How does she get it back?
3 What has Rob decided to do?
4 Is Eddie going to meet her at the airport? Why (not)?
5 Who is Eddie? How old is he?

b Look at the **Social English phrases**. Who says them: **J**enny or **R**ob?

Social English phrases	
I can't believe it!	I'm so happy.
Thank you so much.	Have a good journey.
I'd love to [accept].	See you in [New York].

c 5 43))) Watch or listen and check. How do you say them in your language?

d Watch or listen again and repeat the phrases.

> **Can you...?**
> ☐ ask for a taxi
> ☐ buy a ticket on public transport
> ☐ use common phrases, e.g. *Have a good journey, See you in New York*, etc.

G present perfect
V irregular past participles
P sentence stress

12A Books and films

Have you seen the film?
No, I haven't, but I've read the book.

1 GRAMMAR present perfect

a Look at some images from films. What do the films have in common?

b 🔊 5 44 Listen to Alan and Lucy talking on the phone. What two things are they going to do tonight?

c Listen again and read the conversation. Complete the chart below and answer the questions with a partner.

Alan	Hi, Lucy. Have you finished your report?
Lucy	Yes, I have, finally!
Alan	What do you want to do tonight? Do you want to go out?
Lucy	No, I'm a bit tired.
Alan	Would you like to come here? I can order pizzas and we can watch a film.
Lucy	Good idea. What films do you have?
Alan	How about *Eclipse*? Have you seen it?
Lucy	No, I haven't seen it, but I've read the book.
Alan	Is it good?
Lucy	I loved it! Vampires – perfect for a winter night!
Alan	Great. What pizza topping do you want?
Lucy	Cheese and blood, please...no, cheese and tomato.

+	I've seen the film.
–	I _____ the film.
?	_____ you _____ the film?

1 What is *'ve*? What verb is *seen* from?
2 Change the three sentences in the chart to third person singular (*He* or *She*).
3 Lucy says *I've read the book*. Do we know *when* she read it?

d ▶ p.146 **Grammar Bank 12A.** Learn more about the present perfect and practise it.

e Look at the films in **a** and talk to a partner. Which of the films have you seen? Have you read any of the books?

I've seen Eclipse, but I haven't read the book.
I haven't seen the film of Alice in Wonderland, but I've read the book.

The Lord of the Rings

Eclipse

The Girl who Played with Fire

Alice in Wonderland

2 PRONUNCIATION sentence stress

a 5 46))) Listen and repeat the dialogue. Copy the rhythm.

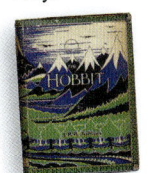

> A **Have** you **seen** The **Hobbit**?
> B **No**, I **haven't**.
> A **Have** you **read** the **book**?
> B **Yes**, I **have**. I've **read** it **twice**.

b Write down the names of three more films from books. Ask and answer with a partner.

Have you seen…?
Have you read the book?
Yes, I have. / No, I haven't.

3 VOCABULARY
irregular past participles

a Look at some irregular past participles. Which verbs do you think they are from? Write the infinitive and the past simple.

	infinitive	past simple	past participle
1	be	was / were	been
2			broken
3			done
4			eaten
5			fallen
6			forgotten
7			gone
8			left
9			sung
10			spoken
11			taken
12			worn

b 5 47))) Listen and check.

c 5 48))) Cover **a**. Listen and say the past simple and past participle.

))) be — was / were, been

d Complete the **Verb** column with a past participle from **a**.

Verb
1 Have you ▨ your homework? _____
2 I'm sorry, I've ▨ your name. _____
3 Have you ever ▨ a photo of an actor? _____
4 Ann's ▨ on holiday. She's going to be away for three weeks. _____
5 Have you ▨ to Mike about the party? _____
6 I've never ▨ that jacket. It was a big mistake. _____
7 Jim's ▨ in love with an Italian girl. _____
8 Oh no! I've ▨ my glasses. _____

e Cover the **Verb** column. Can you remember the sentences?

4 SPEAKING & LISTENING

a Complete the phrases with the past participle of the verb in brackets.

FILM EXPERIENCES
Find someone who has…

	Name	What film was it?
1 _____ asleep watching a film (fall)		
2 _____ the soundtrack of a film (buy)		
3 _____ the cinema before the end of a film (leave)		
4 _____ a film more than three times (see)		
5 _____ in a film (cry)		
6 _____ a film in English with subtitles (see)		
7 _____ in a film (appear)		

b Stand up and move around the class. Ask *Have you ever…?* questions with 1–7. When somebody answers *Yes, I have*, write down their name and ask *What film was it?*

c 5 49))) Listen to three people answering one of the questions from **a**. Which question is it?

d Listen again. Complete the chart for each person.

	Which film?	How many?	Why?
1			
2			
3			

5 5 50))) SONG Flashdance ♪

G present perfect or past simple?
V more irregular past participles
P irregular past participles

> Have you been to New York? — Yes, I have. I went there last year.

12B I've never been there!

1 LISTENING

a Are you following a TV series at the moment? Which one? Why do you like it?

b (5 51) Look at the information about an episode from an American TV series. Listen to part of the episode. Then answer questions 1 and 2.

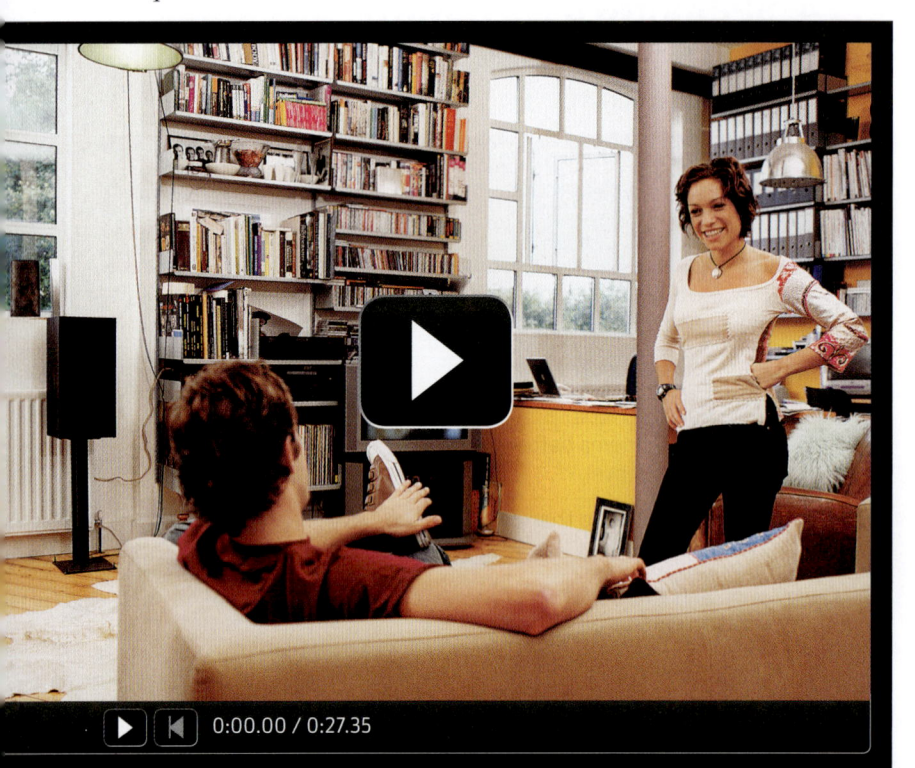

Episode 5
Jess's birthday is on Friday and Matt wants to take her somewhere special...

0:00.00 / 0:27.35

1 Which restaurants has Jess eaten in before? Tick (✓) or cross (✗) the boxes.
☐ The Peking Duck   ☐ Appetito   ☐ Luigi's
2 Do they agree which restaurant to go to?

c Listen again and answer the questions.
1 When did Jess go to *The Peking Duck* and who with?
2 How many times has she been to *Appetito*?
3 What did Matt say happened when they went to *Luigi's*?
4 Why is Jess angry?
5 Who does Jess think Matt went with to *Luigi's*?
6 What does Matt say? Do you believe him?

2 GRAMMAR
present perfect or past simple?

a Look at part of the conversation between Matt and Jess. In pairs, answer the questions.

> **Matt** Have you been to *The Peking Duck*?
> **Jess** Yes, I have.
> **Matt** Oh no! When did you go there?
> **Jess** Last month. I went with the people from work.

1 What tense is Matt's first question?
2 What tense is Matt's second question?
3 Which of the two questions is about a specific time in the past?

b ▶ p.146 **Grammar Bank 12B.** Learn more about the present perfect and past simple and practise them.

c Play *Guess where I've been*.

Guess where I've been

1 Write down the names of **six** cities in your country or abroad (three you **have been to** and three you **haven't been to**.)
2 Swap lists with your partner. Tick (✓) the three cities you think your partner has been to, but don't tell him / her.
3 Ask *Have you been to...?* for each place to check your guesses. Did you guess right?

> Have you been to Oxford?

4 Now ask some past simple questions for the cities your partner *has* been to.

> When did you go to...?
> Did you like it?

3 VOCABULARY & PRONUNCIATION
more irregular past participles

a Look at some more irregular past participles. Write the infinitive and the past simple.

1	_buy_ _bought_	bought
2	_____ _____	drunk
3	_____ _____	found
4	_____ _____	given
5	_____ _____	heard
6	_____ _____	had
7	_____ _____	known
8	_____ _____	lost
9	_____ _____	made
10	_____ _____	met
11	_____ _____	paid
12	_____ _____	sent
13	_____ _____	spent
14	_____ _____	thought
15	_____ _____	won

b (5 54)) Listen and check.

c ▶ p.165 **Irregular verbs** Tick (✓) all the ones you know. Try to learn the new ones.

d (5 55)) Put three irregular past participles in each column. Listen and check.

bought broken done driven drunk
forgotten given gone known lost
made paid spoken sung taken
thought worn written

clock	fish	train

up	phone	horse

e Play past participle *Bingo*.

4 SPEAKING

a Look at question 1 below. What words are missing in the present perfect question? What words are missing in the past simple question? What form do you need of the verb in **bold**?

Recently...

Present perfect	Past simple
1 / **be** to the cinema recently?	What / see? / like it?
2 / **buy** any new clothes recently?	What / buy?
3 / **have** a really good meal recently?	Where / go? What / have?
4 / **be** to a sports match recently?	/ your team win?

In your life...

Present perfect	Past simple
5 / ever **be** on TV?	What programme / it?
6 / ever **lose** your mobile?	Where / lose it? / find it?
7 / ever **win** a cup or medal?	What / win it for?
8 / ever **speak** to a famous person?	Who / it? What / say?

b Work in pairs. **A** ask **B** the questions. If **B** answers *Yes, I have*, ask the past simple questions too. Then change roles.

G revision: question formation
V revision: word groups
P revision: sounds

12C The *English File* questionnaire

1 READING

a Read the information about Sir Ian McKellen. Have you seen any of his films? Did you like them?

> **Sir Ian McKellen** is one of Britain's greatest actors. He was born in Burnley in the north of England on 25 May 1939. He first became well known as an actor for his roles in Shakespeare's plays, e.g. *Hamlet* and *Macbeth*. In recent years he has had many important film roles including James Whale in *Gods and Monsters*, Gandalf in *The Lord of the Rings* trilogy, and Magneto in *X-Men*.

b Sir Ian McKellen agreed to be interviewed especially for *English File*. Read the interview and write a heading from the list below in each section.

YOUR ABILITIES
YOUR WORK EXPERIENCES
YOUR HOME
YOUR LIFESTYLE
YOUR PLACES
~~YOUR TASTES~~

c Read the interview again. Then mark the sentences **T** (true) or **F** (false). Say why the **F** ones are false.

1. He became an actor when he was a student.
2. He lives outside London.
3. He gets up early every day.
4. He's never been to India.
5. He spends a long time on the internet every day.
6. He read *The Lord of the Rings* when he was young.
7. His desk isn't very tidy.
8. He doesn't like animals.
9. He relaxes by playing games.
10. He doesn't have any ambitions.

INTERVIEW WITH SIR IAN MCKELLEN

1 *YOUR TASTES*

What kind of music do you like?
I hardly ever listen to music at home – I prefer going to concerts. I enjoy classical music and pop, but my favourite kind of music is traditional American jazz.

What book are you reading at the moment?
I'm reading *The Hammersteins*, a biography of the American theatre family written by Oscar Andrew Hammerstein.

Who's your favourite historical character?
Perhaps William Shakespeare.

2 _____

What time do you usually get up in the morning?
If I am working, I get up one hour before I have to leave the house. If I am not working, and I went to bed late the night before, I get up at about 10 in the morning.

How much time do you spend a day on the internet?
I can very easily spend three or four hours on the internet, answering emails, reading the news, etc. I think of the internet as a wonderful encyclopaedia of information.

How do you relax?
I enjoy a late night sudoku, but especially being with friends.

3 _____

What's your favourite room in the house?
Perhaps the living room where I cook and eat, and from where I can see the River Thames in London.

What do you always have on your desk?
I always have too many letters, papers, and books which are waiting for me to read.

Do you have any pets? I love dogs, but I can't have one because I'm often away from home.

X-MEN [2000]   GODS AND MONSTERS [1998]   MACBETH [1979]

4 _____

What languages do you speak? I only speak English, but I can remember a little of the French I learned at school.

Can you play a musical instrument? No.

Is there something you would like to learn to do? Yes – many things, e.g. to sing well, to play the piano, and to speak foreign languages.

5 _____

What's your favourite place in London? I love the River Thames and the views from its many bridges.

Where are you going to go for your next holiday? I'm going to go to India for the first time in February.

What's the most beautiful city you've ever visited? I can't choose between Edinburgh, Prague, and Venice.

6 _____

What was your first job? The first money I earned as a professional actor was when I was a student at Cambridge University in 1959. I played small parts in audio recordings of Shakespeare's plays.

When did you first read *The Lord of the Rings*? I read it first when I was preparing to play Gandalf in the movie trilogy.

What was the best and worst thing about filming *The Lord of the Rings*? The best thing about filming was discovering the countryside and people of New Zealand. But the worst thing was living away from home for a year or more.

LORD OF THE RINGS [2003]

2 VOCABULARY revision: word groups

a Put these words from the interview in the right column.

actor   books   desk   go to bed   living room   small

Rooms	Things	Jobs

Furniture	Adjectives	Daily routine

b With a partner, add three more words to each column.

3 PRONUNCIATION revision: sounds

a Look at some words from the interview. Which word has a different sound?

1 uː   school   choose   cook   too
2 ɜː   first   earn   worst   year
3 eɪ   say   wait   can't   favourite
4 e   friends   many   people   ever
5 dʒ   enjoy   bridge   dog   languages
6 h   hour   home   perhaps   hardly
7 θ   thing   three   the   think
8 ʃ   information   school   traditional   professional

b 🔊 5 56 Listen and check. Practise saying the words.

4 GRAMMAR & SPEAKING
revision: question formation

a Without looking back at the interview, try to remember the questions for these answers.
1 Perhaps William Shakespeare.
2 I'm going to go to India for the first time in February.
3 I only speak English…
4 I can't choose between Edinburgh, Prague, and Venice.
5 I read it first when I was preparing to play Gandalf…

b Choose eight questions from the questionnaire to ask a partner.

11 & 12 Revise and Check

GRAMMAR

Circle a, b, or c.

1 You speak _____.
   a very slow
   b very slowly
   c very slower

2 She plays tennis _____.
   a quite well
   b quite good
   c quite goodly

3 My husband works _____.
   a incredible hard
   b incredibly hard
   c incredibly hardly

4 I'd like _____ a Ferrari.
   a drive   b to drive   c driving

5 What do we need _____ next?
   a to do   b do   c doing

6 She wants to pass her exams, but she doesn't like _____.
   a study   b studing   c studying

7 _____ usually drive fast in this country.
   a The men   b Men   c The man

8 I saw _____ good film last night.
   a the   b a   c –

9 It's _____ best place to eat in the city centre.
   a the   b a   c –

10 Do you go to _____ bed late at weekends?
    a the   b a   c –

11 I've read the book, but I _____ the film.
    a don't see
    b haven't saw
    c haven't seen

12 A Have you _____ anyone famous?
    B Yes, I have. A famous film actor.
    a ever met   b ever meet   c met ever

13 _____ he been to New York?
    a Has   b Did   c Have

14 We _____ to Italy last year.
    a have gone   b have been   c went

15 She _____ in a restaurant before.
    a did never worked
    b have never worked
    c has never worked

VOCABULARY

a Write the opposite adjective or adverb.
   1 quickly _____   3 well _____   5 formal _____
   2 safe _____   4 noisy _____ 6 healthily _____

b Complete the sentences with these verbs.

   need   learn   promise   want

   1 I'd like to _____ to dance the tango.
   2 You don't _____ to wash it. You've only worn it once.
   3 I can't _____ to be on time. It depends on the traffic.
   4 Do you _____ to go to a restaurant or to a pub for lunch?

c Complete the sentences with these internet words.

   attachment   wifi   download   online   website

   1 I do a lot of shopping _____ these days.
   2 I can _____ the song for you tonight.
   3 You can find all the information on the hotel's _____ .
   4 Don't open an _____ when you don't know who it's from.
   5 We have _____ at home so I can send emails from my bedroom.

d Complete the sentences with *for*, *in*, *with*, or *up*.
   1 Log _____ with your username and password.
   2 I looked _____ U2 on Wikipedia – they started in 1976.
   3 You can search _____ all kinds of information on the internet.
   4 Have you ever seen a film _____ subtitles?

e Write the past participle of the following verbs.
   1 see saw _____   3 know knew _____   5 fall fell _____
   2 go went _____   4 give gave _____   6 take took _____

PRONUNCIATION

a Circle the word with a different sound.

   1 ʌ   done   sung   gone   won
   2 e   said   been   any   left
   3 ɒ   want   had   what   watch
   4 uː   choose soon   food   book
   5 ɜː   worst   wore   prefer search

b Underline the stressed syllable.
   1 po|lite|ly   2 dan|ge|rous|ly   3 de|cide   4 a|ttach|ment   5 web|site

CAN YOU UNDERSTAND THIS TEXT?

a Read the text and mark the sentences **T** (true) or **F** (false).
   1 It is cheaper to live in the US than in the UK.
   2 It is more expensive to be ill in the US.
   3 Waiters are better in UK restaurants.
   4 It's more difficult to make friends in the US.
   5 The British are less direct than Americans.

b Look at the highlighted words or phrases in the text and guess their meaning.

Amy Johnson is an American who lives and works in England. We asked her to tell us about her first impressions of the UK.

One of my first impressions was that the UK is more expensive than the US. I live in Oxford and the cost of living, (rent, bills, food, etc.) is higher than in Ohio, where I'm from in the US. The only thing that is a lot cheaper here is healthcare – it's free to go to the doctor's or to hospital, whereas in the US it isn't, so you need to have health insurance, which can be very expensive.

I think you can eat very well in England – there's a wide variety of food from all around the world – Chinese, Japanese, Italian, Turkish, etc. – but eating out is more expensive than in the US, and the service is worse. Generally, I'd say British food is healthier than American food, and the portions are a lot smaller, too.

As for the people, I find British people quite pessimistic compared to Americans who are usually very positive and optimistic about the future. Also, when I'm in Ohio I talk to everybody: shop assistants, the person behind me in the supermarket queue, the person sitting next to me in the restaurant, but I can't do that in the UK – people are much more reserved. But, on the other hand, I think it is easier to make real friends here than in the US. I also find British people are not very good at telling you what they really think or (in a work situation) saying something negative about you. Americans just say things as they are!

CAN YOU UNDERSTAND THESE PEOPLE?

5 57))) **In the street** Watch or listen to five people and answer the questions.

Selina   David   Ruth   Ben   Justin

1 Selina was surprised when she arrived in London because it was the summer but _____.
   a the weather was bad
   b there weren't many tourists
   c the weather was good
2 David would like to _____.
   a get a completely new job
   b change the job that he has
   c do a job he did before
3 When Ruth talks about Mamma Mia she doesn't mention _____.
   a the actors   b the soundtrack   c the story
4 Ben thinks that women drive _____ than men.
   a more slowly   b less dangerously   c better
5 Justin went to a karaoke bar _____.
   a a long time ago   b quite recently   c last year

CAN YOU SAY THIS IN ENGLISH?

Do the tasks with a partner. Tick (✓) the box if you can do them.

Can you…?
1 ☐ say how people in your country a) drive b) dress
2 ☐ say three things you would like to do in the future
3 ☐ say which of the following you prefer and why
   • classical music or pop music
   • summer holidays or winter holidays
   • Chinese food or Japanese food
4 ☐ say what things you do on the internet and how often
5 ☐ answer the questions below
   • What city have you been to recently?
   • When did you go there?
   • What did you do there?
   • What's the best / worst thing about your town?

Short films the Electric Cinema
Watch and enjoy a film on iTutor.

Communication

1B WHERE ARE THEY FROM?
Student A

a Ask **B** the questions about person 1.
  - Where's Masako from?
  - Where in (country)?

	1	2	3
Name	Masako	Carlo	Petra
From	( )	( )	( )

b Answer **B**'s questions about person 4.

c Repeat for the other people.

	4	5	6
Name	Ali	Antonia	Oliver
From	Turkey (Ankara)	Mexico (Acapulco)	Germany (Berlin)

1C WHAT'S HIS / HER REAL NAME? Student A

a Look at the names of your four people. Two are their real names and two aren't. Cross (✗) the names you think are not their real names.

Tom Hanks, actor	Bono, singer	Angelina Jolie, actress	Katy Perry, singer
_____	_____	_____	_____

b Check your answers. Tell **B** *I think _____ is / isn't his / her real name.* If **B** says *No, it isn't,* ask **B** *What's his / her real name? How do you spell it?* and write the name under the photo.

c Answer **B**'s questions.

Jude Law, actor	Tina Turner, singer ✗	Eminem, singer ✗	Scarlett Johansson, actress
✓ real name	Anna Mae Bullock	Marshall Mathers	✓ real name

2A WHAT'S ON THE TABLE?
Students A+B

a Look at the picture for one minute. Try to remember the things on the table.

b Close your books and write down the ten things on the table.

c Now compare with your partner. Did he / she remember more things than you?

2C WHAT'S THE MATTER?
Student A

a Read the conversation.

> A What's the matter?
> B I'm sad.
> A Don't be sad. Cheer up.
> B Thanks.

b Have four conversations with **B**. Ask **B** *What's the matter?* **B** answers. Then choose a phrase below.

> Relax.   Have a holiday.   Open the window.
> Have a drink.   Don't worry.

c Change roles. **B** asks you *What's the matter?* You answer with **1** below. **B** responds with a phrase. Then you respond, e.g. *Thanks, OK, Good idea*, etc.

1 I'm bored.
2 I'm cold.
3 I'm tired.
4 I'm hungry.

d Cover the phrases and do all eight conversations again from memory.

PE2 WHAT'S THE TIME?
Student A

Ask and answer questions with **B** to complete the times on the clocks. Then compare your clocks.

Clock 1: What's the time / What time is it?

4B NICO'S DAY Student A

a Ask **B** the questions below. **B** must find the answers in the text.
1 What time does Nico get up? (*He gets up at 6.30.*)
2 What does he have for breakfast? (*He has a coffee and cereal.*)
3 What two things does he check at the restaurant? (*He checks the reservations and his emails.*)
4 What time do all the customers arrive? (*They arrive at 1.30.*)
5 How many customers do they have in the restaurant at lunchtime? (*They have 85 customers.*)
6 What does Nico ask the customers? (*He asks if they are happy with the food.*)
7 What does Nico do after lunch? (*He goes back to the kitchen and plans the food for the evening menu.*)
8 What time does he go home in the afternoon? (*He goes home at 5.30.*)
9 What does Nico do at 7.30? (*He goes back to the restaurant and checks everything is OK.*)
10 What time does Nico go home? (*He goes home at 10 o'clock.*)

b Look at the text. Find the answers to **B**'s questions.

4C SHORT LIFE, LONG LIFE? Students A+B

Interview your partner. **A** ask the questions in the questionnaire. **B** answer and give more information if you can. Then change roles.

How often do you…?
1 have breakfast
   a hardly ever / never
   b sometimes / usually
   c always
2 eat fresh fruit and vegetables
   a hardly ever
   b once a day
   c three times a day
3 eat fast food
   a often
   b sometimes
   c hardly ever / never
4 do exercise
   a hardly ever / never
   b once or twice a week
   c three or four times a week
5 feel tired or stressed
   a always / often
   b sometimes
   c hardly ever / never
6 drink alcohol
   a every day
   b hardly ever / never
   c sometimes
7 see your friends
   a sometimes
   b often
   c very often

How many…?
8 hours do you usually sleep a day
   a 0 to 4
   b 5 to 6
   c 7 to 9
9 cups of coffee do you drink a day
   a more than five
   b usually only one or two
   c I don't drink coffee
10 Which of these is true for you?
   a I'm not very positive about life.
   b I'm usually positive about life.
   c I'm always positive about life.

Now calculate your partner's score.
a = 5   b = 7   c = 10   Total score = number of years you live

Communication

5A DO YOU WANT TO BE FAMOUS? Students A+B

Interview each other with the questionnaire. Ask *Can you…?* If the answer is *Yes, I can*, ask *How well?* Do you think your partner has the X Factor?

You want to be **famous** – but what can you do?

✓ = yes
✗ = no
3 = very well
2 = quite well
1 = not very well

Music	✓/✗	How well?	Words	✓/✗	How well?
sing	☐	☐	write short stories	☐	☐
play an instrument	☐	☐	write poems or song lyrics	☐	☐
dance	☐	☐	speak foreign languages	☐	☐
read or write music	☐	☐	speak in public	☐	☐
Art			**Sport**		
take artistic photos	☐	☐	run a half marathon	☐	☐
draw cartoons	☐	☐	play a team sport	☐	☐
paint pictures	☐	☐	do a winter or water sport	☐	☐
design websites or logos	☐	☐	do an individual sport	☐	☐

5B SPOT THE DIFFERENCES Student A

You and **B** have the same picture but with eight differences.

a   Tell **B** what is happening in flats 1–4 and in the garden on the left. **B** will tell you what is different in his / her picture. Circle the differences.

b   Listen to **B** telling you what is happening in flats 5–8 and in the garden on the right. Look at your picture and tell **B** if it is the same or different. If it is different, tell **B** what is happening. Circle the differences.

c   When you finish, compare the two pictures.

5C WHAT DO YOU DO? WHAT ARE YOU DOING NOW?
Student A

a Ask **B** your questions.
- What do you do?
- What are you doing now?
- Are you wearing a watch today?
- Do you usually wear a watch?
- What kind of books do you usually read?
- What are you reading at the moment?

b Answer **B**'s questions.

6A READING IN ENGLISH
Students A+B

How do you usually read?		
a on paper	b on screen	c on an eReader

What kind of things do you read?	
a books	d websites
b newspapers	e work documents
c magazines	f others (what?)

When and where do you usually read?
a at work / school
b when you are on a bus or train
c on holiday
d before you go to bed

Do you ever need to read in English? What?

7A WHERE WERE YOU? Student A

a Ask **B** your questions. Ask *Where were you at…?*
- 9 o'clock yesterday morning
- 11.30 yesterday evening
- 3 o'clock yesterday afternoon
- 12 o'clock last night
- 6.30 yesterday evening
- 7 o'clock this morning

b Answer **B**'s questions.

> **Useful language**
> **at** home / work / school / university
> **in** bed / the street / my car
> **on** the bus / the train

7B STAMFORD BRIDGE Students A+B

Tourist Information UK
STAMFORD BRIDGE

Stamford Bridge is a small village in the North of England, near York. It is about 230 miles (370 kilometres) from London. It has a population of 3,500 people. It is famous for a battle between the English and the Vikings in 1066.

NB Don't confuse Stamford Bridge near York with Stamford Bridge in London, the stadium of Chelsea Football Club!

7C A NIGHT TO REMEMBER Student A

a Ask **B** the questions about Mehmet's night.

1. When and where was it? (*Last year, in Istanbul.*)
2. Who was he with? Why? (*His friends. It was his best friend's birthday.*)
3. What colour T-shirt did he wear? (*Black.*)
4. What is Cezayir? (*It's an old building with a bar and a restaurant.*)
5. What did they do after dinner? (*They had a coffee and then they went to the beach to have a swim.*)
6. Was the sea cold? (*No, it was warm.*)
7. Why did he go home in his friend's car? (*Because he couldn't find his car keys.*)
8. What time did he get home? (*Really late, at five o'clock in the morning.*)

b Answer **B**'s questions about Maria Julia's night.

c Whose memory is better?

Communication

Communication

8A POLICE INTERVIEW
Student A

Work in pairs with another **A**. You are police officers. There was a robbery last night. **B** and **B** are two friends. You think they were responsible. They say that they went out for dinner and went to the cinema last night. You want to know if this is true.

a Look at the Police interview form and prepare to ask the **B**s the questions. Think of more questions to get more details about the evening, e.g. *What did you wear? What did you eat and drink? What film was it?*

b Interview one of the **B**s. Write down his / her answers in the form. (Your partner interviews the other **B**.)

c Compare with your partner. Did the two **B**s tell exactly the same story? If not, arrest them!

POLICE INTERVIEW FORM

Name: _____ Date: _____

	What time?	Where?	More details:
/ meet?			
/ have dinner?			
/ go to the cinema?			

What / do after the cinema?	
What time / get home?	

8C THE GHOST ROOM Student A

a Look at the picture for a minute. Try to remember what's in the room.

b Ask **B** the questions.
- / a TV? (*No, there wasn't.*)
- / a double or a single bed? (*There was a single bed.*)
- / a mirror? Where was it? (*Yes, there was. It was on the table.*)
- / any plants? (*No, there weren't.*)
- / any books in the room? (*No, there weren't.*)
- How many windows / ? (*There were two.*)

c Close your books. Answer **B**'s questions.

9C QUIZ NIGHT Student A

a Complete your sentences 1–8 with the comparative from the **bold** adjectives.

> 1 **small** Spain is _____ than France.
> (*True. Spain is 505,000 square kilometres and France is 544,000.*)
> 2 **long** The river Amazon is _____ than the river Nile.
> (*False. The Amazon is about 6,400 km long and the Nile is about 6,670 km long.*)
> 3 **old** Oxford University is _____ than Cambridge University.
> (*True. Oxford University was founded in 1170 and Cambridge 40 years later.*)
> 4 **short** The English alphabet is _____ than the Arabic alphabet.
> (*True. There are 26 letters in the English alphabet and 28 in the Arabic alphabet.*)
> 5 **dangerous** K2 is _____ to climb than Mount Everest.
> (*True. 40% of climbers who get to the top of K2 die, but only 9% of climbers of Everest die.*)
> 6 **large** A gigabyte is _____ than a megabyte.
> (*True. A megabyte is 1,000 bytes, but a gigabyte is 1,000 megabytes.*)
> 7 **dry** The Sahara Desert is _____ than the Atacama Desert.
> (*False. Sahara Desert average rainfall = 25 mm; Atacama Desert average rainfall = 0.1 mm.*)
> 8 **far** New Zealand is _____ south than Australia.
> (*True. It's 2,000 km south-east of Australia.*)

b Play *Quiz Night*. You are the presenter.

> - Read your sentence 1 to **B**. **B** must say if it's true or false.
> - Tell **B** if he / she is right and give the extra information in brackets.
> - If **B** is right, he / she wins 500 euros. Then read sentence 2 for 1,000 euros, sentence 3 for 2,000 euros, sentence 4 for 4,000 euros, etc.
> - If **B** gets a question wrong, he / she loses the money, but continues to play. The prize starts again from 500 euros.

c Play *Quiz Night* again. You are the contestant.

10A CITIES QUIZ Student A

a Complete your questions with the superlative of the adjectives in brackets.

1 What's the _____ city in the world? (noisy)
  a **Tokyo**   b Madrid   c Rome
2 What's the _____ city in the world? (hot)
  a Rio de Janeiro   b **Bangkok**   c Nairobi
3 Which city has the _____ monument in the world? (popular)
  a New York   b **Paris**   c Istanbul
4 What's the _____ city in Europe? (foggy)
  a Prague   b London   c **Milan**
5 Which city has the _____ traffic jams in the world? (bad)
  a São Paulo   b **Beijing**   c Mexico City

b Answer **B**'s questions.

c Ask **B** your questions. Does he / she know the answers? (The correct answers are in **bold**.)

> *What's the noisiest city in the world, Tokyo, Madrid, or Rome?*

10B WHAT ARE YOU GOING TO DO?
Student A

a Ask **B** the questions below.

Tonight
- What / do tonight?
- / study English? Why (not)?

Tomorrow
- What time / get up tomorrow?
- Where / have lunch?

Next weekend
- / go away next weekend? Where to?
- What / do on Saturday night?

b Answer **B**'s questions.

Communication

Communication

1B WHERE ARE THEY FROM?
Student B

a Answer **A**'s questions about person 1.

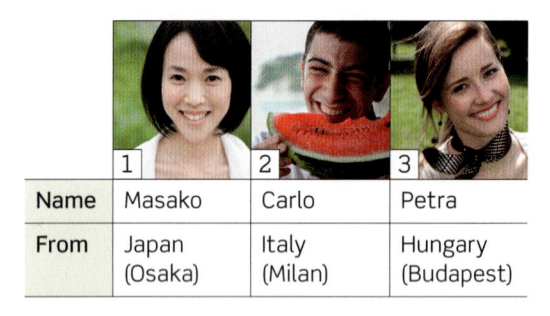

	1	2	3
Name	Masako	Carlo	Petra
From	Japan (Osaka)	Italy (Milan)	Hungary (Budapest)

b Ask **A** the questions about person 4.
- Where's Ali from?
- Where in (country)?

	4	5	6
Name	Ali	Antonia	Oliver
From	_____ ( )	_____ ( )	_____ ( )

c Repeat for the other people.

1C WHAT'S HIS / HER REAL NAME? Student B

a Look at the names of your four people. Two are their real names and two aren't. Cross (✗) the names you think are not their real names.

Jude Law, actor	Tina Turner, singer	Eminem, singer	Scarlett Johansson, actress
_____	_____	_____	_____

b Answer **A**'s questions.

Tom Hanks, actor	Bono, singer ✗	Angelina Jolie, actress	Katy Perry, singer ✗
✓ real name	Paul Hewson	✓ real name	Katheryn Hudson

c Check your answers to **a**. Tell **A** *I think _____ is / isn't his / her real name.* If **A** says *No, it isn't*, ask **A** *What's his / her real name? How do you spell it?* and write the name under the photo.

2C WHAT'S THE MATTER? Student B

a Read the conversation.

> **A** What's the matter?
> **B** I'm sad.
> **A** Don't be sad. Cheer up.
> **B** Thanks.

b Have four conversations with **A**. **A** asks you *What's the matter?* You answer with **1** below. **A** responds with a phrase. Then you respond, e.g. *Thanks, OK, Good idea*, etc.

1 I'm hot.   2 I'm thirsty.   3 I'm worried.   4 I'm stressed.

c Have four more conversations. Ask **A** *What's the matter?* **A** answers. Then choose a phrase below.

> Close the window.
> Have a sandwich.
> Read a book.
> Sit down.

d Cover the phrases and do all eight conversations again from memory.

PE2 WHAT'S THE TIME?
Student B

Ask and answer questions with **A** to complete the times on the clocks. Then compare your clocks.

Clock 2: What's the time / What time is it?

4B NICO'S DAY   Student B

a   Look at the *Father & Daughter* text. Find the answers to **A**'s questions.

b   Ask **A** the questions below. **A** must find the answers in the text.
1   What part of the newspaper does Nico read? (*He reads the sports section.*)
2   Where does he go after breakfast? (*He goes to the market.*)
3   What time does he start cooking the food for lunch? (*He starts cooking at 10.30.*)
4   How many cups of coffee does he have in the morning? (*He has three cups of coffee.*)
5   What time does Nico have lunch? (*He has lunch at 3.30.*)
6   Why doesn't Nico enjoy his lunch? (*Because he doesn't have time to relax.*)
7   How long does he spend with the children in the afternoon? (*He spends a couple of hours / two hours with them.*)
8   What do Nico and the children do between 5.30 and 7.30? (*The children do their homework and Nico makes their dinner.*)
9   What is the first thing Nico does when he gets home? (*He has a shower.*)
10 What time does he go to bed? (*He goes to bed at 11 o'clock.*)

5B SPOT THE DIFFERENCES   Student B

You and **A** have the same picture but with eight differences.

a   Listen to **A** telling you what is happening in flats 1–4 and in the garden on the left. Look at your picture and tell **A** if it is the same or different. If it is different, tell **A** what is happening. Circle the differences.

b   Tell **A** what is happening in flats 5–8 and in the garden on the right. **A** will tell you what is different in his / her picture. Circle the differences.

c   When you finish, compare the two pictures.

Communication

5C WHAT DO YOU DO? WHAT ARE YOU DOING NOW? Student B

a Answer **A**'s questions.

b Ask **A** your questions.
- Do your parents work? What do they do?
- What do you think they are doing now?
- Do you watch a series on TV?
- What TV series are you watching at the moment?
- Is it raining now?
- Does it rain a lot at this time of year?

7A WHERE WERE YOU? Student B

a Answer **A**'s questions.

A Where were you at nine o'clock yesterday morning?
B I was in bed.

b Ask **A** your questions. Ask *Where were you at…?*
- 8.30 yesterday morning
- 6.30 yesterday evening
- 11.30 yesterday morning
- 10 o'clock last night
- 5 o'clock yesterday afternoon
- 6.30 this morning

> **Useful language**
> **at** home / work / school / university
> **in** bed / the street / my car
> **on** the bus / the train

7C A NIGHT TO REMEMBER Student B

a Answer **A**'s questions about Mehmet's night.

b Ask **A** the questions about Maria Julia's night.

> 1 Where was she on holiday? (*In Athens.*)
> 2 Who did she want to see? (*A Greek man that she knew when she was at university.*)
> 3 How did she try to contact him? (*She called him many times, but he didn't answer.*)
> 4 Where did they meet? (*At her hotel.*)
> 5 Why was she embarrassed? (*Because her clothes weren't very special and her hair was a mess.*)
> 6 What did they do? (*They walked round the centre of Athens.*)
> 7 What language did they communicate in? (*They spoke English.*)
> 8 What was the weather like? (*It was a warm night.*)
> 9 What time did she get back to the hotel? (*At three o'clock in the morning.*)

c Whose memory is better?

8A POLICE INTERVIEW Student B

Work in pairs with another **B**. You are friends. Last night you met, had dinner, and went to the cinema. There was a robbery last night. **A** and **A** are police officers. They think you were responsible, and they want to interview you separately. If you both tell the same story, you are innocent!

a Prepare your story. Use these questions. Think of extra details, e.g. *What did you wear? What did you eat and drink? What film was it?*
- What time / where did you meet?
- What time / where did you have dinner?
- What time / where did you go to the cinema?
- What did you do after the cinema?
- What time did you get home?

b Answer **A**'s questions.

c Did you and your friend tell the same story?

8C THE GHOST ROOM Student B

a Look at the picture for a minute. Try to remember what's in the room.

b Close your books. Answer **A**'s questions.

c Ask **A** the questions.
- / a clock? Where was it?
(*Yes, there was. It was next to the window.*)
- / a carpet on the floor? (*No, there wasn't.*)
- / a lamp or light? Where was it?
(*Yes, there was. It was on the wall.*)
- / any pictures on the wall? What of?
(*Yes, there was one. It was of a woman.*)
- / any cupboards? (*No, there weren't.*)
- How many chairs / ? (*There was one.*)

9A GET READY! COOK! Students A+B

Jack's Meal
Starter

carrot and orange soup

Main course

chicken breasts filled with cream cheese

Dessert

pancakes with chocolate sauce

Liz's Meal
Starter

carrot and onion salad

Main course

pasta with creamy chicken sauce

Dessert

chocolate and orange mousse

9B SUGAR AND SALT Students A+B

How much sugar?
According to the American Heart Association, a woman should have no more than 20g (grams) of sugar a day (= 5 teaspoons) and a man no more than 36g (= 9 teaspoons).
- a can of Coke has approximately 35g of sugar
- an apple has approximately 23g of sugar
- a small (40g) bar of dark chocolate has approximately 7g of sugar
- an egg doesn't have any sugar

How much salt?
According to UK Government studies, an adult should eat no more than 6g of salt a day.
- a packet of crisps has approximately 3g of salt
- a slice of white bread has approximately 0.5g of salt
- a bottle of mineral water has approximately 0.0023g of salt
- a bottle of olive oil doesn't have any salt

Communication 109

Communication

9C QUIZ NIGHT Student B

a Complete your sentences 1–8 with the comparative from the **bold** adjectives.

1 **old** The Pyramids in Egypt are _____ than the Parthenon in Greece.
(*True. The Pyramids are about 4,500 years old and the Parthenon is about 2,500 years old.*)

2 **short** The First World War was _____ than the Second World War.
(*True. The First World War lasted four years (1914–1918), but the Second World War lasted six years (1939–1945).*)

3 **high** The mountains on Earth are _____ than the mountains on Mars.
(*False. Olympus Mons on Mars is 25 km high; Everest is about 9 km high.*)

4 **big** China is _____ than Canada.
(*False. Canada is 10,000,000 square kilometres; China is about 9,600,000 square kilometres.*)

5 **popular** In the UK coffee is now _____ than tea.
(*False. On average, the British drink 165,000,000 cups of tea a day and 70,000,000 cups of coffee.*)

6 **warm** The Mediterranean Sea is _____ than the Red Sea.
(*False. Mediterranean Sea average temperature = 24–26 degrees Celsius; Red Sea average = 26–30 degrees Celsius.*)

7 **good** It's _____ to do exercise in the morning than in the afternoon.
(*False. In the afternoon between 4 and 5 p.m. the body temperature is at its maximum, which means it is the perfect time to exercise.*)

8 **hot** The earth is _____ than the moon.
(*False. The average temperature of the moon is about 123 degrees Celsius during the day; the average temperature of the earth is 13–17 degrees Celsius.*)

b Play *Quiz Night*. You are the contestant.

- **A** will read you his / her sentence 1. You must say if it's true or false.
- **A** will tell you if you are right, and give you extra information.
- If you are right, you win 500 euros. **A** then reads you sentence 2 for 1,000 euros, sentence 3 for 2,000 euros, sentence 4 for 4,000 euros, etc.
- If you get a question wrong, you lose all the money, but continue to play. The prize starts again from 500 euros.

c Play *Quiz Night* again. You are the presenter. Use your questions 1–8.

10A CITIES QUIZ Student B

a Complete your questions with the superlative of the adjectives in brackets.

b Ask **A** your questions. Does he / she know the answers? (the correct answers are in **bold**.)

1 Which city has the _____ quality of life in the world? (good)
  a Vienna   b **Copenhagen**   c Miami
2 Which US city has the _____ population? (big)
  a **New York**   b Chicago   c San Francisco
3 Which city has the _____ airport in the world? (busy)
  a London   b **Atlanta**   c Singapore
4 What's the _____ capital city in the world? (high)
  a **La Paz, Bolivia**
  b Kathmandu, Nepal
  c Lima, Peru
5 Which city has the _____ public transport in the world? (expensive)
  a Budapest   b Athens   c **London**

> Which city has the best quality of life in the world, Vienna, Copenhagen, or Miami?

c Answer **A**'s questions.

10B WHAT ARE YOU GOING TO DO? Student B

a Answer **A**'s questions.

b Ask **A** the questions below.

Tonight	• What / have for dinner tonight? • What / do after dinner?
Tomorrow	• / go to work (or school) tomorrow? • What / do in the evening?
Next weekend	• / go out on Friday night? What / do? • What / do on Sunday?

Writing

1 COMPLETING A FORM

a Look at the information about capital letters.

> **Capital letters**
> In English these words start with a CAPITAL letter.
> - names and surnames **M**elissa **R**ogers
> - countries, nationalities, and languages **F**rance, **F**rench
> - towns and cities **N**ew **Y**ork
> - days of the week **M**onday
> - the first word in a sentence **H**er father is from Milan.
> - the pronoun **I** She's Russian and **I**'m Mexican.

b Complete the form with your information.

c Write this text again with capital letters where necessary.

> my name's leos. i'm from brno in the czech republic, and i speak czech, german, and a little english. my teacher is american. her name's kate. my english classes are on mondays and wednesdays.

d Write a similar text about you. Check the capital letters are correct. Then check for any other mistakes.

◀ p.9

APPLICATION FOR A STUDENT VISA

About You

First name

Surname (Family name)

Mr ☐   Mrs ☐   Ms ☐   Gender Male ☐ Female ☐

Date of birth   Day ☐☐   Month ☐☐   Year ☐☐☐☐

Marital status   Married ☐   Single ☐   Divorced ☐   Separated ☐

Nationality

Place of birth

Country   Town / City

Contact Details

Home address   Email address

                         Phone number
                         home
                         mobile

Passport / Identity card number

Signature   Date

2 A PERSONAL PROFILE

a Read Jamie's profile. Do you have similar interests?

b Look at the examples below.

> **and, but, and or**
> **and** I speak English **and** a little Italian.
>   I watch the news **and** football at the weekend.
> **but** I speak English, **but** I don't speak Italian.
>   I'm from Scotland, **but** I live in London.
> **or**   I don't speak English **or** Italian.
>   I don't like classical music **or** jazz.
> **e.g.** *e.g.* = for example. We often use it when we write informally. I like rock music, e.g. Coldplay.

c Write a profile of yourself. Use the same headings (Hometown, Music, etc.). Attach a photo if you can. Use *and*, *but*, and *or* to join your ideas together.

d Check your profile for mistakes (e.g. capital letters and spelling).

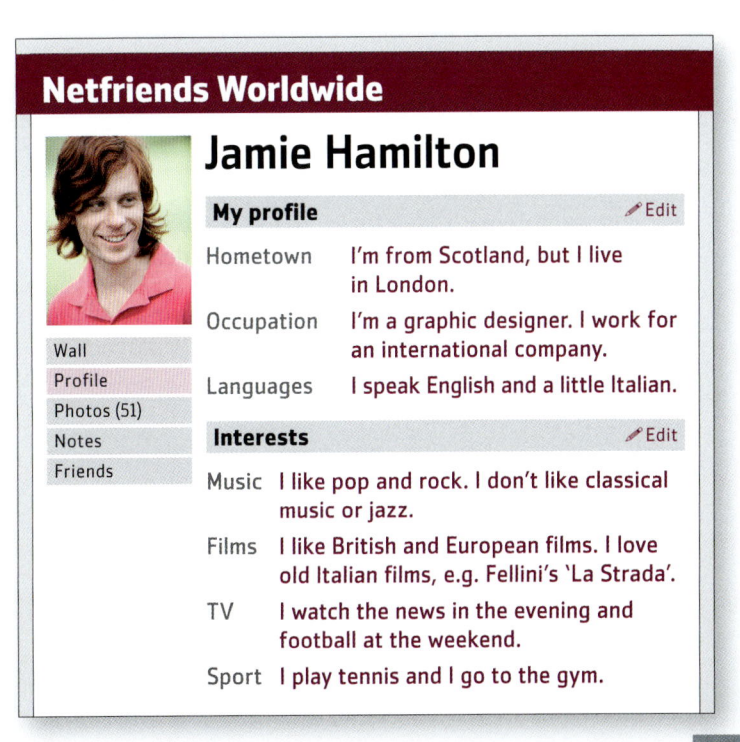

◀ p.25

Netfriends Worldwide

Jamie Hamilton

My profile ✏ Edit

Hometown	I'm from Scotland, but I live in London.
Occupation	I'm a graphic designer. I work for an international company.
Languages	I speak English and a little Italian.

Wall
Profile
Photos (51)
Notes
Friends

Interests ✏ Edit

Music	I like pop and rock. I don't like classical music or jazz.
Films	I like British and European films. I love old Italian films, e.g. Fellini's 'La Strada'.
TV	I watch the news in the evening and football at the weekend.
Sport	I play tennis and I go to the gym.

Writing

3 A MAGAZINE ARTICLE

a Read Cristina's article. Is her Saturday like yours?

b Look at the examples below.

> **after** and **then**
> Use *after* + another word, e.g. **after** *lunch*, **after** *work*, **after** *that*, etc.
> Use *then* to say what happens next, e.g. *I get up and* **then** *I have breakfast*.

c Read her article again and check you understand the highlighted words. Then use them to complete the sentences below.
1 Jack usually gets up at 7.30. _____ he has a shower.
2 _____ lunch I often sleep for half an hour.
3 She always has a bath _____ she goes to bed.
4 _____ the week I work _____ 9.00 _____ 5.00.
5 I usually get home at about midnight, and _____ I go to bed.
6 We usually watch TV _____ it's time to go to bed.

d You are going to write an article for a magazine called **My favourite day**. Write four paragraphs. First, look at the questions and make notes of what you can say.

> 1 What's your favourite day of the week? Why?
> 2 What do you usually do in the morning?
> 3 Where do you have lunch? What do you usually do after lunch?
> 4 What do you usually do in the evening?

e Now write your article. Choose which of your ideas you want to use. Don't forget to use some of the highlighted words to link together your ideas.

f Check your article for mistakes. Show your article to another student. Find one thing in your partner's article that is the same for you.

◀ *p.31*

My favourite day

Cristina,
a university student from Madrid

My favourite day of the week is Saturday, because it's the first day of the weekend!

I get up very early during the week, so on Saturday it's nice to get up late, and I always stay in bed until about 10.30. Then I usually go shopping with a friend. In Spain shops are closed on Sundays, so Saturday is the only day for shopping. We don't always buy anything, but we have fun just looking.

I often have lunch with my mother and my brother. It's great because my mum is a really good cook and she always makes things we like, and my brother and I have time to talk about our week. After lunch I sometimes study from about 4.00 to 6.00, especially if I have exams.

In the evening I usually go out with my friends. We often go to the cinema, and then we have a pizza or tapas. I never go to bed before 1.00, or sometimes later.

4 SOCIAL NETWORKING

a Alain is travelling round the world. He writes posts and puts photos from different places on a social networking site. Read his posts and match them to the photos. What countries do you think he is in?

A		I'm standing above Niagara Falls... Wow! Check out my photos!
B		I'm sitting at a bar looking at the sunset and watching a game of beach volleyball. I have three more days here – paradise!
C		I'm on the bullet train going to Mount Fuji. It's really fast – 300km an hour – just like the trains at home! ha ha ☺
D		I'm having lunch at a little trattoria just one minute from the Trevi fountain. I have my three coins ready to throw in – but my wish is a secret...
E		I'm watching a cricket match in the park in Oxford. A very strange sport – I think they're stopping to have tea now! Can you believe it?

b Imagine you are on holiday in your country or abroad. Write four different posts of about 20–25 words saying what you're doing.

c Check your posts for mistakes.

◀ p.41

5 AN INFORMAL EMAIL

To practise your English you can write to a 'penfriend' in another country. You can find penfriend websites on the internet.

a Read the email. Then cover it. Can you remember what information Chiara gives in the three main paragraphs?

From: Chiara [chiararossi@hitmail.com]
To: Stefan [stefan7541200@moebius.ch]
Subject: Hi from Italy!

Hi Stefan

My name's Chiara. I'm 19, and I'm from Milan, in Italy. I'm a receptionist at a hotel. I'm studing English becuse I need it for my job.

I live with my parents and my brother and sister. My father is an arkitect and my mother works in a clothes shop. My brother and sister are at school.

I don't have very much free time because I work six days a week. I usualy go shoping on my day off. In the evening I like listening to music, or chatting to freinds. I really like hip hop – do you like it?

Please write soon.

Best wishes

Chiara

b Look at the six underlined spelling mistakes. Can you spell these words?

> **Informal emails**
> beginning: *Hi* + name
> middle: Use contractions, e.g. **I'm** *from Milan.*
> end: *Best wishes*, or *Love* (for a good friend)

c You are going to write a similar email to your teacher. First, make notes about the following information.

Paragraph 1	Your name, age, and where you are from. What you do, and why you are studying English.
Paragraph 2	Who you live with. Your family.
Paragraph 3	What you like doing in your free time.

d Now write your email. Use your notes and the language in the information box.

e Check your email for mistakes.

◀ p.49

Writing

Writing

6 DESCRIBING YOUR HOME

a Read the website and the description of a flat in London. Would you like to stay there?

b Number the information in the order it comes in the description.

- [ ] Details about some of the rooms
- [ ] How far it is from the city centre
- [ ] What floor the flat is on
- [ ] What rooms there are
- [ ] What services there are nearby
- [ ] What you can see from the flat
- [ ] Where it is

c Look at the information about *so*.

> **so**
> There's a sofa bed in the study, **so** you can use it as an extra bedroom.
> We can use *so* to express a result or consequence, e.g.
> *I was very tired, so I went to bed early.*
> *My office is near my house, so I walk to work.*

d You are going to write a description of your house or flat for the website. First, make notes on the topics in **b**.

e Now write your description. Choose which of your ideas you want to use. Don't forget to say where you would like to go.

f Check your description for mistakes. Show it to other students. Whose house or flat would you like to stay in?

◀ p.63

---

house swap

Home | How it works | Search | News and views | Join our community | Help

Do you want a cheap holiday? Write a description of your house or flat, and say where <u>you</u> want to go. Post the description on our website, and find someone to swap homes with.

My home
Flat in north London

My flat is in a quiet street in Hampstead, north-west London. It's on the first floor. It has two bedrooms, two bathrooms, a living room, a study, and a kitchen. The kitchen is quite big and there's a table and chairs so you can eat there. There's a sofa bed in the study, so you can use it as an extra bedroom. The bedrooms have a great view and you can see many London landmarks like the London Eye and St Paul's Cathedral. The flat doesn't have a garden, but it's very near Hampstead Heath, a beautiful big park. It's a 5-minute walk from shops, and bus and underground stations, and about a 30-minute train ride from Oxford Street in the centre of London.

Where I want to go
San Francisco, Siena, Palma de Majorca

7 A FORMAL EMAIL

a Read the advertisement and Pascal's email. Complete the email with the words in the list.

| about | confirm | Dear | double | from |
| hope | Regards | reservation | would |

b Look at the information box and then write a similar email to the White Cottage Bed and Breakfast.

- Decide how many nights you want to stay and the kind of room you need.
- Ask an *Is there / Are there…?* question.

🔍 **Formal emails (e.g. to a hotel or Bed and Breakfast, a language school, etc.)**

Beginning
Dear Mr / Mrs / Ms + surname, or
Dear Sir / Madam if you don't know the person's name
Use a comma (,) (or nothing), NOT a colon (:)
Dear Mr Brown, NOT ~~Dear Mr Brown:~~

Middle
Don't use contractions.
I would like to make a reservation
NOT ~~I'd like to…~~

End
Regards
Your first name + surname

◀ p.79

The White Cottage
Bed and Breakfast in West Bexington, Dorset

Mark and Diana Buckingham and their family welcome you to their 200-year-old country home in a small village in Dorset.

Two double bedrooms, one single, and a family suite ☐ TV 📶 WiFi

The White Cottage – reservation
From: Pascal Mercier [pascal80@gomail.com]
To: thewhitecottage@greentomato.co.uk

1_____ Mr and Mrs Buckingham,

I 2_____ like to make a 3_____ for a 4_____ room and a single room for two nights, 5_____ 24th to 26th June.

We 6_____ to arrive by car at 7_____ 5.00 in the afternoon on the 24th. Is there a place where we can park near your house?

Could you please 8_____ the reservation?

9_____

Pascal Mercier

Listening

1 13)))

1 A A cheese and tomato sandwich, please.
   B That's 3 euros and 20 cents.
2 A So Anna, your classes are on Tuesday and Thursday mornings.
   B *Que?* Sorry?
3 British Airways flight to Madrid is now boarding at gate number 9.
4 A Where to, madam?
   B Manchester Road, please. Number 16.
5 A Here's your key, sir. Room 12.
   B Thank you.
6 A Here we are.
   B Oh no. It's closed.
   A Look, it says 'Closed on Mondays'!

1 29)))

1 The train waiting at platform 13 is the Eurostar to Paris.
2 A Excuse me! How far is it to Dublin?
   B It's about 40 kilometres.
   B Thanks a lot.
3 15 love.
4 Will all passengers on flight BA234 to New York please go to gate 60 immediately.
5 A How much is that?
   B A pizza and two cokes. That's 17 euros.
6 A What's your address?
   B It's 80 Park Road.
   A Sorry? What number?
   B 80, 8 oh.
7 **Teacher** OK. Can you be quiet, please? Open your books on page 90.
   Student 1 What page?
   Student 2 Page 90.

1 39)))

Receptionist Hello. Are you a new student?
Darly Yes, I am.
Receptionist Sit down, please. I'm the receptionist and my name's Mark. I'm just going to ask you a few questions.
Darly OK.
Receptionist Right. What's your first name?
Darly Darly.
Receptionist How do you spell that?
Darly D-A-R-L-Y
Receptionist D-A-R-L-Y?
Darly Yes, that's right.
Receptionist And what's your surname?
Darly Bezerra.
Receptionist Bezerra. Is that B-E-Z-E-R-A?
Darly B-E-Z-E-double R-A.
Receptionist B-E-Z-E-double R-A. OK. Where are you from?
Darly I'm from Brazil.
Receptionist Where in Brazil?
Darly From Rio.
Receptionist And how old are you?
Darly I'm 20.
Receptionist What's your address?
Darly In Rio?
Receptionist Yes.
Darly It's 350 Avenida Princesa Isabel.
Receptionist That's 350 Avenida Princesa Isabel.
Darly Yes.
Receptionist What's your postcode?
Darly Sorry?
Receptionist The postcode, you know, a number?
Darly Ah yes. It's 22011-010.
Receptionist 22011-010. Great. What's your email address?
Darly It's dbezerra@mail.com.
Receptionist And what's your phone number?
Darly My mobile number or my home number in Rio?
Receptionist Both – home and mobile.
Darly My phone number in Rio is 55 – that's the code for Brazil – 219 560733.
Receptionist 55 219 560733.
Darly Yes, that's right. And my mobile number is 07621 3784511. It's an English mobile.
Receptionist 07621 3784511. That's great, Darly. Thank you. OK, so you're in level 6. Your first class is on Monday.

1 44)))

Rob Hi. My name's Rob Walker. I live here in London, I work in London, and I write about London! I work for a magazine called *London 24seven*. I write about life in London. The people, the theatre, the restaurants... It's fun! I love London. It's a great city.
Jenny Hi. My name's Jenny Zielinski. I'm from New York. The number one city in the world. I'm the assistant editor of a magazine, *New York 24seven*. I'm the new assistant editor. But this week, I'm on a business trip to London. This is my first time in the UK. It's very exciting!

1 48)))

Waitress Is your tea OK?
Jenny Yes, thank you. It's very quiet this evening.
Waitress Yes, very relaxing! Are you on holiday?
Jenny No, I'm here on business.
Waitress Where are you from?
Jenny I'm from New York. What about you?
Waitress I'm from Budapest, in Hungary.
Jenny Really? Oh, sorry.
Waitress No problem.
—
Jenny Hello?
Rob Is that Jennifer?
Jenny Yes.
Rob This is Rob. Rob Walker...From *London 24seven*?
Jenny Oh, Rob, yes, of course. Hi.
Rob Hi. How are you?
Jenny Oh, I'm fine, thanks. A little tired, that's all.
Rob I can meet you at the hotel tomorrow morning. Is nine OK for you?
Jenny That's perfect.
Rob Great. OK, see you tomorrow at nine.
Jenny Thanks. See you then. Bye.
Waitress Would you like another tea?
Jenny No, thanks. It's time for bed.
Waitress Good night, and enjoy your stay.
Jenny Good night.

1 55)))

1 I have a big table, and on the table I have a computer and a printer, pens and pieces of paper, er, photos, and a lamp. Lots of things. My table isn't tidy. It's very untidy.
2 On my desk I have a lamp, a phone, books, a laptop, a photo of my family, pens and pencils, and a lot of pieces of paper. I think my desk is tidy. Not very tidy, but tidy.
3 On my desk I have a computer, a lamp, a diary, a Spanish-English dictionary, DVDs, and some pens. Oh, and tissues. At the moment my desk is very tidy.

1 70)))

Receptionist Good evening, sir. Good evening, madam.
Dad Good evening. Can we have two double rooms, please?
Receptionist Do you have a reservation?
Dad No, we don't.
Receptionist I'm sorry, sir. The hotel is full.
Mum Oh no!
Dad Come on. Let's go. I know another hotel near here.
Policeman Excuse me, sir. Is this your car?
Dad Yes, it is. What's the problem?
Policeman This is no parking, sir. Look at the sign.
Dad I'm very sorry.
Policeman Can I see your driving licence, please?

2 10)))

Announcer And now on Radio 4, His job, her job.
Presenter Good evening and welcome again to the jobs quiz, His job, her job. And our team tonight are David, a teacher...
David Hello.
Presenter ...Kate, who's unemployed...
Kate Hi.
Presenter ...and Lorna, who's a writer.
Lorna Good evening.

Presenter And our first guest tonight is…
Wayne Wayne.
Presenter Hello, Wayne. Welcome to the programme. What's your wife's name, Wayne?
Wayne Her name's Tanya.
Presenter Tanya? Nice name. OK team, you have one minute to ask Wayne questions about his job and then one minute to ask him about Tanya's job, starting now. Let's have your first question.
David Hi, Wayne. Do you work in an office?
Wayne No, I don't.
Lorna Do you work in the evening?
Wayne It depends. Yes, sometimes.
Kate Do you make things?
Wayne No, I don't.
Lorna Do you wear a uniform or special clothes?
Wayne Er, yes – I wear special clothes.
Kate Do you drive in your job?
Wayne No, I don't.
Lorna Do you work with other people?
Wayne Yes, I do. Ten people.
Kate Do you have special qualifications?
Wayne Qualifications? No, I don't.
David Do you speak foreign languages?
Wayne No, only English.
Presenter You only have time for one more question team.
David Er, do you earn a lot of money?
Wayne Yes, I do.
Presenter Your time's up…

2)11))
Presenter Now you have a minute to ask Wayne about Tanya's job.
Kate Wayne, does Tanya work outside?
Wayne It depends. Outside and inside.
Lorna Does she work at the weekend?
Wayne Yes, she does.
Kate Does she work with computers?
Wayne No, she doesn't.
David Does she wear a uniform or special clothes?
Wayne Yes, she does. She wears special clothes.
Kate Does she travel?
Wayne Yes, she does. A lot.
Lorna Does she earn a lot of money?
Wayne Yes, she does. A lot.
Presenter That's time. OK team…

2)12))
Presenter OK team. So, what's Wayne's job?
Kate OK, so you wear special clothes, you work with ten other people, you earn a lot of money. Are you a footballer, Wayne?
Wayne Yes, I am.
Presenter Very good! And Tanya's job?
David Let's see. She works outside and inside. She works at the weekend. She doesn't work with computers. She wears special clothes. She travels a lot. We think she's a flight attendant.
Presenter Is that right, Wayne?
Wayne No, that's wrong. Tanya is a model.

2)19))
Kevin Do you like Star Wars?
Samantha No, I don't.
Kevin Why not? It's a fantastic film.
Samantha I don't like science fiction.
Kevin What kind of films do you like?
Samantha I love foreign films, French, Italian, Spanish.
Kevin Oh.
Samantha My salad's very nice.
Kevin Good. My burger's nice too.
Samantha What kind of music do you like?
Kevin Music? I love heavy metal. What about you?
Samantha Opera.
Kevin Opera – that's not really my thing!
Kevin What do you do at the weekend?
Samantha I go to the cinema, I go to restaurants, I cook. I love good food. And you?
Kevin Well, I don't cook! I meet friends and we play video games.
Samantha You meet friends and you play video games. Wow.
Kevin Do you want another drink?
Samantha Oh, excuse me. Hi. Oh? Why? Now? OK. See you in a minute. Sorry Kevin. I need to go. Nice to meet you. Bye.
Kevin Oh. Bye.
Waiter The bill, sir.
Kevin The bill! Hey, Samantha. Wait!

2)25))
Rob Erm… Jennifer?
Jenny Rob?
Rob Yes, hello. Nice to meet you, Jennifer.
Jenny Call me Jenny. Good to meet you, too.
Rob Welcome to London. Am I late?
Jenny Erm… just a little.
Rob What time is it?
Jenny Nine fifteen.
Rob I'm really sorry. The traffic is terrible today.
Jenny No problem.
Rob How are you? How's the hotel?
Jenny The hotel's very nice. But breakfast isn't great. I'd like a good cup of coffee. Not hotel coffee, real coffee.
Rob OK, let's get a coffee.
Jenny Do I have time? I have a meeting at nine-thirty.
Rob With Daniel?
Jenny Yes.
Rob Don't worry. We have lots of time, the office is very near. So, Jenny, where do you live in New York?

2)28))
Rob Here we are. This is the office. And this is Karen.
Jenny Hello, Karen.
Rob Karen, this is Jennifer Zielinski from the New York office.
Karen Hello, Jennifer.
Jenny Nice to meet you.
Rob Karen is our administrator. We all depend on her.
Karen Don't listen to Rob.

Rob But it's true!
Karen Is this your first time in the UK, Jennifer?
Jenny Yes, it is. But it isn't my first time in Europe. I have family in Poland.
Karen Really? And where do you live in New York?
Jenny In Manhattan. Do you know New York?
Karen Yes. My sister lives in Brooklyn.
Jenny I have family in Brooklyn, too. Where does your sister live?
Daniel Jennifer!
Jenny Daniel?
Daniel How nice to meet you, at last. Would you like something to drink? Tea, coffee, water?
Jenny No, I'm fine, thanks.
Daniel Great. Oh, Karen. What time is my next meeting?
Karen At twelve o'clock.
Daniel That's good, we have time. OK, come into my office, Jennifer.
Jenny Thank you.
Daniel Talk to you later, Rob.
Rob Yeah. Sure.

2)35))
Anna Who's that?
Isabel That's my boyfriend, Alex.
Anna He's good-looking. How old is he?
Isabel Twenty-six.
Anna What does he do?
Isabel He's a policeman.
Anna Really? Does he like it?
Isabel Yes, he loves it. And this is my dad.
Anna He looks very young.
Isabel Well, he's fifty-five this year.
Anna He doesn't look fifty-five! Is that your mother?
Isabel No, that's Gloria, my stepmother.
Anna Is she nice?
Isabel Yes, she's great. She's a hairdresser – she does my hair for free!
Anna Oh, that's good. Who's that?
Isabel That's Natalie.
Anna Who's she?
Isabel My brother's girlfriend.
Anna She's pretty!
Isabel Do you think so?
Anna Yes. Don't you like her?
Isabel Not very much. She thinks she's very intelligent, but she isn't really.
Anna What does she do?
Isabel She's at university. She studies French – but she can't speak it very well…

2)40))
Interviewer What time do you get up in the morning?
Amelia Me levanto a las seis y media. Nunca me quiero levantar porque es tan temprano. I get up at half past six. I never want to get up because it's very early.
Interviewer Do you have breakfast?
Amelia Yes, a quick breakfast, and then I go to school.
Interviewer How do you go to school?

Listening 117

Amelia By bus. We have these yellow school buses – we call them liebres.
Interviewer What time do you start school?
Amelia At 8 o'clock. In the first lesson everyone is really sleepy.
Interviewer How many lessons do you have?
Amelia In the morning we usually have five but sometimes six.
Interviewer What time do you have lunch?
Amelia At 1 o'clock.
Interviewer That's a very long morning!
Amelia Yes, it is. We're very hungry at lunchtime.
Interviewer Where do you have lunch?
Amelia We have lunch at school in the cafeteria. We only have fifty minutes so we don't have much time to relax. We just eat our food and then run to the next lesson.
Interviewer How many lessons do you have in the afternoon?
Amelia On a good day only three, on a bad day five. After the second lesson everybody is tired and we don't concentrate on what the teacher is telling us.
Interviewer What time does school finish?
Amelia At half past five.
Interviewer Do you go home then?
Amelia It depends. On Mondays and Wednesdays I go to extra classes to prepare for university entrance exams, and on Tuesdays and Thursdays I have basketball practice.
Interviewer What do you do when you get home?
Amelia I just want to relax but it's impossible. I have homework and exams so I need to study! So I sit down at my desk and start working again. After dinner I go back to my room and study until 11 o'clock, or sometimes later.
Interviewer What time do you go to bed?
Amelia About half past eleven. I lie in bed and think about the next day and the lessons I have. Luckily, it's Friday today! No school tomorrow!

2 57)))
GARY
Gary (sings)
Judge 1 Very nice Gary.
Judge 2 Yes, I like it. Well done.
JUSTIN
Justin (sings)
Judge 1 In a word…'terrible!'
Judge 2 Justin, you have a very pretty face, but I'm sorry, you can't sing!
NAOMI
Naomi (sings)
Judge 1 Thank you Naomi. Very nice.
Judge 2 Naomi, you have a beautiful voice, but I can't hear the feeling.
Judge 1 OK. Justin and Naomi. Thank you very much, but no thank you. Gary, congratulations. See you on the show next week.
Gary Fantastic! That's great. Thank you.

3 7)))
Interviewer Do you have a problem with noisy neighbours, Rebecca?
Rebecca No, I don't, not at all. But sometimes my neighbours have problems with me! I live in a block of small flats and the house rules here are really strict.
Interviewer What kind of house rules do you have?
Rebecca Well, for example, during the week you can't make noise between 12.30 and two o'clock because this is when young children are asleep and the same is true after ten o'clock at night. So, for example, after ten o'clock you can't listen to loud music without headphones, or play a musical instrument. I think it's because people in Switzerland get up early in the morning, so they go to bed very early.
Interviewer Can you watch TV after ten o'clock?
Rebecca Yes, you can, just not really loudly. So, I watch TV, but with the volume low and the windows closed so that's not a problem. But the problem is I can't use my bathroom, because the water makes a noise, and my bathroom is next to my neighbour's bedroom.
Interviewer So you can't have a shower or a bath?
Rebecca No, not after ten o'clock. This isn't true in all flats in Switzerland, but in my flat it is. Maybe because the flats are small.
Interviewer What about at the weekend?
Rebecca On Saturday the rules are the same. No noise after ten o'clock in the evening.
Interviewer What happens if you want to have a party?
Rebecca You can have a party but the music can't be loud after ten.
Interviewer What happens if you make a lot of noise after ten?
Rebecca Well, the neighbours complain and if it's really loud, they can call the police.
Interviewer What about on Sunday?
Rebecca Sunday is a day of rest in Switzerland so you can't make any noise in your flat at all. For example, in my building you can't move furniture, or put a picture on the wall, or turn on the washing machine.
Interviewer What do you think of these rules?
Rebecca Well, I like the rules that control noise during the week and on Sunday. I think it's a good idea. But I think they need to be a bit more flexible on Saturdays. I mean if a party is still a little loud after ten, I don't think you need to call the police.
Interviewer Does that really happen?
Rebecca Yes, it happened to me.

3 10)))
The best thing about the weather in London is that it's never extreme. It isn't usually very hot or very cold. In the summer it's sometimes sunny and sometimes cloudy, with temperatures of about 22 degrees. And of course it sometimes rains.
In winter the temperature is usually between zero and ten degrees. It can be windy and cold but it hardly ever snows.
In spring and in autumn the weather is very changeable – you can have all the four seasons in one day! It can be sunny in the morning, cloudy at lunchtime, raining in the afternoon, and then cold and windy in the evening. I always tell tourists to take their sunglasses and their umbrellas when they go out!
But one thing you don't often see these days in London is fog. A lot of tourists come to London and say 'Where's the fog? London is always foggy in films!' Well, it's true that, in the past, that is until the 1950s, London was a very foggy city because the air was really dirty. But today the air is clean and it's hardly ever foggy.

3 15)))
Rob Hey, Jenny!
Jenny Oh hi, Rob. Is that coffee for me?
Rob Yes. A double espresso.
Jenny Oh wow, thanks. That's really nice of you.
Rob No problem. Do you have a meeting with Daniel?
Jenny Yes, another meeting. And you?
Rob I'm going to the office, too. I have an interview in twenty minutes.
Jenny Oh really? With who?
Rob A theatre director.
Jenny Sounds interesting.
Rob What time is your meeting with Daniel?
Jenny At half past nine.
Rob Ugh!
Jenny Oh no. Are you OK? I'm so sorry!
Rob I'm fine!
Jenny I'm really sorry. You can't wear that shirt to an interview!
Rob Don't worry, there's a clothes shop over there. I can buy a new one.
Jenny OK. I can help you choose one.
Jenny Oh, that's my phone. Sorry, I need to answer this. See you in there?
Rob OK.

3 19)))
Eddie So, Jenny, what do you think of London?
Jenny I love it, Eddie! It's so cool!
Eddie What about the people in the office?
Jenny They're really nice. And they're very polite!
Eddie What are you doing right now? You aren't in the office. I can hear traffic.
Jenny Right now? I am standing outside a men's clothing store.
Eddie You're what?
Jenny I'm waiting for Rob.
Eddie Who's Rob? Do you have a new boyfriend already?
Jenny Don't be silly. He's just a guy from the office. He's buying a new shirt.
Eddie Wait a minute. So you're waiting for a guy named Rob outside a men's clothing store?
Jenny Stop it. I don't have time to explain it all now. Oh, here he is now. I have to go.

Eddie OK. Have fun.
Jenny Bye, Eddie. Love you.
Rob So, what do you think?
Jenny You cannot be serious!
Rob What's wrong? You don't like my new shirt?
Jenny No way! You can't wear that to an interview! Come on, let's go back into the store and change it.
Rob OK.

3 33))
Interviewer What's your favourite time of day?
Martin It depends. During the week it's seven in the evening, because that's when I get home from work and when I can relax. But at the weekend my favourite time is breakfast time. I have a big breakfast, and I have time to read the papers and listen to the radio.
Interviewer What's your favourite day of the week?
Martin My favourite day of the week is Friday, because then I know the weekend is near.
Interviewer What's your favourite month?
Martin Probably May. It's when the weather starts to get warm and the evenings are long.
Interviewer What's your favourite season?
Martin Spring, because it means that winter is finally over. I love cycling, and spring is a great time for cycling – not too hot and not too cold.
Interviewer What's your favourite public holiday?
Martin Probably New Year's Eve, because you don't need to worry about buying presents or cooking a big lunch, and everybody's in a good mood.

3 49))
1 He was an English writer.
 He was born in the 16th century.
 He was married with three children.
 He was born in Stratford upon Avon.
 He is famous for his plays, for example *Hamlet* and *Macbeth*.
2 She was born in Los Angeles in 1926.
 She was a famous actress.
 She was blonde and very beautiful.
 Her real name was Norma Jeane Baker.
 There is a famous painting of her by Andy Warhol.

3 52))
… and finally on the news today the story of two football fans who missed the big match.
 Last week Chelsea played Arsenal at Chelsea's famous stadium, Stamford Bridge in west London. It was the match that football fans all over the world wanted to watch. Charles Spencer's daughter and a friend were among the lucky people with tickets. The girls were in Althorp, which is about 140 km from London, and they decided to go by taxi. But when the taxi stopped in a small village, it was clear that something was wrong. They were in Stamford Bridge, but not at the Chelsea stadium. The driver had typed Stamford Bridge into his satnav. But unfortunately, Stamford Bridge is also a small village in the north of England – and that's where they were! Of course, they missed the match.

3 60))
Interviewer When was your memorable night?
David Te puedo decir exactamente, fue el once de julio del dos mil diez. I can tell you exactly, it was the 11th July 2010.
Interviewer Why do you remember the date?
David Because it was the final of the Football World Cup, Spain against Holland.
Interviewer Where were you?
David Well, I'm a flight attendant and that day I was in Acapulco in Mexico.
Interviewer Who were you with?
David I was with three other Spanish flight attendants.
Interviewer Where did you go to watch the match?
David We didn't go out. We watched the match in the hotel bar.
Interviewer And what did you wear to watch the match?
David We wore Spanish football shirts which we bought in a shop and we also had red and yellow scarves.
Interviewer Tell me about the night. What did you do?
David Well, the match was on in the afternoon Mexican time. We went down to the hotel bar early to get a good seat. There was a big screen. The bar was full of Spanish tourists. There was a great atmosphere.
Interviewer And Spain won the match, of course.
David Yes. It wasn't a good match, but when Spain got their winning goal everybody shouted and jumped up. It was amazing! When the match finished we all went out. We wanted to celebrate. We went to another bar near the beach and it was full of Spanish people. Everyone was really happy. We had a great party!
Interviewer What was the weather like? Do you remember?
David Yes, it was a warm night. About 20 degrees, I think.
Interviewer What time did you get back to your hotel?
David I can't remember exactly but very late, about three in the morning. Luckily, I had a free day the next day so I didn't need to get up early.
Interviewer Why was this night so memorable?
David First, of course, because Spain won their first World Cup, but also because of the circumstances – we were very far away from Spain, thousands of kilometres away in another country, but we all felt very Spanish that night!

3 64))
Rob So, Jenny, we have a free morning. What do you want to do?
Jenny Well, you're the expert on London life! What do you suggest?
Rob Well, we can go cycling.
Jenny I don't have a bike.
Rob We can rent bikes. It's easy.
Jenny That's cool.
Rob OK, great. So we can cycle through the parks, and you can see a bit of London. Oh, hang on. Uh oh. It's Daniel. Daniel, hi!
Daniel Hi, Rob. You need to do an interview this morning, with an artist. He's at the Tate Modern.
Rob Can I do the interview on Monday?
Daniel Sorry, he can only do this morning.
Rob OK, send me the details.
Daniel Thank you very much, Rob.
Rob I'm sorry.
Jenny That's OK, I understand. Work is work!
Rob But I can meet you later, outside the Tate Modern. It's on the South Bank.
Jenny I can find it. I have a map, I can cycle there.
Rob Let's meet at twelve o'clock then.
Jenny Great.

3 68))
Rob Sorry about the weather.
Jenny Yeah… but what a view! It's a great bridge too.
Rob It's the Millennium Bridge. It's not for cars, only for people. It was the first new bridge over the Thames in 100 years.
Jenny You sound like a tour guide!
Rob Sorry… I interviewed the architect last year. So what would you like to visit?
Jenny What is there to see?
Rob Well, we could see the Tate Modern first as we're here, and then we could go to the Globe Theatre. Do you like Shakespeare?
Jenny Not really. I studied too much Shakespeare in college. It's Daniel. Sorry. Hi, Daniel.
Daniel Hi, Jennifer. How's your free day? Are you enjoying London?
Jenny Absolutely. It's fantastic.
Daniel Listen, I have some free time today. Would you like to meet for lunch?
Jenny That's really nice of you, Daniel, but I'm sorry, I can't. I'm really far away from the office right now.
Daniel That's OK. No problem. Maybe another time?
Jenny Definitely. Bye.
Rob What did he want? Anything important?
Jenny Not at all. Hey, let's go inside the Tate Modern now.
Rob Yes, of course. There's a great restaurant on the top floor. The view is fantastic. The Tate Modern was a power station until 1981. Did you know that?
Jenny I didn't. Do you know anything else about the Tate Modern?
Rob Thank you for asking. I know a lot about it actually.
Jenny Oh, great!

Listening 119

4 6))

Then the inspector questioned Barbara Travers.
Inspector What did you do after dinner yesterday evening?
Barbara After dinner? I played cards with Gordon, and then I went to bed.
Inspector What time was that?
Barbara It was about half past eleven. I remember I looked at my watch.
Inspector Did you hear anything in your father's room?
Barbara No. I didn't hear anything.
Inspector Miss Travers, did you have any problems with your father?
Barbara No, I didn't have any problems with him at all. My father was a wonderful man and a wonderful father. I'm sorry, Inspector.
Inspector Don't worry, Miss Travers. No more questions.

4 7))

Next, the inspector questioned Gordon Smith.
Inspector What did you do after dinner, Gordon?
Gordon I played cards with Barbara. Then she went to bed.
Inspector Did you go to bed then?
Gordon No. I stayed in the sitting room and I had a glass of whisky. Then I went to bed.
Inspector What time was that?
Gordon I don't remember exactly. I didn't look at the time.
Inspector Did you hear anything during the night?
Gordon No, I didn't. I was very tired. I slept very well.
Inspector You and Mr Travers were business partners, weren't you?
Gordon Yes, that's right.
Inspector And it's a very good business I understand.
Gordon Yes, inspector, it is.
Inspector And now it is your business.
Gordon Listen, inspector, I did not kill Jeremy. He was my partner and he was my friend.

4 8))

Finally, the inspector questioned Claudia Simeone.
Inspector What did you do yesterday evening, after dinner?
Claudia I went to my room and I had a bath and I went to bed.
Inspector What time was that?
Claudia About 11 o'clock.
Inspector Did you hear anything?
Claudia Yes. I heard somebody go into Jeremy's room. It was about 12 o'clock.
Inspector Who was it?
Claudia It was Amanda, his wife.
Inspector Are you sure? Did you see her?
Claudia Well, no, I didn't see her. But I'm sure it was Amanda.
Inspector You were Mr Travers' secretary, Claudia.
Claudia Yes, I was.
Inspector Were you just his secretary?
Claudia What do you mean?
Inspector Were you in love with Mr Travers?
Claudia No, I wasn't.
Inspector The truth please, Claudia.
Claudia Very well, inspector. Yes, I was in love with him and he said he was in love with me. He said he wanted to leave his wife – Amanda – and marry me. I was stupid. I believed him. He used me, inspector! I was very angry with him.
Inspector Did you kill him?
Claudia No, inspector, I loved Jeremy.

4 9))

Before dinner, Gordon had a drink with Jeremy in the library.
Gordon Cheers, Jeremy. Happy birthday.
Jeremy Ah, thanks, Gordon.
Gordon Listen, Jeremy, I want to talk to you about Barbara.
Jeremy Barbara? What's the problem?
Gordon It's not exactly a problem. I am in love with her, and I want to marry her.
Jeremy Marry Barbara? Marry my daughter! Are you crazy? Never! You don't love Barbara. You only want her money!
Gordon That's not true, Jeremy. I love her.
Jeremy Listen to me. If you marry Barbara, when I die all my money goes to Claudia.
Gordon To Claudia? To your secretary?
Jeremy Yes.
Gordon Is that your last word, Jeremy?
Jeremy Yes, it is.
Amanda Dinner everybody!
Reader At midnight Gordon was in the sitting room. He finished his whisky and went upstairs.
Jeremy Who is it? Gordon?

4 14))

Barbara Let's go upstairs. Follow me. Be careful. The ceiling is very low here.
Leo It's a very old house.
Barbara Yes, the house is three hundred years old. My family lived here for nearly eighty years. There are six bedrooms. This was my father's bedroom.
Kim Is there central heating in the house?
Barbara Yes, there is. Why do you ask? Are you cold?
Kim Yes, it's very cold in here.
Leo That's because we're from California.
Barbara Let's go and see the other bedrooms.
Leo Yes, of course.
Leo Well, what do you think, Kim? I love it! Don't you?
Kim I'm not sure. There's something about the house I don't like.
Leo Kim, it's perfect for the kids. Think of the garden. And it's a real authentic English country house. What do you say?
Kim I suppose so. If you're sure.
Leo I am sure! Mrs…er, Barbara. We want it. We want to rent the house.
Barbara Excellent.
Leo When can we move in?
Barbara As soon as you like.

4 15))

Leo Hello.
Barman Good evening, sir, madam. What would you like to drink?
Leo Do you have champagne?
Barman Yes, sir.
Leo Two glasses of champagne, please.
Barman Here you are!
Leo Cheers, Kim.
Kim Cheers. To our new house.
Barman You're Americans, aren't you?
Leo Yes, that's right. We're from California.
Kim We just rented the big house near here.
Barman Which house? The Travers family's house?
Leo Yes.
Barman Oh.
Leo Is something wrong?
Barman Who showed you the house?
Kim Barbara. The old lady who lived there before.
Barman Ahh, Barbara. Old Mr Travers' daughter. Some people thought that she was the one that did it. She never married, of course.
Kim The one who did what? What happened? Why did she never marry?
Barman Didn't she tell you?
Leo Tell us what?
Barman About the murder.
Leo & Kim Murder??
Barman Yes, Mr Travers was murdered in that house in 1958… in his bed.
Kim Oh, how horrible!
Barman The man who killed Mr Travers was Barbara's lover. The family never lived there again. They tried to sell the house, but nobody wanted to buy it. Not after a murder. That's why that house is always rented.
Leo Kim.
Kim Yes.
Leo Are you thinking what I'm thinking?
Kim Yes – I don't want to sleep in a house where somebody was murdered. Come on. Let's go to a hotel.
Barman Hey, your champagne! You didn't drink your champagne! Ah, well.

4 24))

I arrived at Gosforth Hall late in the evening. I don't believe in ghosts, but yes, I felt a little bit nervous. I checked in, and the receptionist gave me the key and showed me to my room.

I left my things in the room and came downstairs. There weren't many other guests in the hotel. There were only three. I sat in the lounge and I talked to the manager, Sara Daniels, about her hotel. Then I had a drink in the bar and at 12 o'clock I went upstairs to my room.

Room 11 was on the top floor. I opened the door and turned on the light.

It was a very big room, quite old, and yes, it was a bit spooky. There was an old TV on a table – but there wasn't a remote control. I turned on the TV.

There was a film on. I was happy to see that it wasn't a horror film. I decided to watch the film, but I was tired after my long journey and after half an hour I went to sleep.

4 25))
Stephen In the middle of the night I suddenly woke up! I looked at my watch. It was two o'clock in the morning. The television was off! But how? There was no remote control, and I didn't get up and turn it off. The light was on, but suddenly the light went off too. Now I was scared! I couldn't see anything strange, but I could feel that there was somebody or something in the room. I got out of bed and turned on the light and TV again. Little by little I started to relax, and I went to sleep again. When I woke up it was morning. I had breakfast and checked out.
Interviewer So the question is, did you see the ghost?
Stephen No, I didn't see the ghost, but I definitely felt something or somebody in the room when I woke up in the night.
Interviewer Were you frightened?
Stephen Yes, I was! Very frightened!
Interviewer Would you like to spend another night in the hotel?
Stephen Definitely, yes.
Interviewer Why?
Stephen Well, I'm sure there was something strange in that room. I can't explain the television and the light. I want to go back because I want to see the ghost.

4 32))
Presenter Good afternoon and welcome to today's edition of Get Ready! Cook! And a big round of applause for today's contestants, Jack and Liz. Hello, Jack. So, do you like cooking?
Jack I love it. I cook dinner every evening at home.
Presenter How about you Liz?
Liz Yes, I'm the cook in my family too. I cook every day of course, but what I really like is cooking for friends at the weekend.
Presenter OK, so you know the rules. In the bag there are six ingredients, just six ingredients. You have an hour to cook three dishes, a starter, a main course, and a dessert. Apart from the ingredients in the bag you can also use basic ingredients like pasta, rice, eggs, sugar, salt, pepper, etc. OK? Are you ready? Let's open the bag. And today's ingredients are a chicken, some carrots, some onions, three oranges, some cream cheese, and some dark chocolate. OK, Jack and Liz. You have five minutes to decide what to make and then it's Get ready! Cook!

4 33))
Presenter Liz and Jack, you have two more minutes, so I hope you're nearly ready. OK, time's up, stop cooking now, please. OK Jack, what did you make?
Jack For the starter there's carrot and orange soup, for the main course I made chicken breasts filled with cream cheese, and for dessert pancakes with chocolate sauce.
Presenter That all looks delicious. And you Liz?
Liz I made a carrot and onion salad with orange dressing, then for the main course pasta with creamy chicken sauce and for dessert chocolate and orange mousse.
Presenter It all looks good too. But now, the moment of truth. Let's taste your dishes…

4 34))
Presenter Right Jack, let's try your soup. Mmm, that's delicious. It's a great combination, carrot and orange. Is there any onion in the soup?
Jack Yes, one onion.
Presenter It's very good, but next time maybe you could add a little cream, not much, just a little. OK, now the chicken. Mmm, that's lovely. Not very original, but very tasty. And finally the pancakes. They look beautiful… and they taste fantastic. Now Liz, let's try your dishes. The salad first. Mmm, it's nice, but the taste of onion is very strong. How many onions did you use?
Liz Three.
Presenter I think perhaps two are enough for this salad. OK, the pasta. Mmm, it's very good but it needs a bit more salt and pepper. And finally the mousse. That's a beautiful mousse, Liz.
Liz Thank you.
Presenter Mmm, and it tastes fantastic, absolutely delicious.
Well, congratulations to you both. I loved all your dishes – but only one of you can win – and today's winner is…Jack!

4 42))
Compere Question 1. What is the approximate population of the UK? Is it a 42 million, b 52 million, or c 62 million?
Contestant 1 I think it's c, 62 million.
Compere c is the right answer! Question 2. How many calories are there in a Big Mac? Is it a 670, b 485, or c 305?
Contestant 2 I think it's a, 670.
Compere Final answer?
Contestant 2 Final answer, 670.
Compere I'm sorry, the right answer is b. A Big Mac has 485 calories. And Question 3. How far is it from New York City to Los Angeles? Is it a about 4,000 km, b about 2,500 km, or c about 5,000 km?
Contestant 3 About 4,000 km.
Compere Are you sure?
Contestant 3 Yes. I'm sure.
Compere a is the right answer!

4 45))
Presenter Good evening. Welcome to Quiz Night. Tonight's show comes from Dublin. And our first contestant is Colleen from London. Hi Colleen. Are you nervous?
Colleen Yes, a bit.
Presenter Well, just try to relax. The rules are the same as always. I'm going to read you some sentences, and you have ten seconds to say if the sentence is true or false. If you get the first answer right, you win 500 euros. Then for each correct answer you double your money, so if you get the second answer right, you win 1,000 euros, and for the third correct answer you win 2,000 euros. For eight correct answers you win 64,000 euros. But if you get an answer wrong, you lose all the money. Remember you can also phone a friend, so if you're not sure about one of the answers, you can phone your friend to help you. Is that OK, Colleen?
Colleen Yes, OK.

4 46))
Presenter OK Colleen, first question for 500 euros. The North Pole is colder than the South Pole. True or false?
Colleen The North Pole is colder than the South Pole. Er, false.
Presenter Correct. The South Pole is much colder, because it's much higher than the North Pole. In the summer the average temperature at the North Pole is zero degrees, but at the South Pole it's minus 26. Now, for 1,000 euros, carrots are sweeter than tomatoes. True or false?
Colleen Er, I think it's true.
Presenter Correct. It's true. Carrots are about five percent sugar, but tomatoes don't have any sugar at all. Right, for 2,000 euros, a proton is heavier than an electron.
Colleen I think it's true.
Presenter Correct. A proton is more than 1,800 times heavier than an electron. Next, for 4,000 euros, The White House is bigger than Buckingham Palace. True or false?
Colleen The White House is bigger than Buckingham Palace. Er, false.
Presenter Correct. Buckingham Palace has 775 rooms, but the White House has only 132 rooms. Next, for 8,000 euros, oranges are healthier than strawberries. True or false?
Colleen Er, true. No, er, false.
Presenter Do you want to phone a friend?
Colleen No, I think it's false.
Presenter Correct. An orange has 70 milligrams of vitamin C, but a cup of strawberries, a normal serving, has 98. OK, for 16,000 euros, female mosquitoes are more dangerous than male mosquitoes.
Colleen Er, true.
Presenter Correct. Female mosquitoes are the ones that bite. Male mosquitoes don't bite. OK Colleen, for 32,000 euros, in judo a green belt is better than a blue belt. True or false?
Colleen Er, I'm sure that's false. My brother does judo. False.
Presenter Correct. The order of belts in the lower stages of judo is white for a beginner, then yellow, orange, green, blue, brown, and black. And finally, the last question. Be very careful, Colleen. If you get it right, you win 64,000 euros, but if you get it wrong, you get nothing. Are you ready?
Colleen Yes, ready.

Presenter OK, for 64,000 euros, hepatitis A is worse than hepatitis B. True or false?
Colleen Er… er…
Presenter Quickly, Colleen, your time is nearly up.
Colleen I want to phone a friend.
Presenter Right, Colleen. So, who do you want to call?
Colleen Kevin.
Presenter Is he your boyfriend?
Colleen Yes, he is.
Presenter OK then. Hello, is that Kevin?
Kevin Yes, it is.
Presenter I'm phoning from Quiz Night. Colleen needs some help. You have 30 seconds, Kevin. Here she is.
Colleen Hi Kevin.
Kevin Hi Colleen.
Colleen Listen, Kevin. It's the last question. Hepatitis A is worse than hepatitis B. True or false?
Kevin Er, I think it's true. Hepatitis A, yes, that's the serious one.
Colleen Are you sure?
Kevin Yes, definitely!
Presenter Time's up. OK Colleen, true or false?
Colleen True.
Presenter Final answer?
Colleen Final answer. True.
Presenter I'm sorry Colleen, it's false. Hepatitis B is much more serious, you can die from it. You had 32,000 euros, but now you go home with nothing.
Colleen Ooh, Kevin. You wait until I see him…

4 49))
Jenny Thanks for showing me around London yesterday. I had a great time.
Rob Me too. So, what did you do last night?
Jenny Nothing really. I had a lot of work to do. Emails, phone calls… What did you do?
Rob I wrote my article about the artist that I interviewed yesterday morning.
Jenny Can I see it?
Rob Sure, it's on my laptop. Hang on a second. There.
Jenny Sorry. Hi, Eddie. Thanks! But listen, I can't talk right now. I'm in the office. Yeah, later. OK. Sorry, but it's my birthday today.
Rob Really?! Happy birthday! Maybe we could have dinner tonight?
Daniel Jennifer.
Jenny Oh, hi Daniel.
Daniel I'd like to take you out for dinner this evening.
Jenny This evening?
Daniel Yes, for a working dinner. We have a lot to talk about before you go back to New York. I know a very good restaurant.
Jenny Oh, erm… yes, of course.
Daniel Great. See you later.
Jenny Yes, sure. Sorry, Rob.

4 55))
Daniel So, Jenny, I hear it's your birthday today.
Jenny Yes, that's right.
Daniel Well, Happy Birthday! How do you normally celebrate?
Jenny Oh, nothing special. Maybe I go out for dinner with friends or see a movie.
Daniel Well, we could go out somewhere, after dinner.
Waiter Would you like a dessert?
Jenny Not for me, thanks.
Daniel OK, no.
Waiter Coffee?
Jenny A decaf espresso.
Daniel The same for me, please.
Waiter Two decaffeinated espressos. Certainly, sir.
Daniel You know Jenny, you've got beautiful eyes.
Jenny I get them from my mother. Anyway, what are your plans for the July edition of the magazine?
Daniel The, er, July edition? I um…
Jenny I have to take this. Sorry.
Daniel No problem.
Jenny Hi, Barbara.
Barbara Jenny, just a quick call. We really like your idea about Rob Walker. He's a great writer.
Jenny So can I ask him?
Barbara Yes. Go ahead.
Jenny That's great.
Barbara Good luck. I hope he says yes.
Jenny Me too.
Daniel Good news?
Jenny Er, yeah. That was Barbara my boss from the New York office. She just gave me a little birthday present.
Daniel So, would you like to go somewhere else?
Jenny I'm sorry, Daniel. I'm a little tired.
Daniel Yes, of course. Waiter, could I have the bill, please?

5 8))
Presenter On today's travel programme Alan Marks is going to tell us about CouchSurfing, a new way of travelling. Alan, what exactly is CouchSurfing?
Alan Well, CouchSurfing is an exciting and cheap way of travelling and seeing new places. It's a very simple idea. When you visit another city, you stay in somebody's flat or house. That person, the host, gives you a room and a bed, and if they don't have a bed, then you can sleep on their couch, or sofa.

5 9))
Presenter Do you have to pay for the bed?
Alan No, you don't. It's completely free. CouchSurfers usually take a small present for the host or maybe they can help with the housework or cook a meal. But you never pay any money.
Presenter How do you find these people?
Alan Well, there is a website called CouchSurfing.org. First, you go there and create a profile. Then you search for the city you want to visit and you look for people there who are offering a bed. When you find somebody you send them an email and then you can agree the day or days that you want to stay. The website is free.
Presenter And do you have to offer a bed in your house?
Alan No, not if you don't want to. You can just be a guest or you can be a host and offer a room in your house, or you can do both things. It's up to you.
Presenter Is CouchSurfing safe?
Alan Yes, it is. You have a lot of information on the website about the person you are going to stay with. Every time a person stays with a host they write a report, either positive or negative and you can read all these reports. Also you can email the person before you go and ask any questions you like.
Presenter Does the host usually show you their city?
Alan Well, it depends on the person. Some hosts take their guests to see some of the sights, but others don't. It depends when you visit too. Some hosts take their guests out at weekends, but are too busy during the week. But hosts usually recommend things to do, so you often see things which tourists don't usually see.
Presenter And can I CouchSurf all over the world?
Alan Of course. In fact you can visit 230 countries and more than 70,000 cities.

5 15))
Part 2
'Well I have a problem with my boyfriend. We argue all the time. I'm not sure that he loves me. I want to know if we're going to stay together.' 'Please choose five cards, but don't look at them.' Jane took five cards. The fortune-teller put them on the table face down. He turned over the first card. 'Ah, this is a good card. This means you're going to be very lucky.' 'But am I going to stay with my boyfriend?' Jane asked. 'Maybe,' said the fortune-teller. 'We need to look at the other cards first.'

5 17))
Part 4
The fortune-teller turned over a card with two rings. 'Now I can see everything clearly. You are going to leave your boyfriend and go away with the other man, with Jim…to another country. And very soon you're going to get married.' 'Married? To Jim? But am I going to be happy with him?' 'You're going to be very happy together. I'm sure of it.' Jane looked at her watch. 'Oh no, look at the time. I'm going to be late for work.' She stood up, left a £50 note on the table, and ran out of the room.

5 30))
One of the first things I noticed in Valencia is that people eat out a lot. They spend a lot of time in cafés and bars. You find people having

breakfast, or tea, in a bar, not just lunch and dinner. People who work go out to a bar to have coffee, they don't have it in their office. In restaurants one thing that really surprised me was that when people go out in big groups, the men all sit at one end of the table and the women at the other.

Another thing I notice, maybe because I'm a woman myself, is what Spanish women are like, or Valencian women maybe. Of course I'm a foreigner, but I find that the women here talk very fast and very loudly, much more than the men. Women dress very well, especially older women, and they always look immaculate!

Finally, there's a myth that the Spanish don't work hard, but I don't think it's true, it's just that they work different hours. People have a long lunch break, but they finish work very late.

5 36)))

Interviewer Today, most people spend a lot of time every day online, but do men and women use the internet in the same way?

Expert Research shows that in general they use the internet in different ways. For example, men and women both use the internet to send emails, but men send more work emails, while women send more personal emails, to friends and family.

Interviewer What about online shopping?

Expert As you can imagine, women do more internet shopping than men. They often use online shops to buy things for the house, clothes, toys, and so on. Men, on the other hand prefer buying things on auction sites like eBay.

Interviewer What other sites are more popular with men?

Expert News sites like the BBC are more popular with men than with women. Men also like visiting sports sites where they can find out, for example, the football results. In general men use the internet a lot for fun. They download music and play games much more than women do.

Interviewer What do women do more than men?

Expert Well, women often use the internet to get information about health and medicine. And they are also more interested in websites which give them advice, for example websites which give advice about how to be good parents, or diet websites which help them to lose weight. They also use the internet for directions much more than men, they use websites like Google maps when they need to go somewhere new. And they use social networks like Facebook more than men do.

Interviewer Are there some things that both men and women do?

Expert Yes, they both use the internet to book tickets for trains and planes, and to book hotels. They also both use online banking, for example to pay bills or make transfers.

5 38)))

Jenny Rob!
Rob Jenny, hi. Sorry I'm a bit late.
Jenny No problem.
Rob Really?
Jenny Really!
Rob I got your message.
Jenny Would you like a coffee or something?
Rob No, I'm fine thanks. So what did you want to talk about? You think London is the best city in the world and you don't want to go home.
Jenny Not exactly. We'd like you to come to New York.
Rob Me? To New York?!
Jenny I talked to Barbara about you. You know, Barbara, my boss? She loves your articles, too. So, would you like to come over to New York and work for us? Just for a month. And write a column for *New York 24seven*. And maybe a daily blog?
Rob Wow, sounds great!? What could I call it? *An Englishman in New York*?
Jenny Why not! Are you interested?
Rob Yes, very. It's amazing! But I need to think about it.
Jenny Of course.
Rob When do I need to decide?
Jenny Before the end of the week?
Rob OK, great. Thank you.
Jenny And now, I really have to go.

5 42)))

Jenny Where is it? Where's my phone?!
Rob Are you looking for this?
Jenny Rob! I can't believe it! My phone! You're a hero, thank you so much.
Rob No problem. It gave me a chance to see you again. And I had more time to think about your offer.
Jenny And?
Rob I'd love to accept. I really want to come and work in New York.
Jenny That's great, Rob! I'm so happy.
Rob Me too. Oh, you had a call from Eddie. I didn't answer it. Is he going to meet you at the airport?
Jenny Eddie? No. He's at college in California.
Rob In California? Does he teach there?
Jenny Teach? No, he's a student.
Rob A student?
Jenny Well, he's only 19. Eddie's my brother.
Announcement Next departure flight 232 to New York is now ready for boarding.
Jenny I need to go.
Rob Well, have a good journey.
Jenny Thanks, Rob. Bye.
Rob Bye. And see you in New York!

5 49)))

1 Yes, I have. I don't usually see films more than once or twice, but I've probably seen It's a Wonderful Life, the old Frank Capra film, at least six or seven times because it's on TV every Christmas and it's usually on just after lunch on Christmas Day, which is when I'm full and a bit sleepy and I want to sit on the sofa and watch a film. Actually, I think it's a great film.

2 Yes, The Empire Strikes Back, the second Star Wars film, well, the fifth episode in the series. I've seen it about twenty times probably. It's my favourite film of all time, and when I meet a girl I always watch it with her. It's a kind of test. If she doesn't like the film, then I think that our relationship isn't going to work.

3 Yes, I have. Flashdance. I've seen it, oh, more than a hundred times. I absolutely love it. I love the music, and the film just makes me feel good. Whenever I feel a bit depressed I think, right, I'm going to watch Flashdance. It always makes me feel better. I've bought the DVD three times because after you've played a DVD a lot it doesn't work properly.

5 51)))

Jess So, where are you going to take me for my birthday?
Matt I want to take you somewhere really nice. Have you been to *The Peking Duck* on 24th Street?
Jess On 24th Street. Yes, I have.
Matt Oh no! When did you go there?
Jess Last month. I went with some people from work.
Matt OK. Somewhere else. Have you ever eaten in *Appetito* on 2nd Avenue? They make fantastic pasta.
Jess I know. I've been there twice. But we could go there. I love Italian food.
Matt No, listen. Why don't we go back to *Luigi's*? We had a lovely meal last time. Do you remember? The Italian waiter sang for you. It was so romantic!
Jess No, I don't remember.
Matt You don't?
Jess No, I don't remember because it wasn't me. I've never been to *Luigi's*.
Matt Oh. My bad memory again.
Jess So, who did you go there with? With your ex-girlfriend?
Matt No, no, I went there with…my sister. Yes, with my sister.
Jess Your sister, huh? Let's forget it. I don't think I want to go out on my birthday.

1A present tense verb be +, subject pronouns: I, you, etc.

+ = positive form		1 5)))
Full form	**Contraction**	
I am your teacher.	**I'm** your teacher.	
You are in room 7.	**You're** in room 7.	
He is Mike.	**He's** Mike.	
She is Hannah.	**She's** Hannah.	
It is a school.	**It's** a school.	
We are students.	**We're** students.	
You are in Class 2.	**You're** in Class 2.	
They are teachers.	**They're** teachers.	

- Always use a subject pronoun (*you, he*, etc.) with a verb, e.g. **It**'s a school. **NOT** *Is a school.* **They**'re teachers. **NOT** *Are teachers.*
- Always use capital *I*, e.g. He's Mike and **I**'m Sally. **NOT** *i'm Sally.* With other pronouns only use a capital letter when it's the first word in a sentence.
- *you* = singular and plural.
- Use *he* for a man, *she* for a woman, and *it* for a thing.
- Use *they* for people and things.

Contractions
- In contractions ' = a missing letter, e.g. *'m = am*.
- We use contractions in conversation and in informal writing, e.g. an email to a friend.

1B present tense verb be − and ?

I**'m not** American.   1 23)))
She **isn't** from London.
They **aren't** Spanish.
Are you Polish? Yes, I **am**.
Is she Russian? No, she **isn't**.

? = question form		
Am I		
Are you		German?
Is he / she / it		Russian?
Are we		Polish?
Are you		
Are they		

✓ = positive short answer			✗ = negative short answer	
Yes,	I am. you are. he / she / it is. we are. you are. they are.		No,	I'm not. you aren't. he / she / it isn't. we aren't. you aren't. they aren't.

− = negative form		
Full form	**Contraction**	
I **am not**	**I'm not**	
You **are not**	You **aren't**	Italian.
He / She / It **is not**	He / She / It **isn't**	Spanish.
We **are not**	We **aren't**	British.
You **are not**	You **aren't**	
They **are not**	They **aren't**	

- Put *not* after the verb *be* to make negatives.
- You can also contract *are not* and *is not* like this: You**'re not** Italian. She**'s not** Spanish.

- In questions, put *am, are, is*, before *I, you, he*, etc. **Are you** German? **NOT** *You are German?* Where **are you** from? **NOT** *Where you are from?*
- Don't use contractions in positive short answers. Are you Russian? Yes, **I am**. **NOT** *Yes, I'm.*

1C possessive adjectives: my, your, etc.

I'm Italian.	**My** family are from Rome.	1 41)))
You're in level 1.	This is **your** classroom.	
He's the director.	**His** name is Michael.	
She's your teacher.	**Her** name is Tina.	
It's a school.	**Its** name is Queen's School.	
We're an international school.	**Our** students are from many different countries.	
They're new students.	**Their** names are David and Emma.	

🔍 **it's or its?**
Be careful with *it's* and *its*.
it's = it is   **It's** a school.
its = possessive   **Its** name is Queen's School.

- *his* = of a man, *her* = of a woman, *its* = of a thing.
- *their* = of plural people or things.
- Possessive adjectives don't change with plural nouns.
  our students **NOT** *ours students*

GRAMMAR BANK

1A

a Complete with *am*, *is*, or *are*.

I *am* Mike.
1 We _____ from London.
2 He _____ early.
3 They _____ teachers.
4 Today _____ Wednesday.
5 I _____ sorry.
6 It _____ a hotel.
7 You _____ in room 402.
8 She _____ a student.
9 My name _____ Carla.
10 I _____ in a taxi.

b Write the sentences with contractions.

He is late. *He's late.*
1 It is Friday. _____
2 They are in school. _____
3 I am very well. _____
4 You are in my class. _____

c Write the sentences with a subject pronoun and a contraction.

Mike and Hannah are students. *They're* students.
1 **John is** in room 5. _____
2 **Sam and I are** early. _____
3 **Julia is** a teacher. _____
4 **The school is** in Madrid. _____

◀ p.5

1B

a Write the sentences in the negative.

She's Australian. *She isn't Australian.*
1 I'm British. _____
2 They're Brazilian. _____
3 It's in South America. _____
4 You're French. _____

b Make questions and short answers.

/ you English?	? *Are you English?*	✓ *Yes, I am.*
1 / I in room 10?	? _____ ?	✓ _____
2 / it Italian?	? _____ ?	✗ _____
3 / they students?	? _____ ?	✗ _____
4 / he from the USA?	? _____ ?	✓ _____
5 / you sure?	? _____ ?	✗ _____

c Complete the dialogue. Use contractions if possible.

A Hi. I'*m* Mark.
B Hello Mark. My name [1]____ Maria.
A [2]____ you Spanish, Maria?
B No. I [3]____ from Mexico.
A [4]____ you from Mexico City?
B No. I [5]____ from Tijuana.
A [6]____ Tijuana near Mexico City?
B No, it [7]____. It [8]____ in the north.
A [9]____ you a student?
B No. I [10]____ a teacher.

◀ p.7

1C

a Complete the sentences with a possessive adjective.

My name's Darly. I'm from Brazil.
1 The students are from Italy. ____ names are Susanna and Tito.
2 She's in my class. ____ name is Rebecca.
3 We're in class 2. ____ teacher is Richard.
4 London is famous for ____ parks.
5 How do you spell ____ surname, Anna?
6 This is my teacher. ____ name is Brad.
7 I'm from London. ____ address is 31, Old Kent Road.
8 Sit down and open ____ books, please.
9 Laura is in my class. ____ desk is near the window.
10 We're from Liverpool. ____ surname is Connor.

b (Circle) the correct word.

Mark and Simon are friends. (*They*) / *Their* are in class 2.
1 She's a new student. *She* / *Her* name's Ipek.
2 Is *they* / *their* teacher British?
3 My name's Soraya. I'm in *you* / *your* class.
4 Where are *you* / *your* friends from?
5 We're French. *We* / *Our* names are Marc and Jacques.
6 Is *she* / *her* German?
7 Peter is a teacher. *He* / *His* is from Ireland.
8 What's *he* / *his* name?
9 I'm Karen. *I* / *My* surname is White.
10 *She* / *Her* is from Barcelona.

◀ p.9

2A a / an, plurals; this / that / these / those

a / an, plurals

It's **a** bag. 🔊 1 52
It's **an** umbrella.
They're **books**.
They're **watches**.

a / an (indefinite article)

It's	a	bag. pen.
	an	identity card. umbrella.

- Use *a / an* with singular nouns.
- Use *an* with a noun beginning with a vowel (*a, e, i, o, u*).
- Use *a* with nouns beginning *u* when *u* = /juː/, e.g. *university*.

regular plurals

Singular	Plural	Spelling
a book a key	books keys	add -s
a watch a box	watches boxes	add -es after *ch, sh, s, x*
a country a dictionary	countries dictionaries	consonant + *y* > *ies*

- Add *-s* (or *-es* or *-ies*) to make plural nouns: *It's a pen. They're pens.*
- Don't use *a / an* with plural nouns: *They're keys.* **NOT** *They're a keys.*

irregular plurals

Singular	Plural
a man /mæn/	men /men/
a woman /ˈwʊmən/	women /ˈwɪmɪn/
a child /tʃaɪld/	children /ˈtʃɪldrən/
a person /ˈpɜːsn/	people /ˈpiːpl/

this / that / these / those

1. What's **this**? It's a ticket. 🔊 1 57
   These watches are Japanese.
2. **That** car is Italian.
   What are **those**? They're headphones.

- Use *this / these* for things near you (*here*).
- Use *that / those* for things which aren't near you (*there*).
- *this / that* = singular; *these / those* = plural.
- *this, that, these,* and *those* can be adjectives (**this** watch) or pronouns (*What's* **this**?).

2B adjectives

1. The **White** House is in the USA. 🔊 1 63
   They're **blue** jeans.
2. He's **strong**.
   It isn't **easy**.
   Is it **American**?
3. It's a **very big** city.
   She's **quite small**.

1. When we use an adjective with a noun, the adjective goes before the noun: *It's a big house.* **NOT** *It's a house big.*
   Adjectives don't change before a plural noun: *They're blue jeans.* **NOT** *They're blues jeans.*
2. We can also use adjectives without a noun, after the verb *be*.
3. We often use *very* and *quite* before adjectives:
   a *He's very tall.*
   b *He's quite tall.*
   c *He isn't very tall.*

2C imperatives, let's

1. **Open** the door. **Turn** right. 🔊 1 71
   Don't worry. Don't stop.
   Be quiet, please. Please **sit down**.
2. **Let's go** home. **Let's wait**.

1. Use imperatives to give orders or instructions.
   - [+] imperatives = verb (infinitive). [–] imperatives = *don't* + verb (infinitive).
   - Add *please* to be polite: *Open the door, please.*
   - We often use *be* + adjective in imperatives: *Be quiet, Be careful,* etc.
   - Don't use a pronoun with imperatives: *Be quiet.*
2. Use *Let's* + verb (infinitive) to make suggestions.
   Use *Let's not* + verb to make a negative suggestion: *Let's not wait.*

GRAMMAR BANK

2A

a Complete with *a* or *an*. Write the plural.

singular	plural
a photo	*photos*
1 ____ city	_____
2 ____ email	_____
3 ____ person	_____
4 ____ box	_____
5 ____ woman	_____

b Write sentences with *It's* or *They're* (and *a* or *an* if necessary).

pen	*It's a pen.*
buses	*They're buses.*
1 children	_____
2 purse	_____
3 men	_____
4 umbrella	_____
5 sunglasses	_____

◀ p.12

c Complete the dialogues with *this*, *these*, *that*, or *those*.

Teacher What's ¹_____, Jenny?
Jenny It's an iPod.
Teacher And what are ²_____, Jenny?
Jenny They're headphones.
Teacher Give them to me, please, Jenny.

Boy 1 Who's ³_____ man over there?
Boy 2 He's my father.
Boy 1 And are ⁴_____ your dogs?
Boy 2 Yes, they are.
Boy 1 Wow!

◀ p.13

2B

a Underline the adjectives in these sentences.

He's a <u>rich</u> man.
1 They're Japanese tourists.
2 It's an international school.
3 That isn't the right answer.
4 We're good friends.
5 Hi, Anna. Nice to meet you.
6 Those animals are dangerous.
7 This is a big country.
8 My phone is very cheap.

b Put the words in the right order.

is Chinese he ?   *Is he Chinese?*
1 a day very it's hot
2 your Australian is teacher?
3 car fast isn't that very
4 a idea bad it's
5 a are student you good?
6 easy is English quite
7 strong my is brother very
8 watch expensive is this an

◀ p.14

2C

a Complete with a verb from the list. Use a ⊞ or a ⊟ imperative.

be   go   have   ~~open~~   park   read   speak   take   turn on   ~~worry~~

A It's hot.   **B** *Open* the window.
A I'm very sorry   **B** *Don't worry*. It isn't a problem.
1 **A** I'm bored.   **B** _____ the TV.
2 **A** *No entiendo.*   **B** This is an English class. Please _____ Spanish.
3 **A** I'm tired.   **B** It's late. _____ to bed.
4 **A** Is this book good?   **B** No, it isn't. _____ it.
5 **A** I'm hungry.   **B** _____ a sandwich.
6 **A** Look at those animals.   **B** _____ careful. They're dangerous.
7 **A** It's raining.   **B** _____ an umbrella.
8 **A** Where is our hotel?   **B** It's over there. _____ here.

b Complete with *Let's* and a verb from the list.

close   go   ~~open~~   sit down   stop   turn off

It's hot. *Let's open* the window.
1 Come on. _____.
2 It's late. _____ the TV and go to bed.
3 I'm tired. _____.
4 It's very cold in here. _____ the window.
5 There's a service station. _____ and have a coffee.

◀ p.17

127

3

3A present simple + and -

> British people **like** animals. (2 4))
> They **live** in houses with gardens.
> My husband **works** from 9.00 to 5.00.
> Ann **has** three children.

+	-
I **work**.	I **don't work**.
You **work**.	You **don't work**.
He / She / It **works**.	He / She / It **doesn't work**.
We **work**.	We **don't work**.
You **work**.	You **don't work**.
They **work**.	They **don't work**.

- We use the present simple for things that are generally true or that habitually happen.

- Contractions: *don't* = do not, *doesn't* = does not.
- To make negatives use *don't* / *doesn't* + verb (infinitive):
  He doesn't **work**. NOT ~~He doesn't works~~.

spelling rules for *he* / *she* / *it*	
I work / play / live.	He work**s** / play**s** / live**s**.
I watch / finish / go / do.	She watch**es** / finish**es** / go**es** / do**es**.
I study.	She stud**ies**.

- The spelling rules for the *he* / *she* / *it* forms are the same as for the plurals (see **Grammar Bank 2A p.126**).

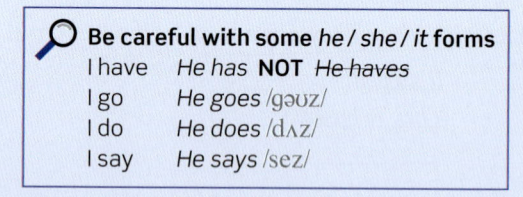

> 🔍 Be careful with some *he* / *she* / *it* forms
> I have   He **has**   NOT ~~He haves~~
> I go   He **goes** /gəʊz/
> I do   He **does** /dʌz/
> I say   He **says** /sez/

3B present simple ?

> **Do** you work in an office? No, I **don't**. (2 14))
> **Does** she work outside? Yes, she **does**.

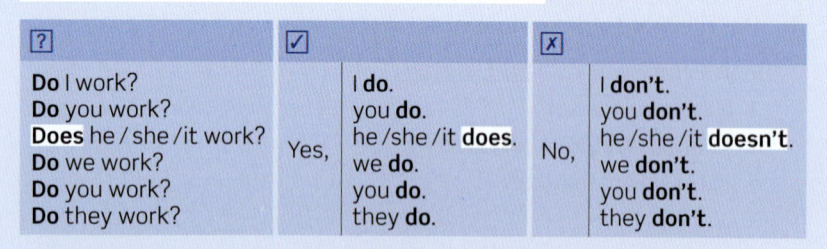

?		✓		✗
Do I work?		I **do**.		I **don't**.
Do you work?		you **do**.		you **don't**.
Does he / she / it work?	Yes,	he / she / it **does**.	No,	he / she / it **doesn't**.
Do we work?		we **do**.		we **don't**.
Do you work?		you **do**.		you **don't**.
Do they work?		they **do**.		they **don't**.

- Use *do* (or *does* with *he*, *she*, *it*) to make questions.

> 🔍 **do and does**
> *do* = /duː/, *does* = /dʌz/
> *Do* and *does* can be:
> 1 the auxiliary verb to make present simple questions. **Do** you speak English? **Does** she live here?
> 2 a normal verb. I **do** my homework in the evening. He **does** exercise every day.

- The word order for present simple questions is **ASI** = **A**uxiliary verb (*do*, *does*), **S**ubject (*I*, *you*, *he*, *she*, etc.), **I**nfinitive (*work*, *live*, etc.).

3C word order in questions

Question word / phrase	Auxiliary	Subject	Infinitive	(2 20))
	Do	you	live near here?	
	Does	your mother	work?	
What	do	you	do?	
Where	does	he	live?	
How many children	do	you	have?	
What kind of music	does	she	like?	
How	do	you	spell your surname?	

> 🔍 **Word order in *be* questions**
> Remember the word order in questions with *be*. Put *be* before the subject. *Where are you from? What's your name? Is he Spanish?*

- The word order for present simple questions with *do* and *does* is:
  ASI (**A**uxiliary, **S**ubject, **I**nfinitive), e.g. *Do you live here?*: OR
  QUASI (**Q**uestion, **A**uxiliary, **S**ubject, **I**nfinitive), e.g. *Where do you live?*
- We often use question phrases beginning with *What*, e.g. *What colour…? What size…? What make…? What time…?*, etc.

GRAMMAR BANK

3A

a Change the sentences.

My mum drinks tea. — *I drink tea.*
1 I go to the cinema. She _____.
2 We live in a flat. He _____.
3 She has two children. They _____.
4 My dad doesn't like cats. I _____.
5 The shops close at 5.30. The supermarket _____.
6 We don't study French. My sister _____.
7 I do housework. My husband _____.
8 I want a guitar. My son _____.
9 I don't work on Saturdays. My friend _____.
10 Our lessons finish at 5 o'clock. Our English lesson _____.

b Complete the sentences with a ⊕ or ⊖ verb.

eat   have   listen   play   read
speak   study   wear   work

⊕ They *study* economics.
1 ⊖ Pedro _____ in an office.
2 ⊕ Eva _____ books in English.
3 ⊕ You _____ Arabic very well.
4 ⊖ I _____ games on my phone.
5 ⊕ Paolo _____ glasses.
6 ⊕ We _____ to music on the bus.
7 ⊖ They _____ fast food.
8 ⊕ Julia _____ two children.

◀ p.20

3B

a Complete the questions with *do* or *does*.

Do you work with a computer?
1 _____ she have any qualifications?
2 _____ you speak a foreign language?
3 _____ Jamie play the guitar?
4 _____ you like Italian food?
5 _____ you study another language?
6 _____ school children wear a uniform?
7 _____ your dad cook?
8 _____ people in your country work long hours?

b Make questions.

A She works at night. B *Does she work* at the weekend?
A I don't play the guitar. B *Do you play the* piano?
1 A He likes sport. B _____ tennis?
2 A She speaks foreign languages. B _____ German?
3 A I don't eat fast food. B _____ pizzas?
4 A They cook Italian food. B _____ lasagne?
5 A Teresa doesn't live in a flat. B _____ in a house?
6 A I want a new phone. B _____ an iPhone?
7 A My dad drives a Ferrari. B _____ fast?

◀ p.22

3C

a Order the words to make questions.

you live where do ?   *Where do you live?*
1 phones how many do you have?
2 interesting is job it an?
3 you drink how do coffee much ?
4 brother your where from is ?
5 you with work computers do?
6 read of what do kind you magazines?
7 do what does weekend he at the?
8 want you do drink another?
9 your where does sister live?
10 do how that you say English in?

b Complete the questions.

What's *your name?* My name's Andrew.
1 How many children _____? Three, two girls and a boy.
2 What kind of films _____? He likes science-fiction films.
3 Where _____? We're from New York.
4 What _____ your father _____? He's a lawyer.
5 What kind of food _____? I like Japanese food.
6 Where _____? She works in an office.
7 Where _____? Our flat is near the market.
8 How many foreign languages _____? I speak French and Spanish.
9 When _____ to the gym? I go on Mondays, Wednesdays, and Fridays.
10 How old _____? I'm 21.

◀ p.25

4A Whose...?, possessive 's

1 He's George Clooney's father. (2) 31))
  It's James's house.
2 They're my parents' friends.
3 **Whose** is this bag? It's Maria's.
4 The end of the film is fantastic. I live in the city centre.

1 We use *'s* with a person to talk about family and possessions:
  George Clooney's mother **NOT** *the mother of George Clooney*
2 We use *s'* not *'s* with regular plural nouns, e.g.
  They're my parents' friends. **NOT** *They're my parent's friends.*
• With irregular plural nouns, e.g. *children, men*, use *'s*:
  the children's room, men's clothes.

3 We use *Whose...?* to ask about possessions.
  We can ask *Whose is this bag?* **OR** *Whose bag is this?*
  You can answer *It's Maria's bag.* **OR** *It's Maria's.*
4 We don't usually use a thing + *'s*, e.g. *the end of the class* **NOT** *the class's end*, *the city centre* **NOT** *the city's centre*.

> 🔍 **'s**
> Be careful with *'s*. It can be two things:
> *Maria's mother* (*'s* = of Maria)
> *Maria's Spanish* (*'s* = is)
> **Whose / Who's**
> *Who's = Who is*, e.g. **Who's** that girl? She's my sister.
> *Whose = of who*, e.g. **Whose** is this bag? It's Jack's.
> *Whose* and *Who's* are pronounced the same.

4B prepositions: (at, in, on, to)

Time

in	on	at	(2) 42))
the morning	Monday	three o'clock	
the afternoon	Tuesday (morning)	midday / midnight	
the evening		lunchtime	
the summer		night	
		the weekend	
		Christmas	

• We use *in* for parts of the day and seasons.
• We use *on* for days.
• We use *at* for times of the day, *night*, *the weekend*, and festivals.

> 🔍 **Other uses of *in* and *on***
> We also use **in** with months and years.
>   e.g. **in** December, **in** 2015
> We also use **on** with dates.
>   e.g. **on** 1 January
> (See **Grammar Bank 7A** p.136)

Movement and place

1 He goes **to** work at 8.00. (2) 43))
2 He has lunch **at** work.
  He works **in** an office.

1 We use *to* for movement or direction: *She goes* **to** *the gym.*
  NOT *She goes at the gym.*
  We don't use *to* before *home*: *go home* **NOT** *go to home*
2 We use *at* and *in* for position.
• We use *at* + *work, home, school, university.*
• We use *in* + other places: *a flat, an office, a room*, etc.
• We can use *in* or *at* with some public places: *a restaurant, the cinema*, etc.
  On Saturdays he usually has lunch **in** / **at** *a restaurant.*

4C adverbs and expressions of frequency

1 I **always** have toast for breakfast. (2) 49))
  Do you **usually** go to work by bus?
  She doesn't **often** go to the cinema.
  They're **sometimes** late.
  She **hardly ever** watches TV.
  He is **never** stressed.

2 I have English classes **twice a week**.
  She doesn't work **every day**.

1 We use adverbs of frequency to say how often you do something.
• Adverbs of frequency go <u>before</u> all main verbs (except *be*).
                          <u>after</u> *be*.
• Use a [+] verb with *never* and *hardly ever*. *He* **never** *smokes*.
  NOT *He doesn't never smoke.*
• In negative sentences the adverb of frequency goes between *don't / doesn't* and the verb.
2 Expressions of frequency usually go at the end of a sentence or verb phrase.

GRAMMAR BANK

4A

a Circle the correct form.

Monica Cruz is *Penelope Cruz's sister* / *sister's Penelope Cruz*.
1 It's *my mother's birthday* / *my birthday's mother*.
2 That's *her house's parents* / *her parents' house*.
3 I'm tired when I go home at *the end of the day* / *the day's end*.
4 Those are *friends' my sister* / *my sister's friends*.
5 That's *Anne's bag* / *Annes' bag*.
6 Those are *the students' desks* / *the student's desks*.

b Look at the pictures. Answer the questions with a short sentence.

Whose is the laptop? *It's Bill's.*
1 Whose are the cars? _____
2 Whose is the wallet? _____
3 Whose are the magazines? _____
4 Whose is the watch? _____
5 Whose are the glasses? _____

c Complete with *Whose* or *Who's*.

Whose car is this?   *Who's* the man with dark hair?
1 _____ book is this?
2 _____ keys are these?
3 _____ your favourite singer?
4 _____ Kevin's girlfriend?
5 _____ bag is this?
6 _____ their English teacher?

◀ p.28

4B

a Complete with *in*, *on*, or *at*.

on Saturday
1 _____ the evening
2 _____ 22nd September
3 _____ the summer
4 _____ 7.30
5 _____ night
6 _____ Monday mornings
7 _____ the weekend
8 _____ January

b Complete with *to*, *at*, *in* or –.

We go *to* school by bus.   They get *–* home late.
1 Sorry, John's not here. He's ____ work.
2 It's a lovely day. Let's go ____ the beach.
3 Sally's boyfriend works ____ an office.
4 My brother studies maths ____ the University of Manchester.
5 I go ____ the gym on Tuesdays and Thursdays.
6 What time do you go ____ home?
7 We live ____ a flat.
8 It's Monday. The children are ____ school.
9 My father's a doctor. He works ____ a hospital.
10 Jack isn't ____ home. He's on holiday.

◀ p.31

4C

a Put the adverb or expression of frequency in the right place.

They drive – they don't have a car. **never**
They never drive – they don't have a car.
1 Do you wear glasses? **usually**
2 I'm bored. **hardly ever**
3 She does housework. **sometimes**
4 We go to the cinema. **once a week**
5 Why are you late? **always**
6 I walk to work. **every day**
7 My girlfriend is stressed. **never**
8 Does it rain in the winter? **often**

b Order the words to make sentences.

always she at six up gets
She always gets up at six.
1 for late never I am class
2 eat ever fast hardly we food
3 what work you usually time do finish ?
4 parents radio often the my listen don't to
5 always brother lunchtime is my hungry at
6 don't homework always our we do
7 you work every day to do drive ?
8 hardly teacher angry is our ever

◀ p.32

5A can / can't

1 **I can** sing, but **I can't** dance. (2 58))
2 **I can** come on Tuesday, but **I can't** come on Wednesday.
3 **You can** park here. **You can't** park there.
4 **Can you** help me? **Can I** open the window?

- can + infinitive has different meanings:
  1 *I can* = I know how to.
    I can't = I don't know how to.
  2 *I can* = It's possible for me.
    I can't = It's impossible for me.
  3 *You can* = It's OK / It's permitted.
    You can't = It's not OK / It's not permitted.
  4 *Can you …?* = Please do it.
    Can I …? = Is it OK if I do it?

+			−		
I / You / He / She / It / We / They	can	swim. come. help.	I / You / He / She / It / We / They	can't	swim. come. help.

?			✓			✗		
Can	I / you / he / she / it / we / they	swim? come? help?	Yes,	I / you / he / she / it / we / they	can.	No,	I / you / he / she / it / we / they	can't.

- *can* and *can't* are the same for all persons (*I, you, he*, etc.). **NOT** ~~He cans.~~
- Contraction: *can't* = *cannot*.
- Don't use *to* after *can*.
  I can swim. **NOT** ~~I can to swim.~~

5B present continuous: be + verb + -ing

They're having a party in Flat 4. (3 4))
Oh no! The baby**'s crying**.
It's raining.
A What **are you doing**?
B **I'm waiting** for my brother.

- We use the present continuous for things that are happening now / at the moment.
- We also use the present continuous with longer periods of time, e.g. *today, this week*.
  I'm working at home **this week** because my daughter's not very well.

+	−	
I'm You're He / She / It 's We're They're	I'm not You aren't He / She / It isn't We aren't They aren't	having a party.

?			✓		✗	
Am I Are you Is he / she / it Are we Are they		having a party?	Yes,	I am. you are. he / she / it is. we are. they are.	No,	I'm not. you aren't. he / she / it isn't. we aren't. they aren't.

spelling rules for the *-ing* form		
infinitive	verb + *-ing*	spelling
cook study	cooking studying	add *-ing*
dance	dancing	ҽ + *-ing*
shop	shopping	one vowel + one consonant = double consonant + *-ing*

5C present simple or present continuous?

present simple	present continuous (3 12))
My sister **works** in a bank.	Today she**'s working** at home.
What **do you** usually **wear** to work?	What **are you wearing** now?
It **rains** a lot here in the spring.	Look! **It's raining**.

- We use the present simple to say what we usually do, or things that are normally true.
- We often use the present simple with adverbs and expressions of frequency, e.g. *always, often, once a week*, etc.
- We use the present continuous to say what is happening now.
- We often use the present continuous with *at the moment, today, this week*.

🔍 **What do you do?** or **What are you doing?**
A What **do you do**? (= What's your job?)
B I'm a teacher.
A What **are you doing**? (= now, at the moment)
B I'm waiting for a friend.

GRAMMAR BANK

5A

a Rewrite the sentences using the correct form of *can* or *can't*.

I know how to play the piano.   I *can play the piano*.
1 It's possible for her to meet me after work.
   She _____.
2 Please open the door.
   _____ you _____, please?
3 My boyfriend doesn't know how to ski.
   My boyfriend _____.
4 Is it OK if I use your car?
   _____ I _____?
5 It isn't possible for us to come to your party.
   We _____.

b Complete the sentences with *can* or *can't* and the verbs.

I'm sorry. I *can't remember* your name. (remember)
1 She _____ French, but not Spanish. (speak)
2 _____ you _____ me? These bags are very heavy. (help)
3 I _____ you tonight. I'm very busy. (see)
4 _____ I _____ the window? It's cold in here. (close)
5 _____ you _____ your address, please? (repeat)
6 It says 'No parking'. We _____ here. (stop)
7 Andy doesn't want to go to the beach because he _____. (swim)
8 _____ I _____ your phone? I want to call my dad. (use)

◀ p.36

5B

a Write a question and answer.

What's she doing?   *She's crying*.
1 _____? _____.
2 _____? _____.
3 _____? _____.
4 _____? _____.
5 _____? _____.

b Put the verbs in brackets in the present continuous.

A (*On the telephone*) Hi, Frank. It's Tina.
B Hello, Tina. It's good to hear from you. Where are you?
A I'm here in Bristol. I'm on holiday so I*'m visiting* (visit) my parents. I ¹_____ (stay) with them all this week. They're retired. Right now they ²_____ (work) in the garden and I ³_____ (sit) in the sun. And you, Frank? What ⁴_____ you _____ these days? (do)
B I ⁵_____ (look) for a job.
A Good luck! What about your parents. How are they?
B Fine. My mum ⁶_____ (learn) to drive! She ⁷_____ (not enjoy) it much because she's very nervous. At the moment she ⁸_____ (make) the dinner and my dad ⁹_____ (help) her.
A It's great to speak to you, Frank. Can we meet?
B Yes. Let's have dinner tonight.

◀ p.39

5C

a Circle the correct form.

A What *do you cook* / *are you cooking*? I'm really hungry.
B Spaghetti. We can eat in ten minutes.
1 A Hello. Is Martin at home?
   B No, *he plays* / *he's playing* football with his friends.
2 A *Do your parents live* / *Are your parents living* near here?
   B Yes. They *have* / *are having* a flat in the same building as me.
3 A How often *do you go* / *are you going* to the hairdresser's?
   B About once a month. When *I think* / *I'm thinking* my hair's very long.
4 A Don't make a noise! Your father *sleeps* / *is sleeping*!
   B Is he OK? He *doesn't usually sleep* / *isn't usually sleeping* in the afternoon.

b Put the verbs in brackets in the present simple or continuous.

Look. It*'s raining*. (rain)
1 A Hi, Sarah! What _____ you _____ here? (do)
   B I _____ for a friend. (wait)
2 A Let's have lunch. _____ you _____ hamburgers? (like)
   B No, sorry. I'm a vegetarian. I _____ meat. (not eat)
3 A Listen! The neighbours _____ a party again. (have)
   B They _____ a party every weekend! (have)
4 A What _____ your boyfriend _____? (do)
   B He's a teacher. He _____ at the local school. (work)
5 A Hi, Lisa. Where _____ you _____? (go)
   B To the gym. I _____ to the gym every evening. (go)

◀ p.41

6

6A object pronouns: me, you, him, etc.

subject pronoun	object pronoun		3 21
I	me	Can you help **me**?	
you	you	I know **you**.	
he	him	She isn't in love with **him**.	
she	her	He phones **her** every day.	
it	it	I don't like **it**.	
we	us	Wait for **us**!	
they	them	Call **them** this evening.	

- Pronouns take the place of nouns.
- We use **subject** pronouns when the noun is the subject of a verb (i.e. the person who does the action): *John is a doctor. **He** lives in London.*
- We use **object** pronouns when the noun is the object of a verb (i.e. the person who receives the action): *Anna meets **John**. She invites **him** to a concert.*
- Object pronouns go after the verb:
  I love you. NOT *I you love.*
- We also use object pronouns after prepositions (*with, to, from*, etc.):
  *Listen to **me**! I'm in love with **her**.* NOT *I'm in love with she.*

He loves her but she doesn't love him.

6B like (+ verb + -ing)

			3 34
😊😊	I love	shopping.	
😊	I like	going to the cinema.	
😐	I don't mind	getting up early.	
🙁	I don't like	doing housework.	
🙁🙁	I hate	driving at night.	

- We use verb + *-ing* after *like, love, don't mind,* and *hate*.

spelling rules for the -ing form		
infinitive	verb + -ing	spelling
cook study	cook**ing** study**ing**	add -ing
dance	danc**ing**	*e* + -ing
shop	sho**pp**ing	one vowel + one consonant = double consonant + -ing

6C be or do?

be

1 Hi. **I'm** Jim.   3 36
  She **isn't** very friendly.
  Are you German?
2 I can't talk. **I'm** driving.
  They **aren't** working today.
  Is it raining?

1 We use *be* as a main verb.
2 We also use *be* to form the present continuous. *Be* here is an auxillary verb.

do / does

Do you speak English?   3 37
Where **do** they live?
They **don't** have children.

Does your sister have a job?
What **does** your father do?
Alan **doesn't** like jazz.

- We use *do / does* and *don't / doesn't* to make questions and negatives in the present simple.
- Remember **ASI** and **QUASI** (See **Grammar Bank 3C** p.128).

> 🔍 **do as a main verb**
> Remember, we also use *do* as a main verb.
> *I'm **doing** my homework.*
> *Does he **do** the housework?*

GRAMMAR BANK

6A

a Change the highlighted words to object pronouns.

I call my mother once a week.
I call her once a week.

1 I can't find my wallet.
  _____

2 She speaks to her father in German.
  _____

3 He meets his friends after work.
  _____

4 Can you help my friend and me?
  _____

5 Ivan is in love with his girlfriend.
  _____

6 My son doesn't like cats.
  _____

b Complete the sentences with a subject pronoun (*I*, *he*, etc.) or object pronoun (*me*, *him*, etc.).

John is American. <u>He</u> lives in California, with his parents. <u>He</u> argues with <u>them</u> a lot.

1 Susan has a big flat. _____ likes _____ a lot. We often visit _____ on Sundays because she invites _____ for lunch.
2 I am very happy with my neighbours. _____ often help _____ with my children. They often take _____ to school when I'm working.
3 Mark loves Ruth but she doesn't love _____. He calls _____ every day but _____ doesn't want to speak to _____.
4 My brother has two dogs. _____ takes _____ for a walk twice a day. I don't like _____ very much because _____ bark at _____.
5 We often take my grandfather some magazines, but _____ never reads _____. _____ watches TV all day and never turns _____ off.

◀ p.44

6B

a Write the *-ing* form of the verbs in the chart.

come cook dance eat get have
run sleep stop study swim ~~write~~

work > work**ing**	
live > liv**ing**	writing
shop > shop**ping**	

b Write sentences about Bob with *love*, *not like*, *like*, *not mind*, or *hate* and a verb.

☺☺ ~~in an office~~ a computer
☺   the newspaper housework
😐   lunch at work home late
☹   tennis to the cinema
☹☹ TV music

He loves working in an office.

1 _____   6 _____
2 _____   7 _____
3 _____   8 _____
4 _____   9 _____
5 _____

◀ p.47

6C

a Put the phrases in the correct column.

~~hungry~~   like heavy metal   tired
waiting for a friend   stressed
have a car   speak Russian
listening to me   know those people

Are you...?	Do you...?
hungry	

b Complete the dialogues with *do/does* or *am/is/are*.

A <u>Do</u> you speak German?   **B** Yes, but I <u>don't</u> speak it very well.

1 **A** Where _____ Gemma going?   **B** She _____ going to the gym.
2 **A** _____ you live in a house?   **B** Yes, but it _____ have a garden.
3 **A** _____ Matt like shopping?   **B** He _____ mind it.
4 **A** Why _____ you crying?   **B** Because I _____ feeling sad.
5 **A** _____ your boyfriend cook?   **B** Yes. He _____ making dinner now.
6 **A** _____ you busy?   **B** Yes. We _____ doing our homework.
7 **A** How old _____ your father?   **B** He's 66, but he _____ want to retire.
8 **A** _____ you watching TV?   **B** No. I _____ playing a video game.

◀ p.48

7A past simple of be: was / were

King Edward VIII's wife **was** American.
She **wasn't** in class yesterday. **Was** she ill?
The Beatles **were** famous in the 1960s.
Where **were** you last night? You **weren't** at home.

(3 44)

+			−		
I / He / She / It	**was** there.		I / He / She / It	**wasn't** there.	
You / We / They	**were** there.		You / We / They	**weren't** there.	

?			✓		✗
Was	I / he / she / it	famous?	Yes, I **was**.		No, I **wasn't**.
Were	you / we / they		Yes, you **were**.		No, you **weren't**.

- We use *was / were* to talk about the past.
- We often use *was / were* with past time expressions, e.g. *yesterday, last night, in 1945*, etc.
- We use *was / were* with *born*: *I was born in Hungary.*

7B past simple: regular verbs

I **played** tennis this morning.
We **watched** a good film on TV last night.
My grandfather **lived** in Vienna when he was young.
I **studied** German when I was at school.

(3 53)

+		−	
I / You / He / She / It / We / They	**worked** yesterday.	I / You / He / She / It / We / They	**didn't work** yesterday.

?			✓			✗		
Did	I / you / he / she / it / we / they	**work** yesterday?	Yes,	I / you / he / she / it / we / they	**did**.	No,	I / you / he / she / it / we / they	**didn't**.

- We use the past simple for finished actions in the past.

spelling rules for regular verbs		
infinitive	past	spelling
watch play	watch**ed** play**ed**	add -ed
live	live**d**	add -d
stop	stop**ped**	one vowel + one consonant = double consonant
study	stud**ied**	consonant + y > ied

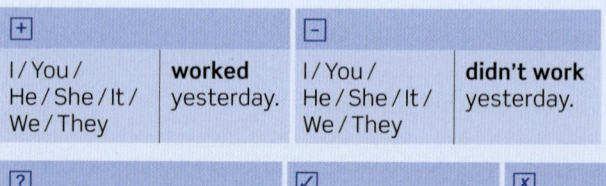

- **Contraction:** *didn't* = *did not*.
- Regular verbs in the past + end in *-ed*, e.g. *worked, lived, played*.
- The past simple is the same for all persons (*I, you, she*, etc.).
- Use auxiliaries *did / didn't* + infinitive for past simple ? and −. *Did* is the past of *do*.

7C past simple: irregular verbs

I **went** to Spain last month.
I **didn't go** to Madrid.
Did you **go** to Barcelona?

(3 59)

infinitive	past +	past −
go	went	didn't go
have	had	didn't have
get	got	didn't get
teach	taught	didn't teach
hear	heard	didn't hear
feel	felt	didn't feel
leave	left	didn't leave
lose	lost	didn't lose
meet	met	didn't meet
see	saw	didn't see
wear	wore	didn't wear
speak	spoke	didn't speak
do	did	didn't do

- Use the irregular past form only in + sentences: *I saw a film last night.*
- Use the infinitive after *did / didn't*: *Did you see a film last night?* NOT *Did you saw...?* *I didn't go out last night.* NOT *I didn't went...*
- Remember word order in questions = **ASI** (Auxiliary, Subject, Infinitive), e.g. *Did you go out last night?* or **QUASI** (Question word, Auxiliary, Subject, Infinitive), e.g. *Where did you go?*
- There is a list of irregular verbs on page 165.

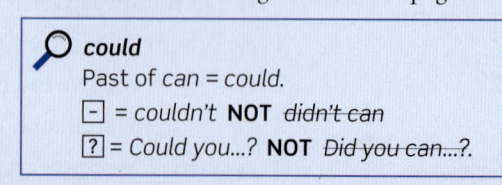

🔎 **could**
Past of *can* = *could*.
− = *couldn't* NOT *didn't can*
? = *Could you...?* NOT *Did you can...?*

GRAMMAR BANK

7A

a Complete the past simple sentences with *was / wasn't* or *were / weren't*.

present simple	past simple
My father's a painter.	My grandfather <u>was</u> a painter, too.
1 Today is Monday.	Yesterday _____ Sunday.
2 Where are you now?	Where _____ you yesterday?
3 I'm in Italy.	I _____ in Germany last month.
4 Is it hot today?	_____ it hot yesterday?
5 The café isn't open now.	It _____ open this morning.
6 My neighbours aren't at home.	They _____ at home yesterday.
7 We're in Rome now.	We _____ in Venice yesterday.
8 They're tired.	They _____ tired last week.

b Complete the dialogues with *was, wasn't, were,* or *weren't*.

A <u>Were</u> you and Charlie at the concert last night?
B Yes, we ¹_____.
A ²_____ it good?
B No, it ³_____. The singer ⁴_____ terrible.
A ⁵_____ the tickets expensive?
B Yes, they ⁶_____.
A Where ⁷_____ your mother born?
B She ⁸_____ born in Argentina in 1955.
A ⁹_____ her parents Argentinian?
B No, they ¹⁰_____. Her father ¹¹_____ German and her mother ¹²_____ from Italy.

◀ p.52

7B

a Rewrite the sentences in the past simple with *yesterday*.

Present	Past
I watch TV.	<u>I watched TV yesterday.</u>
1 We study English.	_____
2 Do you listen to the news?	_____
3 He doesn't cook dinner.	_____
4 Does she play sport?	_____
5 They work late.	_____
6 I use the internet at work.	_____
7 She chats to her friends.	_____
8 My brother doesn't dance.	_____

b Complete the sentences with a verb in the past simple.

not call   cry   dance   finish   not listen   play

We <u>finished</u> work late yesterday.
1 I _____ my mother on her birthday.
2 The film was very sad. _____ you _____?
3 My brother _____ video games all day yesterday.
4 I _____ to the news this morning because I was late.
5 _____ Sarah _____ with Martin at the party?

◀ p.54

7C

a Complete the text with the verbs in brackets in the past simple.

Last weekend, I <u>went</u> (go) to London with some friends. We ¹_____ (meet) at the train station at 7.30 a.m. Our train ²_____ (leave) at 7.45 a.m. In the morning, we ³_____ (buy) some souvenirs. Then, we ⁴_____ (have) lunch in an Italian restaurant. In the evening, we ⁵_____ (see) a Shakespeare play at the Globe Theatre. We ⁶_____ (get) home very late that night. We all ⁷_____ (feel) very tired but very happy.

b Complete the questions in the past simple.

<u>Did you go out</u> last night? Yes, I did.
1 What _____? I wore jeans.
2 Where _____ your friends? We met in a café.
3 What time _____? We got home late.
4 How _____ home? We went home by taxi.
5 _____ a good time? Yes, we had a great time.

c Correct the information using the word in brackets.

They got home at midnight. (11 p.m.)
<u>They didn't get home at midnight. They got home at 11.</u>
1 She wore a red dress. (blue)
_____
2 I left work early. (late)
_____
3 We went by train. (bus)
_____
4 He lost his mobile phone. (wallet)
_____
5 You had a sandwich. (salad)
_____

◀ p.57

8A past simple: regular and irregular verbs

1 be 🔊 4 11
- [+] I **was** born in Japan. They **were** late for class yesterday.
- [−] She **wasn't** at home last night. You **weren't** very nice to her.
- [?] **Were** you ill yesterday? When **was** he born?

2 regular verbs
- [+] I really **liked** the present. She **wanted** to be a doctor.
- [−] She **didn't enjoy** the concert. They **didn't arrive** until very late.
- [?] **Did** you **watch** the match last night? When **did** you **finish** the book?

3 irregular verbs
- [+] I **went** to Paris last summer. She **slept** on the sofa.
- [−] He **didn't come** home last night. They **didn't hear** the music.
- [?] **Did** you **speak** to your sister yesterday? Where **did** you **have** lunch?

1 The past of *be* is *was/were*. We add *not* to make negatives and invert the subject and verb to make questions.
2 Regular verbs add *-ed* or *-d* in the past simple [+], e.g. *like–liked*, *want–wanted*.
3 Irregular verbs change their form in the past simple [+], e.g. *go–went*, *see–saw*.
- Regular and irregular verbs (except *can*) use:
  - *didn't* + infinitive to make negatives, e.g. *I didn't like it. She didn't see him.*
  - *did* + subject + infinitive to make questions, e.g. *Did you want to come? Where did she go?*

> 🔍 **can / could**
> The past of *can* is *could*. We add *not* to make negatives (*I couldn't find my glasses*.) and reverse the subject and verb to make questions (*Could you use your mobile on the mountain?*).

8B there is / there are, some / any + plural nouns

Singular	Plural	🔊 4 16
[+] **There's** a garage.	**There are** some pictures on the wall.	
[−] **There isn't** a swimming pool.	**There aren't** any plants in the room.	
[?] **Is there** a bathroom downstairs?	**Are there** any neighbours with children?	
[✓] Yes, **there is**.	Yes, **there are**.	
[✗] No, **there isn't**.	No, **there aren't**.	

there is / there are
- We use *there is / there are* to say that somebody or something exists. We use *there is* + a singular noun and *there are* + plural nouns.
- *There is* is often contracted to *There's*. *There are* is not usually contracted.
- When we talk about a list of things we use *there is* if the first word in the list is singular or *there are* if the first word in the list is plural:
  In my bedroom **there's a** *bed, two chairs, and a desk.*
  In the living room **there are** *two armchairs and a sofa.*

a / an, some and any
- We often use *there is / there are* with *a / an*, *some*, and *any*.
- Use *some* and *any* with plural nouns. *Some* = not an exact number.
- Use *some* in [+] sentences and *any* in [−] and [?].

> 🔍 **There is or It is?**
> Be careful. *There is* and *It is* are different.
> **There's** a key on the table. **It's** the key to the kitchen.

8C there was / there were

Singular	Plural	🔊 4 27
[+] **There was** an old TV.	**There were** only three guests.	
[−] **There wasn't** a remote control.	**There weren't** any more people.	
[?] **Was there** a ghost?	**Were there** any windows?	
[✓] Yes, **there was**.	Yes, **there were**.	
[✗] No, **there wasn't**.	No, **there weren't**.	

- *there was / were* is the past of *there is / are*.

GRAMMAR BANK

8A

a Complete the dialogue using the past simple of the verbs in brackets.

A Where _were_ (be) you last night at 8.00?
B I [1]_____ (be) at home, Inspector. With my wife. We [2]_____ (be) at home all evening.
A What [3]_____ you _____ (do)?
B We [4]_____ (watch) TV and then we [5]_____ (have) a light dinner. We [6]_____ (not be) hungry. After that, we [7]_____ (go) to bed.
A What time [8]_____ you _____ (go) to bed?
B About 10 o'clock.
A [9]_____ you _____ (hear) a noise during the night?
B No, I [10]_____ (not hear) anything.

b Complete the text with the past simple of the verbs in brackets.

Last night I _was_ (be) asleep in my room when a strange noise [1]_____ (wake) me up. I [2]_____ (not want) to leave my room because I [3]_____ (feel) very scared. Then I [4]_____ (hear) the noise again, so I [5]_____ (decide) to go and investigate. When I [6]_____ (turn on) the light in the kitchen, a bird [7]_____ (fly) out of the window. I [8]_____ (close) the window so that the bird [9]_____ (not can) come in again and then I [10]_____ (go) back to bed.

◀ p.61

8B

a Complete with + or ? of *There's* or *There are*.

There's a dishwasher in the kitchen.
Are there any people in the room?

1 _____ any books on the shelf?
2 _____ a toilet downstairs?
3 _____ some stairs over there.
4 _____ a carpet on the floor.
5 _____ some pictures on the wall.
6 _____ a shower in the bathroom?
7 _____ some chairs in the garden.
8 _____ a lamp in the bedroom?
9 _____ a motorbike in the garage.
10 _____ any glasses in the cupboard?

b Write +, -, or ? sentences with *there is/are + a/an*, *some* or *any*.

+ trees / the garden   _There are some trees in the garden._
1 + table / the kitchen   _____.
2 ? fireplace / the living room   _____?
3 - plants / your flat   _____.
4 ? people / the hall   _____?
5 + pictures / your bedroom   _____.
6 - TV / the kitchen   _____.
7 + computer / the study   _____.
8 - chairs / the dining room   _____.
9 ? mirror / the bathroom   _____?
10 - car / the garage   _____.

◀ p.63

8C

a Complete the dialogue with the correct form of *there was* or *there were*.

A How many guests _were there_ in the hotel?
B [1]_____ _____ four including me. [2]_____ _____ a French tourist and [3]_____ _____ two businessmen.
A [4]_____ _____ a restaurant?
B No, [5]_____ _____, but [6]_____ _____ a bar.
A [7]_____ _____ a minibar in your room?
B Yes, [8]_____ _____ but [9]_____ _____ any drinks in it.
A How many beds [10]_____ _____?
B One. A double bed.

b Complete the sentences with *there was/were/wasn't/weren't + a/an*, or *some/any*.

There were some ghosts in the haunted castle I stayed in.
1 My sister didn't have a shower because _____ spider in the bath.
2 We couldn't watch the news because _____ TV in our room.
3 I couldn't sleep on the plane because _____ noisy children behind me.
4 They couldn't play tennis because _____ tennis balls.
5 She didn't have a coffee because _____ cups.
6 He took a photo because _____ beautiful view.
7 They couldn't park near the restaurant because _____ car park.
8 I couldn't work in the hotel because _____ computer.

◀ p.65

iTutor 139

9

9A countable / uncountable nouns

an apple *three apples* *rice* *meat*

- There are two kinds of nouns in English; countable (C) and uncountable (U).
  C = things you can count, e.g. *apples*. C nouns can be singular (*an* apple) or plural (*apples*).
  U = things you can't count.
  butter, meat **NOT** *two butters, three meats*
  U nouns are normally singular.
- Some nouns can be C or U but the meaning is different.

an ice cream (C)   *some ice cream* (U)

a / an, some / any

	countable	uncountable
+ We need	**an** apple. **some** apples.	**some** butter.
− We don't need	**a** tomato. **any** tomato**es**.	**any** rice.
? Do we need	**an** orange? **any** orange**s**?	**any** sugar?

- We use *a / an* with singular C nouns; *a / an* = one.
- We use *some* + with plural C nouns and with U nouns; *some* = not an exact number or quantity.
- We use *any* in − and ? with plural C nouns and with U nouns.

🔍 **some in ?**
We use *some* in ? to ask for and offer things.
*Can I have **some** apples, please?*
*Would you like **some** coffee?*

9B quantifiers: how much / how many, a lot of, etc.

uncountable (singular)	short answers	full answers
How much sugar do you eat?	A lot. Quite a lot. A little. Not much. None.	I eat **a lot of** sugar. I eat **quite a lot of** sugar. I eat **a little** sugar. I don't eat **much** sugar. I don't eat **any** sugar.
countable (plural)		
How many sweet**s** do you eat?	A lot. Quite a lot. A few. Not many. None.	I eat **a lot of** sweets. I eat **quite a lot of** sweets. I eat **a few** sweets. I don't eat **many** sweets. I don't eat **any** sweets.

- We use *How much…?* with uncountable (U) nouns and *How many…?* with plural countable (C) nouns.
- We use:
  a lot (of) with C and U nouns for a **big quantity**.
  quite a lot (of) for **a medium quantity**.
  a little / not…much with U nouns for a **small quantity**.
  a few / not…many with C plural nouns for a **small quantity**.
  not…any (*none* in short answers) for **zero quantity**.

a lot of and much / many

- In + sentences we usually use *a lot of*.
- In − sentences and ?, we usually use *much* and *many*:
  *I don't drink **much** water. Do you drink **much** coffee?*
- It is also possible to use *a lot of* in − and ?: *Do you drink **a lot of** coffee? I don't eat **a lot of** vegetables.*

9C comparative adjectives

*Is your sister **older than** you?*
*Buckingham Palace is **bigger than** the White House.*
*Female mosquitoes are **more dangerous than** males.*
*My new job is **better than** my old one.*
*The traffic is always **worse** in the evening.*

- Use comparative adjectives + *than* to compare two things, people, etc.

adjective	comparative	
old cheap	old**er** cheap**er**	one-syllable adjectives: add *-er*
big hot	big**ger** hot**ter**	adjectives ending one vowel + one consonant: double consonant, add *-er*
dry healthy	dr**ier** health**ier**	one- or two-syllable adjectives ending consonant + *y* > *-ier*
famous expensive	**more** famous **more** expensive	two- or more syllable adjectives: *more* + adjective
good bad far	better worse further	irregular

GRAMMAR BANK

9A

a Write *a*, *an*, or *some* + a food / drink word.

some bread
1 _____
2 _____
3 _____
4 _____
5 _____
6 _____
7 _____
8 _____

b Complete the dialogue with *a*, *an*, *some*, or *any*.

A What can we cook for your brother and his girlfriend?
B Let's make *a* lasagne.
A Good idea. Are there ¹____ onions?
B Yes. And there are ²____ tomatoes, too.
A Great!
B Oh no! There isn't ³____ pasta!
A Oh. Wait a minute. I bought ⁴____ fish yesterday. Are there ⁵____ potatoes?
B Yes, there are.
A Good. So we can have fish and chips. Do we have ⁶____ fruit?
B Yes. I think we have ⁷____ oranges. Why?
A You can make ⁸____ fruit salad for dessert. There's ⁹____ apple and ¹⁰____ bananas, too.
B OK. Let's start cooking.

◀ p.69

9B

a Complete with *How much* / *How many*.

How much sugar do you put in your tea?
1 _____ butter do you use?
2 _____ cans of cola did she drink?
3 _____ oil do I need?
4 _____ chocolates were in that box?
5 _____ rice do you want?
6 _____ coffee does he drink?
7 _____ bottles of water did you buy?
8 _____ tins of tuna do we have?
9 _____ orange juice is there in that carton?
10 _____ biscuits did you eat?

b (Circle) the correct word or phrase.

I don't put (much) / many salt on my food.
1 We don't eat *a lot of* / *a lot* sweets.
2 **A** How much chocolate do you eat? **B** *A little* / *A few*.
3 My friends don't drink *much* / *many* coffee.
4 **A** How much fruit do you buy? **B** *Quite a lot* / *Quite a lot of*.
5 We eat *a lot of* / *much* fish. We love it!
6 **A** Do your children drink any milk? **B** No. *Not much* / *Not many*.
7 Donna ate her hamburger, but she didn't eat *much* / *many* chips.
8 **A** How many vegetables do you eat? **B** *Any* / *None*. I don't like them.
9 I have a cup of tea and *a few* / *a little* cereal for breakfast.
10 **A** Do you eat *much* / *many* meat?
   B No, I don't eat *no* / *any* meat. I'm a vegetarian.

◀ p.70

9C

a Write the comparative form of these adjectives.

big — *bigger*
1 high — _____
2 dirty — _____
3 dangerous — _____
4 good — _____
5 thin — _____
6 slow — _____
7 healthy — _____
8 far — _____
9 comfortable — _____
10 bad — _____

b Complete with a comparative adjective + *than*.

My sister is *younger than* me. She's only 18. (young)
1 The market is _____ the supermarket for vegetables. (cheap)
2 Italian is _____ for Spanish students _____ it is for English students. (easy)
3 It rains a lot in the spring. April is _____ July. (wet)
4 This restaurant is _____ when it first opened. (busy)
5 Come in the summer. The weather is _____ in the spring. (good)
6 I love science. I find it _____ history. (interesting)
7 Milan is _____ from the sea _____ Rome. (far)
8 I'm _____ my brother. He's very tall. (short)
9 The situation is _____ it was last year. (bad)
10 Skiing is _____ I thought it was. (difficult)

◀ p.73

10

10A superlative adjectives

It's **the hottest** month of the year.
It's **the most dangerous** road in the world.
She's **the best** student in the class.
Monday is **the worst** day of the week.

adjective	comparative	superlative	
cold high	cold**er** high**er**	**the** cold**est** **the** high**est**	add -est
big hot	big**ger** hot**ter**	**the** big**gest** **the** hot**test**	double consonant, add -est
dry sunny	dr**ier** sunn**ier**	**the** dr**iest** **the** sunn**iest**	> -iest
dangerous	**more** dangerous	**the most** dangerous	the most + adjective
good bad far	better worse further	the best the worst the furthest	irregular

- Use *the* + superlative adjective to say which is the (*biggest*, etc.) in a group.
- After superlatives, we use *in* (not *of*) + places, e.g. *the world*, *the class*.

10B be going to (plans)

I'm going to have a holiday next month.
I'm not going to study English.
Are you **going to have** a holiday too?

	full form	contraction		
+	I am You are He / She / It is We are They are	I'm You're He / She / It's We're They're	going to	have a holiday next month. study English tonight.
−	I am not You are not He / She / It is not We are not They are not	I'm not You are'nt He / She / It isn't We aren't They aren't	going to	have a holiday next month. study English tonight.

?		
Am I Are you Is he / she / it Are we Are they	going to	have a holiday next month. study English tonight.

✓		✗	
Yes,	I am. you are. he / she / it is. we are. they are.	No,	I'm not. you aren't. he / she / it isn't. we aren't. they aren't.

- We use *be going to* + verb (infinitive) to talk about future plans.
- We often use future time expressions with *going to*:
  tomorrow, *next week*, *next year*, etc.

10C be going to (predictions)

- We can use *be going to* + verb (infinitive) to make predictions (= to say what you think or can see is going to happen in the future).

I think it**'s going to** rain.
You**'re going to be** very happy.
I'm sure they**'re going to win**.

GRAMMAR BANK

10A

a Write the opposite.

the smallest	*the biggest*
1 the coldest	_____
2 the most expensive	_____
3 the best	_____
4 the most difficult	_____
5 the driest	_____
6 the shortest	_____
7 the nearest	_____
8 the cleanest	_____

b Complete the sentences with a superlative. Use the adjectives in brackets.

The tigers are <u>the most dangerous</u> animals in the zoo. (dangerous)
1. Our house is _____ house in the street. (big)
2. For me, Saturday is _____ day of the week. (good)
3. My bedroom is _____ room in our house. (small)
4. July is _____ month in my country. (hot)
5. My neighbours upstairs are _____ people in the world. (noisy)
6. _____ driver in my family is my dad. (bad)
7. Sophie is _____ student in our English class. (young)
8. _____ building in my town is the castle. (beautiful)

◀ p.76

10B

a Complete the sentences with the correct form of *be going to* and the verb in brackets.

She doesn't have a car. <u>She's going to travel by train.</u> (travel)
1. We need a holiday. We _____ a hotel near the beach. (book)
2. Tomorrow is Saturday. I _____ in bed. (stay)
3. My sister wants to be a doctor. She _____ medicine. (study)
4. Laura and David are in love. They _____ married. (get)
5. Ian is busy. He _____ late tonight. (work)
6. Their house isn't very tidy. They _____ the housework this afternoon. (do)
7. It's raining. We _____ an umbrella. (take)
8. I have a problem at work. I _____ to my boss. (speak)

b Complete the sentences with *be going to* + a verb.

| not buy | call | not come | eat |
| go | not see | sleep | watch |

I'm staying with a friend. <u>I'm going to sleep</u> on the couch.
1. I need to talk to my mum. I _____ her tonight.
2. There isn't any food. What _____ we _____ ?
3. My friend is ill. She _____ to the party.
4. They don't have any money. They _____ any new clothes.
5. Germany are playing England. _____ you _____ the match?
6. Our friends are away. We _____ them this week.
7. The children are tired. They _____ to bed.

◀ p.78

10C

a Write predictions for the pictures.

A	be	catch	make	play	send
B	the bus	an email	a nice day	an omelette	tennis

<u>He's going to play tennis.</u>
1. _____ .
2. _____ .
3. _____ .
4. _____ .

b Complete the predictions with *be going to* and a verb.

| be | break | not finish | forget | have |
| not like | not pass | tell | win |

I'm a fortune-teller. <u>I'm going to tell</u> you about your future.
1. You're driving very fast! I'm sure we _____ an accident!
2. She's a very bad student. She _____ the exam.
3. Be careful with that glass! You _____ it!
4. We have a lot of homework. I'm sure we _____ it.
5. They're playing very well. I think they _____ .
6. Look at the time. We _____ late.
7. Oh no, it's a horror film. I'm sure I _____ it.
8. He didn't put her number in his phone. He _____ it.

◀ p.81

11

11A adverbs (manner and modifiers)

adverbs of manner

They drive **dangerously**. (5 25)
He dresses **fashionably**.
She eats very **quickly**.
I work **hard**.
We speak English **well**.

adjective	adverb	
slow	slow**ly**	
quick	quick**ly**	+ -ly
bad	bad**ly**	
careful	careful**ly**	
healthy	health**ily**	consonant + y
easy	eas**ily**	> -ily
possible	possib**ly**	le > -ly
good	well	
fast	fast	irregular
hard	hard	

- We use adverbs of manner to say <u>how</u> people do things.
- Adverbs usually go after the verb.
  I speak English very well.
  NOT *I speak very well English.*

- Remember the difference between adjectives and adverbs:
  *I'm a **careful** driver.* (*careful* is an adjective. It describes the noun, *driver*.)
  *I drive **carefully**.* (*carefully* is an adverb. It describes the verb, *drive*.)

modifying adverbs: *very, quite,* etc.

It isn't **very** expensive. (5 26)
People are **quite** formal.
She drives **incredibly** fast.
They speak **really** slowly.

- We use modifying adverbs with adjectives or other adverbs.
- They always go <u>before</u> the adjective or adverb.

🔍 **words ending in -ly**
Not all words that end in *-ly* are adverbs, e.g. *friendly* = adjective.
*He's a **friendly** person.*

11B verbs + *to* + infinitive: *want to, need to,* etc.

I **want to find** a new job. (5 31)
You **need to practise** every day.
When did you **learn to play** the guitar?
Would you like to be famous?

- Many verbs are followed by a verb in the infinitive with *to*.
- These include: *want, need, learn, promise, decide, plan,* and *hope*.

would like to

- *I would like to* = *I want to* (now or in the future).
- **Contractions**: *'d* = *would*; *wouldn't* = *would not*.
- Use the infinitive with *to* after *would like*. *I **would like to** learn.* **NOT** *I would like learn.*
- Remember you can also use *Would you like…?* to offer:
  Would you like a drink?
- *would like* is the same for all persons.

🔍 **would like and like**
I'd like to dance. = I want to dance.
I like dancing. = I enjoy it; I like it in general.

11C articles

1 a / an

A What's this? **B** It's **a** photo of my daughter. (5 37)
A What do they do? **B** Jim's **a** doctor. Sally's **an** engineer.
A How often do they have classes? **B** Three times **a** week.

2 the

Can you close **the window**, please?
Can you check their address on **the internet**?
It's **the best** restaurant I know.

3 a or the?

Let's have **a** pizza. **The** pizzas are very good here.

4 no article

Men are usually more interested in sport than **women**.
She's **my mother's cousin**. That's **Tom's chair**!
Jim goes to **school** by **bus**.

1 We use *a / an*
  - to say what something is or what job people do.
  - in expressions of frequency.
2 We use *the*
  - when the speaker and hearer know the thing we are talking about: *Close **the window**.* = the one that is open.
  - when there is only one of something: *the internet, the sun,* etc.
  - before superlative adjectives: *the biggest, the best,* etc.
3 We often use *a* the first time we mention a person or thing and then *the* the next time because it is now clear who or what we are talking about.
4 We don't usually use *the*
  - when we talk about people or things in general:
    ***Men** are more interested in sport than **women**.* (general)
    ***The women** in this class work harder than **the men**.* (specific)
  - before possessive *'s*. *She's my mother's cousin.* **NOT** *She's the my mother's cousin.*
  - with the following:
    meals: *breakfast, lunch, dinner,* etc.
    places: *work, school, university, bed, home,* etc.
    by **+ transport**: *go by car, travel by train,* etc.

GRAMMAR BANK

11A

a Adjective or adverb? Circle the correct form.

People drive quite *dangerous* / *dangerously*.
1. He wrote down the phone number *careful* / *carefully*.
2. My neighbour's children aren't very *polite* / *politely*.
3. My niece plays the piano *beautiful* / *beautifully*.
4. Fast food is incredibly *unhealthy* / *unhealthily*.
5. Old people often walk very *slow* / *slowly*.
6. I bought a *real* / *really* cheap bag in the sales.
7. My friend sings very *good* / *well*.
8. My sister speaks Spanish *perfect* / *perfectly*.
9. We wear *casual* / *casually* clothes to work.
10. The view from the top is *incredible* / *incredibly* beautiful.

b Complete with adverbs from these adjectives.

| bad | careful | easy | fast | good |
| hard | healthy | perfect | quiet |

The buses and trains in Malmö run *perfectly* when it snows.
1. Can you talk _____, please? I'm trying to sleep.
2. Don't drive _____ when it's raining.
3. I don't like the sea because I can't swim very _____.
4. She picked up the baby _____ and put him in the bath.
5. We're working _____ because we have an exam.
6. People who do sport usually eat very _____.
7. We played _____ in the semi-final and we lost 5–1.
8. She was the best athlete so she won the race _____.

◀ p.85

11B

a Complete the sentences with *to* + a verb from the list.

| be | buy | call | climb | drive | get married |
| go | leave | pass | see | stay |

Sam loves Africa. He wants *to climb* Mount Kilimanjaro.
1. I learned _____ a car when I was 17. I passed my test first time!
2. Our fridge is broken. We need _____ a new one.
3. I wouldn't like _____ famous. I'm happy as I am.
4. He promised _____ his girlfriend after work.
5. The weather was terrible. We decided _____ at home.
6. My friend would like _____ Radiohead live. She loves them.
7. They're planning _____. Their wedding is on 12th July.
8. I studied hard last week. I hope _____ the exam.
9. Do you like animals? Would you like _____ on a safari?
10. She's enjoying the party. She doesn't want _____.

b Circle the correct form.

I hate *fly* / *flying* so I usually travel by train.
1. Would you like *have* / *to have* dinner with me tonight?
2. My grandmother learned *to drive* / *driving* when she was 62.
3. I'd like *to travel* / *travelling* around Europe.
4. I like *relax* / *relaxing* at the weekend.
5. Do you want *to play* / *playing* football?
6. He's hoping *to have* / *having* more time when he retires.
7. Most people hate *to go* / *going* to the dentist.
8. I love *to read* / *reading* detective stories.
9. It's cold. You need *wear* / *to wear* a coat.
10. My mum doesn't like *to cook* / *cooking*.

◀ p.86

11C

a Circle the correct word or phrase.

How much time do you spend on *internet* / *the internet*?
1. My brother is *at university* / *at the university* studying Maths.
2. I'd like *cup of tea* / *a cup of tea*, please.
3. We're going to visit my aunt *at weekend* / *at the weekend*.
4. We have English classes *twice a week* / *twice week*.
5. I love reading *novels* / *the novels*.
6. Yolanda is *best* / *the best* student in our class.
7. My mum's *lawyer* / *a lawyer*.
8. He's *the man* / *a man* that I told you about yesterday.
9. Can you open *a door* / *the door* for me, please?
10. He had *breakfast* / *the breakfast* late this morning.

b Complete with *the*, *a* / *an*, or –.

I'm going to buy *a* new laptop next week.
1. What time do you finish ____ work?
2. We usually go to the cinema once ____ month.
3. ____ children behaved very badly yesterday.
4. Lorena doesn't like ____ dogs.
5. I want to be ____ engineer when I finish studying.
6. ____ sun came out so we went for a walk.
7. Can you pass ____ salt, please?
8. My mum chose ____ most expensive dessert.
9. Last year we went on holiday by ____ train.
10. This is Joanne. She's ____ very good friend.

◀ p.89

12

12A present perfect

1. **A Have you seen** his new film? 5 45))
   B Yes, **I've seen** all his films.
   She hasn't read any Harry Potter books.
2. **Have you ever read** a Russian novel?
   Sarah's never worked in a big company.
3. **Have you finished** the exercise?
   Your parents **have arrived**. They're in the living room.

1. We use the present perfect when we talk or ask about things that have happened in the past, but when we don't say when.
2. We often use the present perfect with *ever* (= at any time in your life) and *never* (= at no time in your life).
3. We also use the present perfect to talk about something that has recently happened.

	full form of *have*	contraction	past participle of main verb
+	I **have** You **have** He / She / It **has** We **have** They **have**	I**'ve** You**'ve** He / She / It**'s** We**'ve** They**'ve**	**seen** that film.
–	I **have not** You **have not** He / She / It **has not** We **have not** They **have not**	I **haven't** You **haven't** He / She / It **hasn't** We **haven't** They **haven't**	

?		
Have **Has**	I / you / we / they he / she / it	**seen** that film?

✓		
Yes,	I / you / we / they he / she / it	**have.** **has.**

✗		
No,	I / you / we / they he / she / it	**haven't.** **hasn't.**

- To make the present perfect use *have / has* + the past participle of the verb.
- *'s* = *has* in present perfect.
- Past participles of regular verbs are the same as the past simple.

infinitive	past simple	past participle
like	liked	liked
want	wanted	wanted

- Past participles of irregular verbs are sometimes the same as the past simple, e.g. *read*, but sometimes different, e.g. *seen*.

infinitive	past simple	past participle
read /riːd/	read /red/	read /red/
see	saw	seen

(There is a list of irregular past participles on p.165)

12B present perfect or past simple?

A Have you been to Luigi's? **B** Yes, **I have**. 5 52))
A When **did you go** there? **B I went** last weekend.
A Who **did you go** with? **B I went** with some people from work.
I've been to New York twice. **I went** to visit my sister – she's married to an American.

- We often use the **present perfect** to ask about or tell somebody about a past action for the first time. We don't ask / say when the action happened: **Have you been** to Luigi's? **I've been** to New York twice.
- We then use the **past simple** to ask / talk about specific past details: When **did you go** there? **I went** to visit my sister.
- We use the past simple **NOT** the present perfect with *when* and past time expressions, e.g. *yesterday, last week*:
  When did you see it? **NOT** ~~When have you seen it?~~
  I saw it **last week**. **NOT** ~~I've seen it last week.~~

been or *gone*?

I've **been** to Italy. 5 53))
My sister's **gone** to Italy to study Italian.

- *been to* and *gone to* have different meanings. *been* is the past participle of *be*, and *gone* is the past participle of *go*.
- In the present perfect we use *been to* (**NOT** ~~gone to~~ or ~~been in~~) to say that somebody has visited a place.
  I've **been to** the USA three times. Have you **been to** the new Italian restaurant in George Street?
- We use *gone to* when somebody goes to a place and is still there:
  My parents **have gone** to the USA for their holidays. They don't come back until Saturday.
- Compare: Nick has **been to** Paris = He visited Paris and came back at some time in the past.
  Nick has **gone to** Paris = He went to Paris and he is in Paris now.

GRAMMAR BANK

12A

a Write the sentences with contractions.

I have seen the film. *I've seen the film.*
1 She has not read the book.
2 You have not washed the dishes.
3 We have done the housework.
4 He has been ill.
5 They have not eaten Japanese food before.

b Write +, −, and ? sentences in the present perfect.

+ I / meet a famous actor.
I've met a famous actor.
1 + I / forget your name
2 − my boyfriend / wear his new shirt
3 ? you / speak to your boss
4 − they / do their homework
5 ? your brother / work in New York
6 + the train / leave the station
7 − we / take any photos
8 ? the children / eat all the biscuits
9 − my girlfriend / call me today
10 + Janet / leave her book at home

c Write a sentence in the present perfect for each picture. Use the verbs in the box.

break   buy   fall   go   read   ~~win~~

They've won the cup.
1 _____ his leg.
2 _____ to the beach.
3 _____ off his motorbike.
4 _____ the newspaper.
5 _____ a new car.

◀ p.92

12B

a Circle the correct form.

(Have you ever eaten) / *Did you ever eat* in 'Appetito'?
1 I *haven't bought* / *didn't buy* any new clothes recently.
2 My boyfriend *has given* / *gave* me a ring for my last birthday.
3 They *'ve spent* / *spent* a lot of money yesterday.
4 *Have you ever won* / *Did you ever win* a competition?
5 My friends *have had* / *had* a party last weekend.

b Circle the correct form.

Let's go to the 'Peking Duck'. I've never (been) / *gone* there.
1 The secretary isn't here. She's *gone* / *been* to the bank.
2 I've never *gone* / *been* to the USA.
3 My neighbours aren't at home. They've *gone* / *been* on holiday.
4 Have you ever *gone* / *been* abroad?
5 We have lots of food. We've *gone* / *been* to the supermarket.

c Put the verbs in brackets in the present perfect or past simple.

A *Have you ever travelled* abroad? (travel)
B Yes, I *went* to Portugal last year. (go)
A [1]_____ you ever _____ any countries outside Europe? (visit)
B Yes, I have. I [2]_____ to Morocco a few years ago. (go)
A Who [3]_____ you _____ with? (go)
B My husband. It was a work trip and his company [4]_____ for everything. (pay)
A How wonderful! How [5]_____ you _____ there? (get)
B We [6]_____. (fly)
A Where [7]_____ you _____? (stay)
B We [8]_____ a suite in a five-star hotel. It was beautiful! (have)
A [9]_____ the company _____ you on any other trips recently? (take)
B No. My husband [10]_____ working there a year later, so that was our only trip. (stop)
A What a pity!

◀ p.94

Days and numbers

VOCABULARY BANK

1 DAYS OF THE WEEK

a Complete the days of the week with the letters.

| W | Fr | S | S | Th | T | M |

<u>M</u>onday /ˈmʌndeɪ/   __iday /ˈfraɪdeɪ/
__uesday /ˈtjuːzdeɪ/   __aturday /ˈsætədeɪ/
__ednesday /ˈwenzdeɪ/   __unday /ˈsʌndeɪ/
__ursday /ˈθɜːzdeɪ/

b ▶ 1 10))) Listen and check.

c Cover the days of the week. Say them in order.

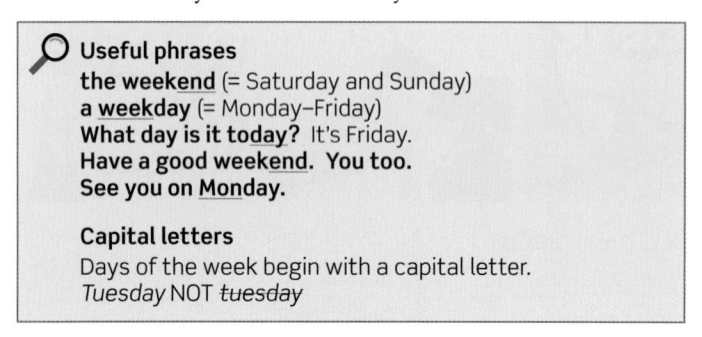

> **Useful phrases**
> the week<u>end</u> (= Saturday and Sunday)
> a <u>week</u>day (= Monday–Friday)
> What day is it to<u>day</u>? It's Friday.
> Have a good weekend. You too.
> See you on <u>Mon</u>day.
>
> **Capital letters**
> Days of the week begin with a capital letter.
> Tuesday NOT tuesday

2 NUMBERS 0-20

a Match the words with the numbers.

| twelve | twenty | eleven | ~~three~~ |
| eighteen | five | fifteen | seven |

0	zero /ˈzɪərəʊ/	11	_____ /ɪˈlevn/
1	one /wʌn/	12	_____ /twelv/
2	two /tuː/	13	thir<u>teen</u> /θɜːˈtiːn/
3	<u>three</u> /θriː/	14	four<u>teen</u> /fɔːˈtiːn/
4	four /fɔː(r)/	15	_____ /fɪfˈtiːn/
5	_____ /faɪv/	16	six<u>teen</u> /sɪksˈtiːn/
6	six /sɪks/	17	seven<u>teen</u> /sevnˈtiːn/
7	_____ /ˈsevn/	18	_____ /eɪˈtiːn/
8	eight /eɪt/	19	nine<u>teen</u> /naɪnˈtiːn/
9	nine /naɪn/	20	_____ /ˈtwenti/
10	ten /ten/		

b ▶ 1 11))) Listen and check.

c Cover the words. Say the numbers.

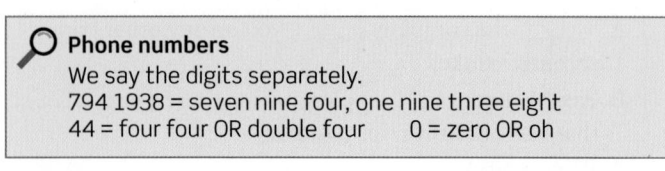

> **Phone numbers**
> We say the digits separately.
> 794 1938 = seven nine four, one nine three eight
> 44 = four four OR double four   0 = zero OR oh

◀ p.5

3 NUMBERS 21-100

a Write the numbers.

_21_	twenty-<u>one</u> /twenti ˈwʌn/
_____	thirty /ˈθɜːti/
_____	thirty-<u>five</u> /θɜːti ˈfaɪv/
_____	forty /ˈfɔːti/
_____	forty-<u>three</u> /fɔːti ˈθriː/
_____	fifty /ˈfɪfti/
_____	fifty-<u>nine</u> /fɪfti ˈnaɪn/
_____	sixty /ˈsɪksti/
_____	sixty-<u>seven</u> /sɪksti ˈsevn/
_____	seventy /ˈsevnti/
_____	seventy-<u>two</u> /sevnti ˈtuː/
_____	eighty /ˈeɪti/
_____	eighty-<u>eight</u> /eɪti ˈeɪt/
_____	ninety /ˈnaɪnti/
_____	ninety-<u>four</u> /naɪnti ˈfɔː/
_____	a / one hundred /ˈhʌndrəd/

b ▶ 1 26))) Listen and repeat.

> **Pronunciation**
> 13 and 30, 14 and 40, etc. are similar, but the stress is different, e.g. thir<u>teen</u>, <u>thir</u>ty, four<u>teen</u>, <u>for</u>ty, etc.
> -een is a long sound /iː/, but -y is a short sound /i/.

◀ p.7

4 HIGH NUMBERS

a Write the missing words or numbers.

_105_	a / one hundred and five
_____	two hundred
350	three hundred and _____
875	eight hundred _____ seventy-five
1,000	a / one thousand /ˈθaʊznd/
_____	one thousand five hundred
2,012	two thousand and _____
5,420	five thousand four _____ and twenty
_____	twenty-five thousand
100,000	a / one hundred _____
1,000,000	a / one million /ˈmɪljən/
2,300,000	two million _____ hundred thousand

b ▶ 4 43))) Listen and check.

◀ p.72

148

The world

VOCABULARY BANK

1 CONTINENTS

a Match the words and continents.

Continent	Adjective
☐ Africa /ˈæfrɪkə/	African /ˈæfrɪkən/
☐ Asia /ˈeɪʒə/	Asian /ˈeɪʒn/
☐ Australia /ɒˈstreɪliə/	Australian /ɒˈstreɪliən/
☐ Europe /ˈjʊərəp/	European /jʊərəˈpiːən/
1 North America	North American
☐ South America	South American

b 1 15)) Listen and check.

c Cover the words and look at the map. Can you remember the continents and their adjectives?

2 COUNTRIES AND NATIONALITIES

a 1 16)) Match the words and countries. Then listen and check.

Country /ˈkʌntri/	Nationality adjective
	-ish
☐ England /ˈɪŋglənd/	English /ˈɪŋglɪʃ/
☐ Ireland /ˈaɪələnd/	Irish /ˈaɪrɪʃ/
☐ Poland /ˈpəʊlənd/	Polish /ˈpəʊlɪʃ/
☐ Scotland /ˈskɒtlənd/	Scottish /ˈskɒtɪʃ/
☐ Spain /speɪn/	Spanish /ˈspænɪʃ/
☐ Turkey /ˈtɜːki/	Turkish /ˈtɜːkɪʃ/
	-an
☐ Germany /ˈdʒɜːməni/	German /ˈdʒɜːmən/
☐ Mexico /ˈmeksɪkəʊ/	Mexican /ˈmeksɪkən/
1 the (United) States / the US(A)	American /əˈmerɪkən/
	-ian
☐ Argentina /ɑːdʒənˈtiːnə/	Argentinian /ɑːdʒənˈtɪniən/
☐ Brazil /brəˈzɪl/	Brazilian /brəˈzɪliən/
☐ Egypt /ˈiːdʒɪpt/	Egyptian /iˈdʒɪpʃn/
☐ Hungary /ˈhʌŋgəri/	Hungarian /hʌnˈgeəriən/
☐ Italy /ˈɪtəli/	Italian /ɪˈtæliən/
☐ Russia /ˈrʌʃə/	Russian /ˈrʌʃn/
	-ese
☐ China /ˈtʃaɪnə/	Chinese /tʃaɪˈniːz/
☐ Japan /dʒəˈpæn/	Japanese /dʒæpəˈniːz/
☐ the Czech Republic /tʃek rɪˈpʌblɪk/	Czech /tʃek/
☐ France /frɑːns/	French /frentʃ/
☐ Switzerland /ˈswɪtsələnd/	Swiss /swɪs/
☐ _____	

b Cover the words and look at the maps. Can you remember the countries and nationalities?

> 🔍 **Capital letters**
> Use CAPITAL letters for countries, continents, nationalities, and languages, e.g. Japan NOT japan; Spanish NOT spanish.

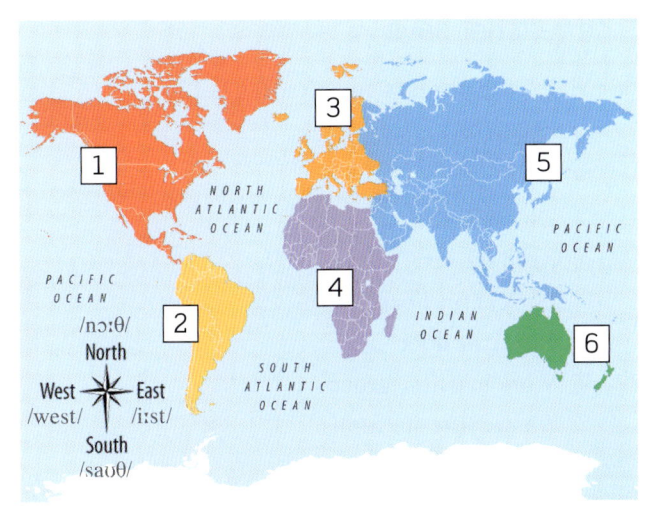

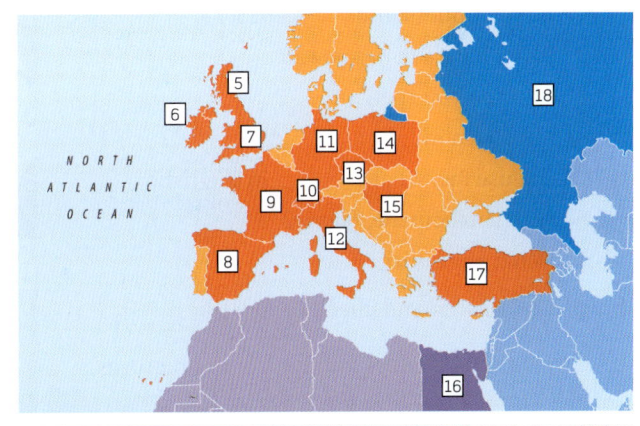

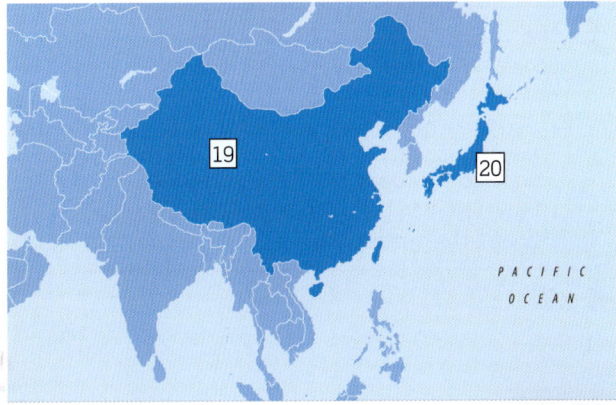

◀ p.6

Classroom language

VOCABULARY BANK

The teacher says

a Match the phrases and pictures 1–13.

- ☐ Open your books, please.
- ☐ Go to page 84.
- ☐ Do exercise a.
- ☐ Read the text.
- ☐ Look at the board.
- ☐ Close the door.
- 1 Work in pairs / groups.
- ☐ Answer the questions.
- ☐ Listen and repeat.
- ☐ Stand up.
- ☐ Sit down.
- ☐ Turn off your mobile.
- ☐ Please stop talking!

b 1 32)) Listen and check.

You say

a Match the phrases and pictures 14–22.

- ☐ Sorry, can you repeat that, please?
- 14 Sorry I'm late.
- ☐ I don't understand.
- ☐ Can I have a copy, please?
- ☐ How do you spell it?
- ☐ I don't know.
- ☐ Excuse me, what's _____ in English?
- ☐ Can you help me, please?
- ☐ What page is it?

b 1 33)) Listen and check.

c Cover the sentences and look at the pictures. Say the sentences.

> 🔍 **the**
> Look at **the** board.
> Answer **the** questions.
> - Use *the* when we know which (board, questions, etc.).
>   Look at **the** board. NOT ~~Look at a board.~~
> - Use *the* with singular and plural nouns (the board, the questions).

◀ p.8

Things

VOCABULARY BANK

a   Match the words and pictures.

- [ ] a book /bʊk/
- [1] a coin /kɔɪn/
- [ ] a credit card /ˈkredɪt kɑːd/
- [ ] a diary /ˈdaɪəri/
- [ ] a dictionary /ˈdɪkʃənri/
- [ ] a file /faɪl/
- [ ] glasses /ˈɡlɑːsɪz/
- [ ] headphones /ˈhedfəʊnz/
- [ ] an identity card /aɪˈdentəti kɑːd/
- [ ] an iPod /ˈaɪpɒd/
- [ ] a key /kiː/
- [ ] a laptop /ˈlæptɒp/
- [ ] a magazine /mæɡəˈziːn/
- [ ] a mobile (phone) /ˈməʊbaɪl/
- [ ] a newspaper /ˈnjuːzpeɪpə/
- [ ] a pen /pen/
- [ ] a pencil /ˈpensl/
- [ ] a photo /ˈfəʊtəʊ/
- [ ] a piece of paper /piːs əv ˈpeɪpə/
- [ ] a purse /pɜːs/
- [ ] scissors /ˈsɪzəz/
- [ ] a stamp /stæmp/
- [ ] sunglasses /ˈsʌnɡlɑːsɪz/
- [ ] a ticket /ˈtɪkɪt/
- [ ] a tissue /ˈtɪʃuː/
- [ ] an umbrella /ʌmˈbrelə/
- [ ] a wallet /ˈwɒlɪt/
- [ ] a watch /wɒtʃ/

b   **1 51**)) Listen and check.

> 🔍 **Plural nouns**
> Some words for things are plural,
> e.g. *glasses*, *headphones*, *trousers*.
> Don't use *a / an* with plural nouns.
> NOT *a glasses*, *a headphones*.

c   Cover the words and look at the pictures. In pairs, ask and answer.

What is it?   It's a watch.

What are they?   They're glasses.

◀ p.12

Adjectives

VOCABULARY BANK

1 COMMON ADJECTIVES

a Match the words and pictures 1–16.

- ☐ bad /bæd/ _____
- ☐ big /bɪg/ _____
- ☐ **1** dangerous /ˈdeɪndʒərəs/ _safe_
- ☐ dirty /ˈdɜːti/ _____
- ☐ easy /ˈiːzi/ _____
- ☐ empty /ˈempti/ _____
- ☐ expensive /ɪkˈspensɪv/ _____
- ☐ far /fɑː/ _____
- ☐ fast /fɑːst/ _____
- ☐ high /haɪ/ _____
- ☐ hot /hɒt/ _____
- ☐ long /lɒŋ/ _____
- ☐ old /əʊld/ _____
- ☐ rich /rɪtʃ/ _____
- ☐ strong /strɒŋ/ _____
- ☐ wrong /rɒŋ/ _____

b 🔊 1 60 Listen and check.

c Match these adjectives with their opposites in **a**.

cheap /tʃiːp/	low /ləʊ/	short /ʃɔːt/
clean /kliːn/	near /nɪə/	slow /sləʊ/
cold /kəʊld/	new /njuː/	small /smɔːl/
difficult /ˈdɪfɪkəlt/	poor /pɔː/	weak /wiːk/
full /fʊl/	right /raɪt/	
good /gʊd/	safe /seɪf/	

d 🔊 1 61 Listen and check. Then test your partner. **A** say an adjective and **B** say the opposite.

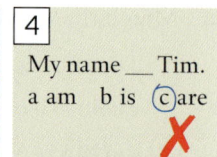

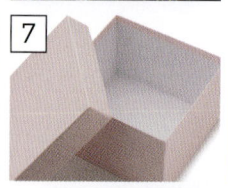

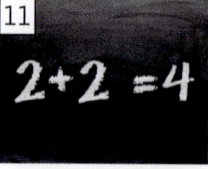

> 🔍 **Modifiers: very / really, quite**
> We often use these words before adjectives.
> A Ferrari is **very / really fast**.
> It's **quite cold** today. (= It's cold, but not very cold)

e Look at the things in the list. Say two adjectives for each one. Use modifiers.

A Ferrari   Mount Everest   Bill Gates
The Pyramids   Africa   Your town / city

> A Ferrari – It's really fast and very expensive.

◀ p.14

2 APPEARANCE

a Match the opposite adjectives and the pictures.

- ☐ blonde /blɒnd/   dark /dɑːk/
- ☐ beautiful /ˈbjuːtɪfl/   ugly /ˈʌgli/
- ☐ fat /fæt/   thin /θɪn/
- ☐ old /əʊld/   young /jʌŋ/
- ☐ tall /tɔːl/   short /ʃɔːt/

b 🔊 1 67 Listen and check.

c Cover the adjectives and look at the pictures. Test yourself or a partner.

> 🔍 **Positive adjectives for appearance**
> **Beautiful**, **good-looking**, **pretty**, and **attractive** can all be used for women, but for men we only use **good-looking** or **attractive**.

◀ p.15

152

Verb phrases

VOCABULARY BANK

a Match the verbs and pictures.

    cook /kʊk/
    do /duː/
    drink /drɪŋk/
    eat /iːt/
    go /gəʊ/
    have /hæv/
    like /laɪk/
    listen /ˈlɪsn/
  1 live /lɪv/
    play /pleɪ/
    read /riːd/
    say /seɪ/
    speak /spiːk/
    study /ˈstʌdi/
    take /teɪk/
    want /wɒnt/
    watch /wɒtʃ/
    wear /weə/
    work /wɜːk/

b **2 2))** Listen and check.

> 🔍 **work**
> *Work* has two meanings.
> 1 *She works in a museum.*
>   = it's her job
> 2 *The phone doesn't work.*
>   = it's broken
>
> **have or eat?**
> *Have* can be used with both food and drink, and is common with meals, e.g. *have a sandwich, have a coffee, have lunch.*
>
> *Eat* can only be used with food, e.g. *eat fast food.*

c Cover the verbs and look at the pictures. Test yourself or a partner.

◀ p.20

1  in a flat
2  in an office
3  children
4  economics
5  German
6  a new car
7  a newspaper
8  animals
9  to the cinema
10  TV
11  to music
12  tennis
13  an umbrella
14  homework / housework
15  the guitar
16  sorry
17  mineral water
18  fast food
19  dinner
20  exercise
21  glasses

Jobs

VOCABULARY BANK

a Match the words and pictures.

- ☐ an ad<u>min</u>istrator /ədˈmɪnɪstreɪtə/
- 1 an <u>arch</u>itect /ˈɑːkɪtekt/
- ☐ a <u>build</u>er /ˈbɪldə/
- ☐ a chef / a cook /ʃef/ /kʊk/
- ☐ a <u>dent</u>ist /ˈdentɪst/
- ☐ a <u>doc</u>tor /ˈdɒktə/
- ☐ an engi<u>neer</u> /endʒɪˈnɪə/
- ☐ a <u>fac</u>tory <u>work</u>er /ˈfæktəri wɜːkə/
- ☐ a flight at<u>tend</u>ant /ˈflaɪt ətendənt/
- ☐ a <u>foot</u>baller /ˈfʊtbɔːlə/
- ☐ a <u>hair</u>dresser /ˈheədresə/
- ☐ a <u>journ</u>alist /ˈdʒɜːnəlɪst/
- ☐ a <u>law</u>yer /ˈlɔːjə/
- ☐ a (bank) <u>man</u>ager /(ˈbæŋk) mænɪdʒə/
- ☐ a <u>mod</u>el /ˈmɒdl/
- ☐ a mu<u>sic</u>ian /mjuˈzɪʃn/
- ☐ a <u>nurse</u> /nɜːs/
- ☐ a <u>pi</u>lot /ˈpaɪlət/
- ☐ a po<u>lice</u>man / a po<u>lice</u>woman /pəˈliːsmən/ /pəˈliːswʊmən/
- ☐ a re<u>cep</u>tionist /rɪˈsepʃənɪst/
- ☐ a <u>shop</u> as<u>sist</u>ant /ˈʃɒp əsɪstənt/
- ☐ a <u>sold</u>ier /ˈsəʊldʒə/
- ☐ a <u>teach</u>er /ˈtiːtʃə/
- ☐ a vet /vet/
- ☐ a <u>wait</u>er / a <u>wait</u>ress /ˈweɪtə/ /ˈweɪtrəs/

> **🔍 Pronunciation**
> In multisyllable words, final -er / -or is pronounced /ə/, e.g. doctor, teacher.
> Final -ian is pronounced /ʃn/, e.g. musician.
>
> **a / an + jobs**
> We use a / an + job words.
> She's a model. NOT She's model.

b 🔊 2 8 Listen and check.

c Cover the jobs. In pairs, say what the people do.
> *She's a vet. He's an engineer.*

d 🔊 2 9 Listen and repeat the sentences. What do *you* do?

What do you do?

I'm **a** musician.	I work **for** a	I'm **a** student.	I'm un**em**ployed.
I'm **an** engineer.	French company.	I'm **at** university.	I'm re**tired**.
	I work **in** a shop.	I'm **at** school.	

◀ p.22

The family

VOCABULARY BANK

a Look at the two family trees. Number the people in relation to Richard.

1 aunt /ɑːnt/
2 brother /ˈbrʌðə/
3 cousin /ˈkʌzn/
4 daughter /ˈdɔːtə/
5 father /ˈfɑːðə/
6 grandfather /ˈɡrænfɑːðə/
7 grandmother /ˈɡrænmʌðə/
8 mother /ˈmʌðə/
9 nephew /ˈnefjuː/
10 niece /niːs/
11 sister /ˈsɪstə/
12 son /sʌn/
13 uncle /ˈʌŋkl/
14 wife /waɪf/

b Complete 1–3 with *children*, *grandparents*, *parents*.

1 my father and my mother = my _____ /ˈpeərənts/
2 my grandfather and my grandmother = my _____ /ˈɡrænpeərənts/
3 my son and my daughter = my _____ /ˈtʃɪldrən/

c ② 32)) Listen and check your answers to **a** and **b**.

> **More family words**
> My wife's mother = my **mother-in-law**; My sister's husband = my **brother-in-law**, etc.
> My mother's second husband = my **stepfather**
> My father's daughter from another wife = my **stepsister**

d Cover the words. In pairs, ask and answer.

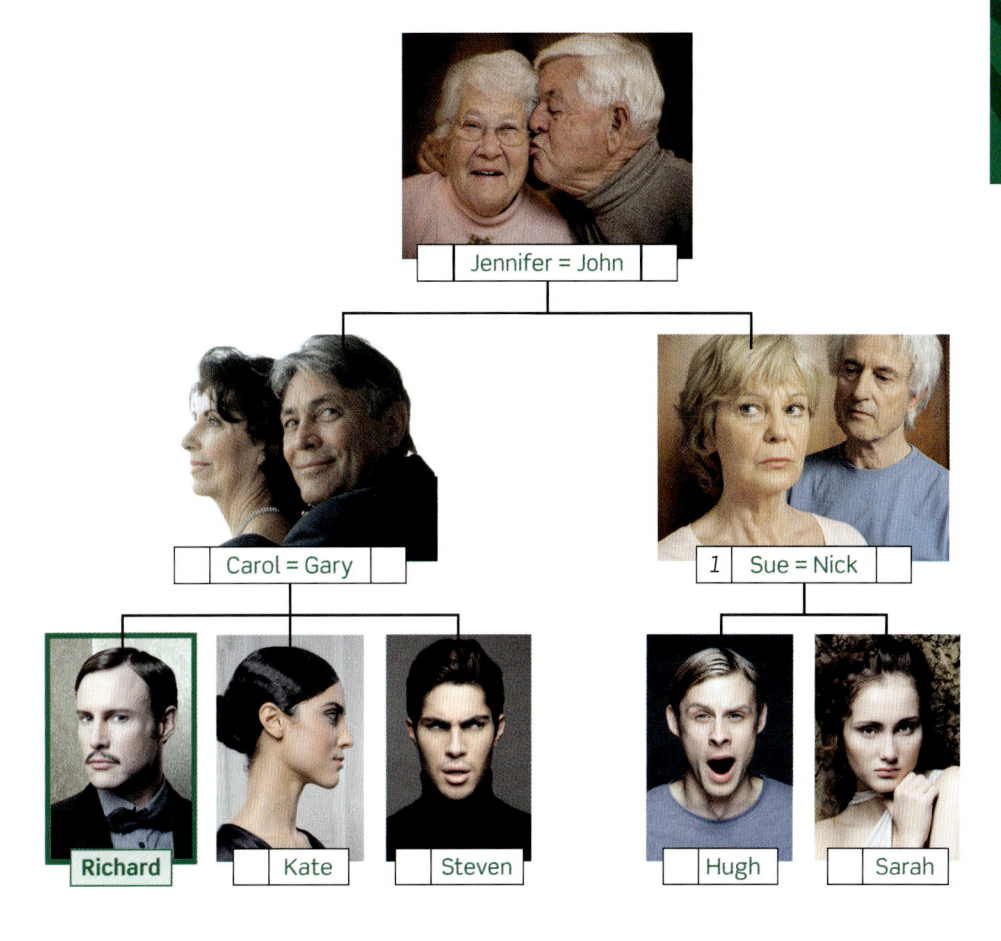

Who's Jennifer? She's Richard's grandmother.

Who are Sue and Nick? They're Richard's aunt and uncle.

◀ p.28

Jennifer = John

Carol = Gary   1 Sue = Nick

Richard | Kate | Steven   Hugh | Sarah

Richard = Emma   Kate = Christopher

Cathy | Jake   Oliver | Sally

Everyday activities

VOCABULARY BANK

a Match the verbs and pictures.

Suzy Stressed
- have a <u>sh</u>ower
- have a <u>c</u>offee
- do the <u>h</u>ousework
- start work at 8.30
- <u>fi</u>nish work at 6.30
- get dressed
- 1 wake up at 7.00
- have lunch at work
- go <u>sh</u>opping
- go to bed late
- have <u>p</u>izza for <u>d</u>inner
- get home late
- go to work by bus
- watch TV and check <u>e</u>mails

Henry Healthy
- go to <u>I</u>talian <u>c</u>lasses
- do <u>I</u>talian <u>h</u>omework
- 1 get up at 8.00
- have <u>br</u>eakfast
- do <u>e</u>xercise
- go home <u>e</u>arly
- walk to work
- re<u>lax</u>
- take the dog for a walk
- sleep for eight hours
- make the <u>d</u>inner
- have a bath

b 2 37)) Listen and check.

c In pairs, cover the phrases and look at the pictures. **A** describe Suzy's day, then **B** describe Henry's day. Then swap.

> **have**
> *Have* has two meanings.
> 1 For family and possessions, e.g. *I have three children. He has a big house.*
> 2 For activities, e.g. *I have lunch at 1.30. She has a shower in the morning.*

◀ p.30

Time

VOCABULARY BANK

1 TELLING THE TIME

a Match the clocks and phrases.

1 2 3
4 5 6
7 8 9

- ☐ It's a quarter past six.
- ☐ It's six o'clock.
- 1 It's a quarter to seven.
- ☐ It's ten past six.
- ☐ It's five to seven.
- ☐ It's twenty-five to seven.
- ☐ It's half past six.
- ☐ It's three minutes past six.
- ☐ It's twenty past six.

b 🔊 2 24 Listen and check.

> 🔍 **Time**
> You can ask for the time in two different ways:
> *What time is it?* OR *What's the time?*
> For times which are not multiples of five we use *minutes*,
> e.g. 6.03 = It's three minutes past six.

c Cover the phrases. Ask and answer with a partner.

What time is it? *It's...*

◀ p.26

2 EXPRESSIONS OF FREQUENCY

a Complete the expressions.

How often do you see your friends?

1 every /'evri/ *day*	M, T, W, Th, F, S, S
2 every w_____	week 1, week 2, week 3, etc.
3 every m_____	January, February, March, etc.
4 every y_____	2001, 2002, 2003, etc.
5 once /wʌns/ a _____	only on Mondays
6 twice /twaɪs/ a _____	on Mondays and Wednesdays
7 three times a _____	on Mondays, Wednesdays, and Fridays
8 four times a _____	in January, April, July, and October

b 🔊 2 46 Listen and check.

c Cover the left-hand column. Test yourself.

3 ADVERBS OF FREQUENCY

a Match sentences 1–6 with a–f. What do the highlighted words mean?

1 ☐ I **always** /'ɔːlweɪz/ get up at 7.00 during the week.
2 a I **often** /'ɒfn/ go to the cinema after work.
3 ☐ I **usually** /'juːʒuəli/ finish work at 6.00.
4 ☐ I **sometimes** /'sʌmtaɪmz/ meet a friend for lunch.
5 ☐ I **hardly ever** /'hɑːdli evə/ go to the theatre.
6 ☐ I **never** /'nevə/ have coffee.

a About seven or eight times a month.
b I start work at 8.00 every day.
c But on Fridays we stop at 3.00.
d I don't like it.
e Only once or twice a year.
f About once or twice a month.

b 🔊 2 47 Listen and check.

> 🔍 **normally**
> *Normally* is the same as *usually*. I normally get
> up early = I usually get up early.

c Cover sentences 1–6 and look at a–f. Can you remember the sentences?

d 🔊 2 48 Listen and repeat the highlighted adverbs of frequency.

◀ p.32

More verb phrases

VOCABULARY BANK

a   Match the verbs and pictures.

1. buy (*a ticket*) /baɪ/
   call / phone (*your mum*) /kɔːl/ /fəʊn/
   dance (*the tango*) /dɑːns/
   draw (*a picture*) /drɔː/
   drive (*a car*) /draɪv/
   find (*a parking space*) /faɪnd/
   forget (*somebody's name*) /fəˈget/
   give (*somebody flowers*) /gɪv/
   hear (*a noise*) /hɪə/
   help (*somebody*) /help/
   look for (*your keys*) /lʊk fɔː/
   meet (*for a coffee*) /miːt/
   paint (*a picture*) /peɪnt/
   play (*chess*) /pleɪ/
   remember (*somebody's name*) /rɪˈmembə/
   run (*a race*) /rʌn/
   see (*a film*) /siː/
   sing (*a song*) /sɪŋ/
   swim (*in the sea*) /swɪm/
   take (*photos*) /teɪk/
   talk (*to your teacher*) /tɔːk/
   tell (*somebody a secret*) /tel/
   use (*a computer*) /juːz/
   wait for (*a bus*) /weɪt fɔː/

b   **2 54**))) Listen and check.

c   Cover the verbs and look at the pictures. Test yourself or a partner.

◀ *p.36*

The weather and dates

VOCABULARY BANK

1 THE WEATHER

a Complete the chart with words from the list.

cloudy /ˈklaʊdi/   hot /hɒt/   raining /ˈreɪnɪŋ/
cold /kəʊld/   snowing /ˈsnəʊɪŋ/ windy /ˈwɪndi/
foggy /ˈfɒgi/   sunny /ˈsʌni/

What's the weather like?

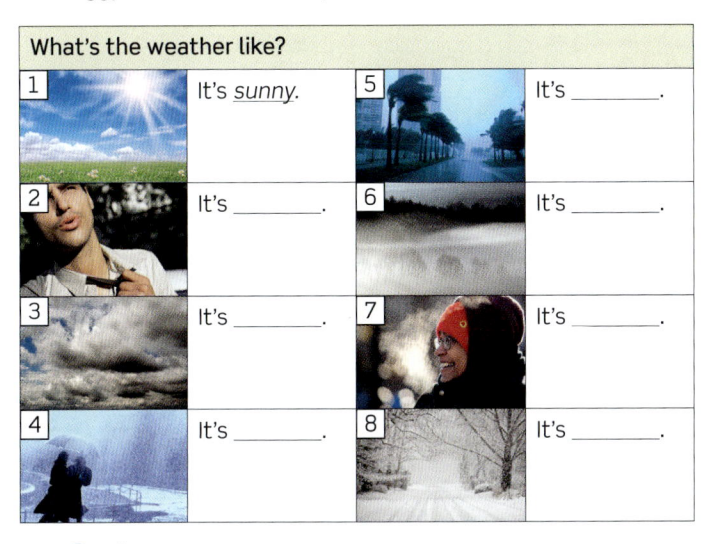

#		#	
1	It's _sunny_.	5	It's _____.
2	It's _____.	6	It's _____.
3	It's _____.	7	It's _____.
4	It's _____.	8	It's _____.

b 3 8))) Listen and check.

🔍 **Other adjectives for temperature**
warm /wɔːm/ = a nice temperature, not <u>very</u> hot (opposite = cool /kuːl/)

c Cover the chart and look at the pictures. Ask and answer with a partner.

What's the weather like?   It's sunny.

The four seasons

d 3 9))) Match the words and pictures. Listen and check.

☐ spring /sprɪŋ/   ☐ autumn /ˈɔːtəm/
☐ summer /ˈsʌmə/   ☐ winter /ˈwɪntə/

e What's the weather like today? What season is it where you are?

◀ p.40

2 THE DATE

a Complete the months. Remember to use CAPITAL letters!

_J_anuary   __pril   __uly   __ctober
__ebruary   __ay   __ugust   __ovember
__arch   __une   __eptember __ecember

b 3 29))) Listen and check.

c Complete the numbers and words.

1st	first	/fɜːst/
2nd	second	/ˈsekənd/
3rd	third	/θɜːd/
4th	fourth	/fɔːθ/
_5th_	fifth	/fɪfθ/
6th	_____	/sɪksθ/
7th	_____	/ˈsevnθ/
_____	eighth	/eɪtθ/
_____	ninth	/naɪnθ/
10th	_____	/tenθ/
11th	_____	/ɪˈlevnθ/
_____	twelfth	/twelfθ/
13th	_____	/θɜːˈtiːnθ/
14th	_____	/fɔːˈtiːnθ/
_____	twentieth	/ˈtwentiəθ/
21st	_____	/twenti ˈfɜːst/
_____	twenty-second	/twenti ˈsekənd/
23rd	_____	/twenti ˈθɜːd/
_____	twenty-fourth	/twenti ˈfɔːθ/
30th	_____	/ˈθɜːtiəθ/
_____	thirty-first	/θɜːti ˈfɜːst/

d 3 30))) Listen and check.

🔍 **Writing and saying the date**
We write	We say
12th March	**the** twelfth **of** March
22/1	**the** twenty-second **of** January

Prepositions with years, months, and dates
Use **in** + years, e.g. _The Rio Olympics are_ **in** _2016._
Use **in** + months, e.g. _My birthday's_ **in** _February._
Use **on** + dates, e.g. _The meeting is_ **on** _Friday 5th September._

Saying years
1807   eighteen oh seven
1936   nineteen thirty-six
2008   two thousand and eight (for years 2000–2010)
2011   two thousand and eleven OR twenty eleven

e What's the date today? What's the date tomorrow? What year is it?

◀ p.46

go, have, get

VOCABULARY BANK

a Match the verbs and pictures.

- [ ] by bus / by car / by plane /bʌs/ /kɑː/ /pleɪn/
- [1] for a walk /wɔːk/
- [ ] home (*from school*) /həʊm/
- [ ] out (*on Friday night*) /aʊt/
- [ ] shopping /ˈʃɒpɪŋ/
- [ ] to a restaurant /ˈrestrɒnt/
- [ ] to bed (*late*) /bed/
- [ ] to church / to mosque /tʃɜːtʃ/ /mɒsk/
- [ ] to the beach /biːtʃ/
- [ ] back (*to work*) /bæk/
- [ ] on holiday /ˈhɒlədeɪ/

- [ ] a car / a bike /kɑː/ /bɪk/
- [ ] long hair /lɒŋ ˈheə/
- [ ] breakfast / lunch / dinner /ˈbrekfəst/ /lʌntʃ/ /ˈdɪnə/
- [ ] a drink /drɪŋk/
- [ ] a good time /gʊd taɪm/
- [ ] a sandwich /ˈsænwɪdʒ/
- [ ] a shower / a bath / a swim /ˈʃaʊə/ /bɑːθ/ /swɪm/

- [ ] a newspaper (= buy) /ˈnjuːzpeɪpə/
- [ ] a taxi / a bus / a train (= take) /ˈtæksi/ /bʌs/ /treɪn/
- [ ] an email / a letter (= receive) /ˈiːmeɪl/ /ˈletə/
- [ ] dressed /drest/
- [ ] home (= arrive) /həʊm/
- [ ] to the airport (= arrive) /ˈeəpɔːt/
- [ ] up (*early*) /ʌp/

b 🔊 3 61 Listen and check.

c Cover the expressions and look at the pictures. Test yourself or a partner.

d Take turns to say three things you did yesterday and three you did last week with *went*, *had*, or *got*.

> Yesterday I got up early. I had breakfast in a café. I went shopping...

◀ p.57

160

The house

VOCABULARY BANK

1 ROOMS

Match the words and pictures 1–10.

- a <u>bath</u>room /ˈbɑːθruːm/
- a <u>bed</u>room /ˈbedruːm/
- a <u>din</u>ing room /ˈdaɪnɪŋ ruːm/
- a <u>gar</u>age /ˈɡærɑːʒ/
- a <u>gar</u>den /ˈɡɑːdn/
- a <u>hall</u> /hɔːl/
- a <u>kit</u>chen /ˈkɪtʃɪn/
- a <u>liv</u>ing room /ˈlɪvɪŋ ruːm/
- 1 a <u>stud</u>y /ˈstʌdi/
- a <u>toi</u>let /ˈtɔɪlət/

2 PARTS OF A ROOM

Match the words and pictures 11–15.

- a <u>bal</u>cony /ˈbælkəni/
- the <u>ceil</u>ing /ˈsiːlɪŋ/
- the <u>floor</u> /flɔː/
- the <u>stairs</u> /steəz/
- the <u>wall</u> /wɔːl/

3 THINGS IN A ROOM

a Match the words and pictures 16–31.

- an <u>arm</u>chair /ˈɑːmtʃeə/
- a <u>bath</u> /bɑːθ/
- a bed /bed/
- a <u>car</u>pet /ˈkɑːpɪt/
- a <u>cook</u>er /ˈkʊkə/
- a <u>cup</u>board /ˈkʌbəd/
- a <u>fire</u>place /ˈfaɪəpleɪs/
- a <u>fridge</u> /frɪdʒ/
- a <u>lamp</u> /læmp/
- a <u>light</u> /laɪt/
- a <u>mir</u>ror /ˈmɪrə/
- a <u>plant</u> /plɑːnt/
- a <u>shelf</u> (shelves) /ʃelf/
- a <u>show</u>er /ˈʃaʊə/
- a <u>so</u>fa / a couch /ˈsəʊfə/ /kaʊtʃ/
- a <u>wa</u>shing ma<u>chine</u> /ˈwɒʃɪŋ məʃiːn/

> 🔍 **Central heating and air conditioning**
> <u>Central</u> <u>heat</u>ing is a system that makes a house warm, usually using radiators.
> <u>Air</u> conditioning is a system that makes a house cool.

b 🔊 **12** Listen and check **1–3**.

c Cover the words and look at the pictures. Test yourself or a partner.

◀ p.62

Prepositions: place and movement

VOCABULARY BANK

1 PLACE

a Match the words and pictures.

- ☐ in /ɪn/
- ☐ in front of /ɪn frʌnt əv/
- ☐ on /ɒn/
- ☐ under /ˈʌndə/
- ☐ 1 behind /bɪˈhaɪnd/
- ☐ between /bɪˈtwiːn/
- ☐ opposite /ˈɒpəzɪt/
- ☐ next to /ˈnekst tu/
- ☐ over /ˈəʊvə/

b 4 21))) Listen and check.

c In pairs, ask and answer about the pictures.

Where's the ghost?

It's under the bed.

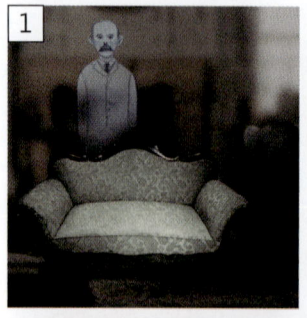

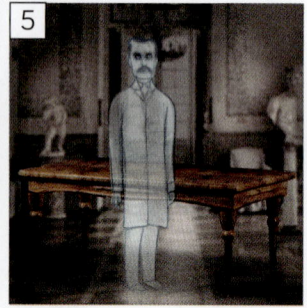

2 MOVEMENT

a Match the words and pictures.

- ☐ from…to /frəm/ /tu/
- ☐ into /ˈɪntu/
- ☐ out of /ˈaʊt əv/
- ☐ up /ʌp/
- ☐ down /daʊn/
- ☐ 1 towards /təˈwɔːdz/

b 4 22))) Listen and check.

c In pairs, ask and answer about the pictures.

Where's the ghost going?

It's going from the bar to room 11.

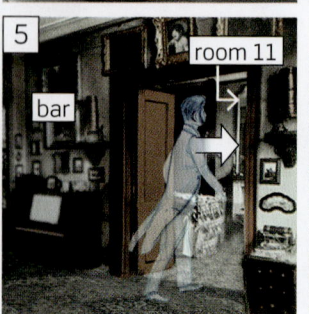

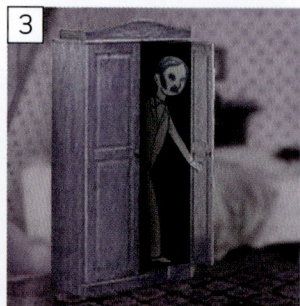

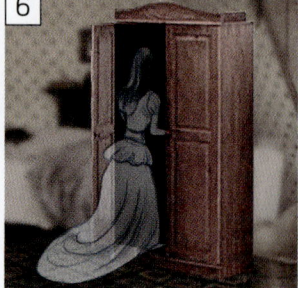

◀ p.65

162

Food

VOCABULARY BANK

a Match the words and pictures.

Breakfast /ˈbrekfəst/
- bread /bred/
- butter /ˈbʌtə/
- cereal /ˈsɪəriəl/
- cheese /tʃiːz/
- coffee /ˈkɒfi/
- eggs /egz/
- jam /dʒæm/
- (orange) juice /dʒuːs/
- milk /mɪlk/
- sugar /ˈʃʊgə/
- 1 tea /tiː/
- toast /təʊst/

Lunch / dinner /lʌntʃ/ /ˈdɪnə/
- fish /fɪʃ/
- meat (steak, chicken, sausages, ham) /miːt/
- (olive) oil /ɔɪl/
- pasta /ˈpæstə/
- rice /raɪs/
- salad /ˈsæləd/

Vegetables /ˈvedʒtəblz/
- carrots /ˈkærəts/
- chips (French fries) /tʃɪps/
- a lettuce /ˈletɪs/
- mushrooms /ˈmʌʃrʊmz/
- onions /ˈʌnjənz/
- peas /piːz/
- potatoes /pəˈteɪtəʊz/
- tomatoes /təˈmɑːtəʊz/

Fruit /fruːt/
- apples /ˈæplz/
- bananas /bəˈnɑːnəz/
- oranges /ˈɒrɪndʒɪz/
- a pineapple /ˈpaɪnæpl/
- strawberries /ˈstrɔːbəriz/

Desserts /dɪˈzɜːts/
- cake /keɪk/
- fruit salad /fruːt ˈsæləd/
- ice cream /aɪs ˈkriːm/

Snacks /snæks/
- biscuits /ˈbɪskɪts/
- chocolate /ˈtʃɒklət/
- crisps /krɪsps/
- sandwiches /ˈsænwɪdʒɪz/
- sweets /swiːts/

b **4 29))** Listen and check.

c Cover the words and look at the pictures. Test yourself or a partner.

◀ p.68

Places and buildings

VOCABULARY BANK

a Match the words and pictures.

- an <u>art</u> gallery /ˈɑːt ɡæləri/
- a <u>bridge</u> /brɪdʒ/
- a <u>bus</u> station /ˈbʌs steɪʃn/
- a <u>car</u> park /ˈkɑː pɑːk/
- a <u>cas</u>tle /ˈkɑːsl/
- a <u>chemist's</u> / a <u>pharmacy</u> /ˈkemɪsts/ /ˈfɑːməsi/
- a <u>church</u> /tʃɜːtʃ/
- a de<u>part</u>ment store /dɪˈpɑːtmənt stɔː/
- a <u>hos</u>pital /ˈhɒspɪtl/
- a <u>mar</u>ket /ˈmɑːkɪt/
- a <u>mos</u>que /mɒsk/
- a mu<u>se</u>um /mjuˈziːəm/
- a po<u>lice</u> station /pəˈliːs steɪʃn/
- a <u>post</u> office /ˈpəʊst ɒfɪs/
- a <u>railway</u> station /ˈreɪlweɪ steɪʃn/
- a <u>river</u> /ˈrɪvə/
- a road /rəʊd/
- a <u>shopping centre</u> / a mall /ˈʃɒpɪŋ sentə/ /mɔːl/
- a <u>square</u> /skweə/
- a <u>street</u> /striːt/
- a <u>super</u>market /ˈsuːpəmɑːkɪt/
- a <u>temple</u> /ˈtempl/
- a <u>theatre</u> /ˈθɪətə/
- 1 a town <u>hall</u> /taʊn ˈhɔːl/

b 5 3))) Listen and check.

c Cover the words and look at the pictures. Test yourself or a partner.

◀ p.76

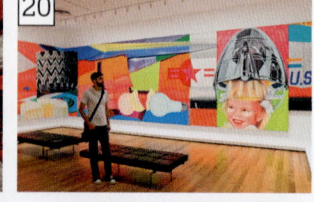

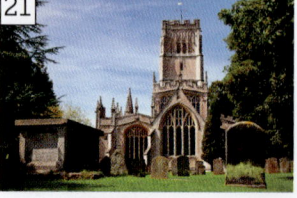

164

Irregular verbs

🔊 5 58

Present	Past simple	Past participle
be /biː/	was /wɒz/ were /wɜː/	been /biːn/
become /bɪˈkʌm/	became /bɪˈkeɪm/	become
begin /bɪˈgɪn/	began /bɪˈgæn/	begun /bɪˈgʌn/
break /breɪk/	broke /brəʊk/	broken /ˈbrəʊkən/
bring /brɪŋ/	brought /brɔːt/	brought
build /bɪld/	built /bɪlt/	built
buy /baɪ/	bought /bɔːt/	bought
can /kæn/	could /kʊd/	—
catch /kætʃ/	caught /kɔːt/	caught
come /kʌm/	came /keɪm/	come
cost /kɒst/	cost	cost
do /duː/	did /dɪd/	done /dʌn/
drink /drɪŋk/	drank /dræŋk/	drunk /drʌŋk/
drive /draɪv/	drove /drəʊv/	driven /ˈdrɪvn/
eat /iːt/	ate /eɪt/	eaten /ˈiːtn/
fall /fɔːl/	fell /fel/	fallen /ˈfɔːlən/
feel /fiːl/	felt /felt/	felt
find /faɪnd/	found /faʊnd/	found
fly /flaɪ/	flew /fluː/	flown /fləʊn/
forget /fəˈget/	forgot /fəˈgɒt/	forgotten /fəˈgɒtn/
get /get/	got /gɒt/	got
give /gɪv/	gave /geɪv/	given /ˈgɪvn/
go /gəʊ/	went /went/	gone /gɒn/
have /hæv/	had /hæd/	had
hear /hɪə/	heard /hɜːd/	heard
know /nəʊ/	knew /njuː/	known /nəʊn/

Present	Past simple	Past participle
leave /liːv/	left /left/	left
lose /luːz/	lost /lɒst/	lost
make /meɪk/	made /meɪd/	made
meet /miːt/	met /met/	met
pay /peɪ/	paid /peɪd/	paid
put /pʊt/	put	put
read /riːd/	read /red/	read /red/
run /rʌn/	ran /ræn/	run
say /seɪ/	said /sed/	said
see /siː/	saw /sɔː/	seen /siːn/
send /send/	sent /sent/	sent
sing /sɪŋ/	sang /sæŋ/	sung /sʌŋ/
sit /sɪt/	sat /sæt/	sat
sleep /sliːp/	slept /slept/	slept
speak /spiːk/	spoke /spəʊk/	spoken /ˈspəʊkən/
spend /spend/	spent /spent/	spent
stand /stænd/	stood /stʊd/	stood
swim /swɪm/	swam /swæm/	swum /swʌm/
teach /tiːtʃ/	taught /tɔːt/	taught
take /teɪk/	took /tʊk/	taken /ˈteɪkən/
tell /tel/	told /təʊld/	told
think /θɪŋk/	thought /θɔːt/	thought
understand /ˌʌndəˈstænd/	understood /ˌʌndəˈstʊd/	understood
wake /weɪk/	woke /wəʊk/	woken /ˈwəʊkən/
wear /weə/	wore /wɔː/	worn /wɔːn/
win /wɪn/	won /wʌn/	won
write /raɪt/	wrote /rəʊt/	written /ˈrɪtn/

Vowel sounds

SOUND BANK

		usual spelling		! but also
fish		i	his this film six big swim	English women busy
tree		ee ea e	meet three speak eat me we	people police key niece
cat		a	thanks flat black Japan have stamp	
car		ar a	garden party start father glasses dance	aunt
clock		o	hot stop coffee long not box	what watch want
horse		or al aw	sport door talk small saw draw	water four bought thought
bull		u oo	full put good book look room	could would woman
boot		oo u* ew	school food June use new flew	do fruit juice shoe
computer		Many different spellings. /ə/ is always unstressed. teacher umbrella America famous second ago		
bird		er ir ur	her verb first third nurse turn	learn work world word
egg		e	yes help ten pet very red	friend bread breakfast any said

		usual spelling		! but also
up		u	bus lunch ugly run lucky cut	come brother son does young
train		a* ai ay	name make rain paint play day	break steak great eight they grey
phone		o* oa	home close old don't road toast	slow low
bike		i* y igh	nine twice my why high night	buy
owl		ou ow	out thousand house count how brown	
boy		oi oy	coin noise toilet toy enjoy	
ear		eer ere ear	beer engineer here we're year hear	really idea
chair		air are	airport stairs fair hair square careful	their there wear
tourist		A very unusual sound. euro Europe poor sure plural		
/i/		A sound between /ɪ/ and /iː/. Consonant + y at the end of words is pronounced /i/. happy any thirsty		
/u/		An unusual sound. education usually situation		

* especially before consonant + e

○ short vowels   ○ **long** vowels   ○ diphthongs

Consonant sounds

SOUND BANK

	usual spelling		! but also
parrot /p/	p pp	paper pilot Poland sleep apple happy	
bag /b/	b bb	be table job builder number rubber	
key /k/	c k ck	credit card actor kitchen like black back	Christmas chemist's
girl /g/	g gg	green get angry big eggs bigger	
flower /f/	f ph ff	Friday fifteen wife photo elephant office coffee	
vase /v/	v	very eleven live travel river love	of
tie /t/	t tt	tea take student sit letter bottle	liked dressed
dog /d/	d dd	dance understand bad read address middle	played tired
snake /s/	s ss ci/ce	sister stops stress actress city cinema centre nice	
zebra /z/	z s	zero Brazil music please dogs watches	
shower /ʃ/	sh ti (+ vowel)	shopping shoes Spanish fish station information	sugar sure
television /ʒ/	si (+on)	revision decision confusion	usually garage
thumb /θ/	th	think thirty throw bathroom fourth tenth	
mother /ð/	th	the these then other that with	
chess /tʃ/	ch tch t (+ure)	cheap children church watch match picture adventure	
jazz /dʒ/	j dge	January juice July enjoy bridge fridge	German manager
leg /l/	l ll	like little plane girl small spelling	
right /r/	r rr	red rich problem try sorry terrible	write wrong
witch /w/	w wh	window twenty Wednesday win why when	one once
yacht /j/	y before u	yellow yesterday young yes use university music student	
monkey /m/	m mm	man Monday money swim summer swimming	
nose /n/	n nn	no never nine ran dinner thinner	know
singer /ŋ/	ng	song England language thing long going	think bank
house /h/	h	happy hungry hotel behind hall head	who whose

○ voiced   ○ unvoiced

OXFORD
UNIVERSITY PRESS

Great Clarendon Street, Oxford, OX2 6DP,
United Kingdom

Oxford University Press is a department of the University of Oxford. It furthers the University's objective of excellence in research, scholarship, and education by publishing worldwide. Oxford is a registered trade mark of Oxford University Press in the UK and in certain other countries

© Oxford University Press 2012

The moral rights of the author have been asserted

First published in 2012

2020 2019 2018
17 16 15 14

No unauthorized photocopying

All rights reserved. No part of this publication may be reproduced, stored in a retrieval system, or transmitted, in any form or by any means, without the prior permission in writing of Oxford University Press, or as expressly permitted by law, by licence or under terms agreed with the appropriate reprographics rights organization. Enquiries concerning reproduction outside the scope of the above should be sent to the ELT Rights Department, Oxford University Press, at the address above

You must not circulate this work in any other form and you must impose this same condition on any acquirer

Links to third party websites are provided by Oxford in good faith and for information only. Oxford disclaims any responsibility for the materials contained in any third party website referenced in this work

ISBN: 978 0 19 459856 9

Printed in China

This book is printed on paper from certified and well-managed sources.

ACKNOWLEDGEMENTS

The authors would like to thank all the teachers and students round the world whose feedback has helped us to shape English File.

The authors would also like to thank: all those at Oxford University Press (both in Oxford and around the world) and the design team who have contributed their skills and ideas to producing this course.

Finally very special thanks from Clive to Maria Angeles, Lucia, and Eric, and from Christina to Cristina, for all their support and encouragement. Clive would also like to thank her children Joaquin, Marco, and Krysia for their constant inspiration.

The publisher and authors would also like to thank the following for their invaluable feedback on the materials: Jane Hudson, Beatriz Martin, Gill Hamilton, Wayne Rimmer, Elif Barbaros, Joanna Sosnowska, Brian Brennan, Rachel Godfrey, Gustavo Viale, Romina Arcaro, Washington Jorge Mukarzel Filho, Emilie Řezníčková, Eva Formanova, Pavlína Zoss, Manuela Gazzola, Rebecca Lennox, Robert Anderson, Anne Parry, Mariusz Mirecki, Belén Sáez Hernáez, Edelweis Fernandez Elorz, Isabel Orgillés Trol, Kieran Donaghy, Paolo Jacomeli, Laura Villiger, Gabriela Fischer, Cassandra Wagg, Jonathan Clarke.

The Publisher and Authors are very grateful to the following who have provided information, personal stories, and/or photographs: David Rodriguez Gimeno and Orbest airline, p.23 (flight attendant text and photograph); Nicholas Baudrand, pp.30/31 ('Father & Daughter'); Margaret Oertig, p.39 ('The sound of silence'); Susana Sena and the students at the Whales Institute, Puerto Madryn, Argentina (Maria Julia) and Peter Lobley and the students at SNT International College Bournemouth (Mehmet), p.56 ('Why do we remember…?'); Joaquin Cogollos for the story 'It's written in the cards' p.80/81; Jemma Thompson, p.85 (Jemma in Valencia); Sir Ian McKellen, p.96 (interview); Cristina Cogollos, p.112 ('My Favourite Day')

The authors and publisher are grateful to those who have given permission to reproduce the following extracts and adaptations of copyright material: p.21 Adapted from 'Starbucks, summer and other unlikely reasons to love Britain' by Mark Vanhoenacker, 17 August 2010, *The Times*. Reproduced by permission of NI Syndication; p.33 Extract from 'Secrets of the isles of eternal youth' by Cherry Norton, 10 June 2001, *The Sunday Times*. Reproduced by permission of NI Syndication; p.35 Extracts from 'How to spot if your husband is average' from 'So THIS is Britain's Mr Average?' by Tim Wardle, 10 November 2007, *The Mail on Sunday*. Reproduced by permission of Solo Syndication; p.37 Adapted from 'X Factor winners and runners up: where are they now?' *The Telegraph* © Telegraph Media Group Limited 2010. Reproduced by permission; p.44 Extracts from Oxford Bookworms Library Starters: *Red Roses* and *Sally's Phone* by Christine Lindop, *New York Café* by Michael Dean. Reproduced by permission; p.51 Extract adapted from 'A grand time in the world's friendliest city' by Nick McCarthy, 26 October 2010, www.coventrytelegraph.net.

Reproduced by permission of Trinity Mirror Midlands Ltd; p.64 Information about Gosforth Hall reproduced by kind permission of Rod and Barbara Davies; p.65 Extract adapted from 'Friday Nights: Gosforth, Cumbria' by Stephen Bleach, 28 October 2001, *The Sunday Times*. Reproduced by permission of NI Syndication; p.68 Extracts from 'What I ate yesterday: Laura Bailey', 15 July 2010, 'What I ate yesterday: James DeGale', 2 December 2010, 'What I ate yesterday: Lionel Shriver' 4 March 2010 from *The Times*. Reproduced by permission of NI Syndication; p.79 Adapted from 'Couch-surfing: going it alone' by Daniel Thomas, 14 August 2008, *The Telegraph* © Telegraph Media Group Limited 2008. Reproduced by permission.

Sources: p.77 www.bbc.co.uk/news

The publisher would like to thank the following for their kind permission to reproduce photographs: Alamy Images pp.14 (plane/Richard Michael Pruitt/Dallas Morning News), 14 (balloon/D.Hurst), 14 (jeans/ignazuri), 21 (Boots/Roger Bamber), 21 (bicycle/Jeffrey Blackler), 33 (fishing/John Warburton-Lee Photography), 33 (Ogliastra/CuboImages srl), 33 (Okinawa/Chris Willson), 35 (Biscuits/latham & holmes), 35 (Ford Focus/Motoring Picture Library), 39 (Switzerland/Patrick Syww), 41 (rink/Travelshots.com), 41 (pond/David Pearson), 42 (Jeans/D.Hurst), 42 (Jacket/Leonid Nyshko), 43 (Jeans/D.Hurst), 47 (Asparagus/Tig Photo), 47 (egg/Samuel Whitton), 54 (Althorp/Trinity Mirror), 54 (stadium/Neil Tingle), 56 (Greece/Vova Pomortzeff), 60 (book/Brownstock), 60 (Woman office/Westend61 GmbH), 64 (Ghost/John Robertson), 68 (cake/Keith Leighton), 69 (Strawberry/Brownstock), 69 (Biscuits/Helen Sessions), 73 (Mastermind/Gerry Yardy), 76 (Mona Lisa/Iain Masterton), 77 (Death Road/Travelscape Images), 78 (CouchSurfing/NetPhotos), 83 (basket/Image Source), 84 (Diners/Lonely Planet Images), 85 (restaurant/Kevin Foy), 88 (Google/Ian Dagnall), 88 (iTunes/Ian Dagnall), 88 (Ebay/Ian Dagnall), 88 (Twitter/zetastock), 88 (Flickr/StfW), 88 (BBC News/Chris Batson), 88 (Facebook/Ian Dagnall), 88 (Barclays/pixelbully), 88 (Slim Secrets/NetPhotos), 88 (World of Warcraft/Ian Dagnall), 88 (Google maps/Ian Dagnall), 89 (iPhone/Alex Segre), 96 (*Gods and Monsters*/Moviestore Collection Ltd.), 97 (*The Lord of the Rings*/Moviestore Collection Ltd.), 100 (watermelon/ableimages), 100 (woman outside/Dorota Szpil), 100 (Smiling man/Adrian Muttitt), 100 (Smiling woman/David Young-Wolff), 100 (Teen/I love images), 100 (Jude Law/MARKA), 100 (Scarlett Johansson/Allstar Photo Library), 113 (Cricket/CountryCollection – Homer Sykes), 113 (Niagara/Mark A.Johnson), 113 (Trevi Fountain/PhotoStock-Israel), 114 (Kitchen/Graham Jepson), 115 (Cottage/incamerastock), 151 (Train ticket/Kevin Wheal), 151 (Binder/Richard Heyes), 151 (Wallet/L A Heusinkveld), 151 (Tissue/PhotoAlto), 151 (iPod/D. Hurst), 151 (FT/Geoffrey Kidd), 152 (Shark/Stephen Frink Collection), 152 (Coffee/Leigh Prather), 152 (Box/Mode Images Limited), 152 (Elephant/Mike Hill), 152 (Muddy hands/Craig Holmes Premium), 152 (Maths sum/incamerastock), 152 (Signpost/Stefano Politi Markovina), 152 (Fat and skinny/Catchlight Visual Services), 152 (Running beach/BE&W agencja fotograficzna Sp. zoo), 153 (Man sofa/UpperCut Images), 153 (Woman files/moodboard), 153 (Man relaxing/Cultura Creative), 153 (Nissan Micra/izmostock), 154 (Businesswoman/David Young-Wolff), 154 (Nurse/Monty Rakusen), 154 (TV crew/imac), 154 (Charlie Adam/AhmadFaizal Yahya), 154 (Shop assistant/Ace Stock Limited), 154 (Police/Janine Wiedel Photography), 154 (Receptionist/ACE STOCK LTD), 157 (Watch/musk), 158 (Subway ticket/Sami Sarkis), 158 (Drawing/Shepic), 158 (Teacher student/Blend Images), 158 (Car/Motoring Picture Library), 158 (Man singing/Image Source), 159 (Cloudy/HAWKEYE), 159 (Outside cold/Enigma), 159 (Stalactites/Paolo Gislimberti), 159 (Sun road/redbrickstock.com), 159 (Bluebells/Organics Image Library), 159 (Leaves/Jon Arnold Images Ltd), 164 (Town hall/Les. Ladbury), 164 (Pharmacy/graficart.net), 164 (Bus station/Peter Titmuss), 164 (Post office/PBstock), 164 (Arcade/David Bagnall), 164 (Police station/Justin Kase ztwoz), 164 (Paternoster Square/Peter Crome), 164 (Mosque/Paul Doyle), 164 (Department store/Robert Stainforth), 164 (Car park/Jonathan Howell Photography), 164 (Street/Alex Segre), 164 (Temple/ephotocorp), 164 (Toll bridge/Motoring Picture Library), 164 (Hospital/Justin Kase z12z), 164 (Dalyan River/dk), 164 (Theatre/Kirsty McLaren), 164 (MOMA/Patrick Batchelder), 164 (Church/incamerastock), 164 (Market/Homer Sykes), 164 (Castle/BL Images Ltd), 164 (Rail station/incamerastock), Ballygally Castle pp.104, 109 (hotel room); Camera Press p.53 (Helena Bonham-Carter/John Swannell); Castro Café p.79 (Castro Café, Budapest); Comlongon Castle p.65 (hotel room); Corbis pp.9 (Woman reception/Lucas Lenci), 14 (Statue of Liberty/Cameron Davidson), 14 (Empire State Building/Jean-Pierre Lescourret), 21 (ATM/Andy Rain/epa), 25 (Couple cafe/Mika), 28, 29 (Jack Nicholson and daughter/Hubert Boesl/dpa), 28, 29 (Lionel Messi/GUSTAU NACARINO/Reuters), 46 (deckchairs/Barry Lewis/In Pictures), 48 (Placido Domingo/Fernando Aceves/epa), 48 (Beyoncé/James Palmer/Retna Ltd.), 49 (Gustavo Dudamel/Sigi Tischler/epa), 49 (SB Youth Orchestra/Jennifer Taylor), 56 (Fans/Justin Lane/epa), 60, 62 (Newark Park/Philippa Lewis/Edifice/Arcaid), 61 (businessman/Awilli), 61 (Disapproving woman/Robert Recker), 67 (Sir Arthur Conan Doyle/Hulton-Deutsch Collection), 76 (Tiananmen Square/Victor Fraile), 76 (Shinjuku station/Robert Holmes), 79 (Man in city/Josef Lindau), 79 (Cinema/Tatiana Markow/Sygma), 79 (Cafe/René Mattes/Hemis), 93 (J.R.R. Tolkien's *The Hobbit*/HO/REUTERS/Bonhams), 100 (Tom Hanks/John A. Angelillo), 100 (Bono/David Silpa), 100 (Angelina Jolie/Ron Sachs/CNP), 100 (Katy Perry/Jared Milgrim), 111 (Smiling man/Westend61), 113 (Volleyball/Alexander Hubrich), 152 (Ring/James Noble), 152 (Bank notes/Jamie Grill), 152 (TV/Motofish Images), 152 (Basketball/Patrik Giardino), 153 (Mother children/Kevin Dodge), 153 (Women pets/Dan Tardif/LWA), 153 (Burger/Max Wanger), 153 (Yoga/Jetta Productions/Walter Hodges/Blend Images), 154 (Dentist/Benelux), 154 (Construction worker/Rick Gomez), 154 (Engineer/Andrew Brookes), 154 (Production line/Monty Rakusen/Cultura), 154 (Barrister/Ocean), 154 (Violinist/Tim Pannell), 155 (Man kissing wife/Rick Chapman), 155 (Happy couple/Bernd Vogel), 155 (Unhappy couple/Christopher Weidlich), 155 (Wealthy man/Robert Recker), 155 (Couple champagne/Robert Recker), 155 (Irritated man/Robert Recker), 155 (Man yawning/Robert Recker), 155 (Shy woman/Robert Recker), 155 (Wealthy couple/Robert Recker), 155 (Messy baby/Bernd Vogel), 155 (Child chocolate/Annie Engel), 158 (Man searching/Randy Faris), 158 (Tango/Jim Naughten),

158 (Swimming/Frank and Helena/Cultura), 158 (Marathon/JLP/Jose L. Pelaez), 158 (Whispering), 159 (Running rain/Robert Dowling), 159 (Fog/Gary W. Carter); Eammon McCabe p.12 (Roald Dahl's shed); Getty Images pp.7 (Jacket/James Whitaker/Digital Vision), 7 (Woman shopping/Frederic Lucano), 7 (Couple walking/Nick Dolding), 9 (Office workers/Leigh Schindler), 14 (Cheeseburger fries/James and James/Photodisc), 14 (New York/Buena Vista Images), 15 (Johnny Depp/WireImage), 15 (Penelope Cruz/Alberto E.Rodriguez), 20 (Pedestrians/Alan Copson), 21 (Starbucks/ChinaFotoPress), 23 (Schoolgirl/Ron Levine), 28 (Justin Bieber and mother/Larry Busacca), 29 (Man beach/Jordan Siemens/Photodisc), 29 (iPhone/Bloomberg via Getty Images), 29 (Family/Jupiterimages), 29 (Stressed boy/Peter Cade), 35 (Queen CD/AFP), 37 (Steve Brookstein/Jo Hale), 37 (Leona Lewis/Indigo), 37 (Leon Jackson/Dave Hogan), 37 (Alexandra Burke/Robert Heathcote), 40 (Rain London/Daniel Berehulak), 41 (London Eye/Richard Newstead), 42 (Shirt/Jonathan Kantor/Lifesize), 42 (Shoes/Thomas Northcut/Photodisc), 42 (Grey pants/Jonathan Kantor/Lifesize), 42, 43 (T-shirt/Tom Schierlitz), 42 (Denim skirt/Howard Shooter), 43 (Leather jacket/Tom Schierlitz), 48 (Guitar/Jonathan Kitchen/Photodisc), 48 (Louis Armstrong/Popperfoto), 48 (Drum/Stockbyte), 48 (Violin/Dorling Kindersley), 54 (Spencer family/Dave Thompson), 56 (Couple beach/Stockbyte), 60 (Businessman/Jason Hetherington), 60 (Book/Eric van den Brulle), 68 (Laura Bailey/Gareth Cattermole), 68 (James De Gale/Andrew Redington), 68 (Lionel Shriver/Ulf Andersen), 69 (Tomato/Michael Blann/Digital Vision), 71 (Scales/Stockbyte), 76 (Mountain road/Sergio Ballivian), 76 (Avenida 9 de Julio/Chad Ehlers), 76 (Vasco da Gama bridge/Paulo Ferreira), 79 (Man/Westend61), 79 (Listen music/Gregg Bucken-Knapp), 84 (Happy woman/Westend61), 89 (Web chat/David Malan), 94 (Couple/Digital Vision), 96 (Sir Ian McKellan/WireImage), 99 (Waitress/Andersen Ross/Stockbyte), 99 (Waiter/Andersen Ross), 100 (Tina Turner/Frederick M. Brown), 100 (Eminem/Larry Busacca/Getty Images For The Recording Academy), 113 (Bullet train/Keren Su), 152 (Angel devil/Vincent Besnault), 152 (F1 car/Colin Anderson), 152 (Mountain climbers/Mario Colonel), 152 (Grandmother grandson/Photo and Co), 152 (Woman bulldog/Elena Korenbaum/Vetta), 153 (Woman radio/Kactus), 153 (Tennis player/David J Spurdens/Digital Vision), 153 (Businesspeople/Chris Ryan/OJO Images), 153 (Friends homework/Jupiterimages), 153 (Guitar/Newton Daly), 153 (Boy marigold/Cheyenne Glasgow), 153 (Cooking/Karina Mansfield), 153 (Happy man/Fyza Hashim), 154 (Doctor/Thomas Tolstrup), 154 (Vet/Malcolm MacGregor), 154 (Soldier/Garry Wade/Photodisc), 154 (Piggy bank/Stephen Hoeck), 154 (Model/Stefan Gosatti), 154 (Doctor/Thomas Tolstrup), 154 (Haircut/Frank Gaglione/Stockbyte), 154 (Pilot/AAGAMIA/Iconica), 154 (Teacher/Taxi), 157 (Watch/Mark Harwood), 158 (Man helping/Tara Moore), 158 (Businessman using computer/sot/Digital Vision), 158 (Man painting/Mark Romanelli), 158 (Woman taking photo/Oliver Rossi), 158 (Women coffee/Ghislain & Marie David de Lossy), 159 (Snow storm/David Sacks); Gosforth Hall Hotel p.65 (Hotel room); Kobal Collection pp.92 (*The Lord of the Rings*/New Line Cinemá), 92 (*Girl who Played with Fire*/Nordisk Film/SVT/ZDF), 92 (*Alice in Wonderland*/Walt Disney Pictures); Masterfile pp.69 (onion), 71 (sugar/Photocuisine); Moviestore Collection p.92 (*Twilight*); National Portrait Gallery Picture Library pp.53 (Henry VIII/The National Portrait Gallery, London), 53 (Brontë Sisters by Patrick Branwell Brontë/National Portrait Gallery, London); Oxford University Press pp.14 (Cloudy sky/Corbis), 14 (White House/Photodisc), 19 (American flag/Image Farm), 41 (Dinosaur museum/Nigel Reed QEDimages), 84 (Dreadlocks/Photodisc), 86 (Man/Radius Images), 86 (Manga cartoon/Digital Vision), 86 (Asian woman/GLOW ASIA), 86 (Shaking hands/Photodisc), 86 (Brain waves/Digital Vision), 112 (College student/Fancy), 152 (Man dumbbell/Photodisc), 154 (Chef/Tetra Images), 154 (Waiter/Corbis), 158 (Teen laptop/White), 158 (Woman lunch/Photodisc), 158 (Couple cinema/Image Source), 159 (Sunny day/Katrina Brown), 159 (Windy day/Stockbyte), 164 (Country highway/Digital Vision), 164 (Supermarket shopping/Photographer's Choice), 164 (Dinosaur exhibit/BananaStock); Photolibrary pp.14 (School hallway/Design Pics Inc), 21 (Crossing road/Jacques Loic/Photononstop), 23 (Pharmacists/Cultura), 30 (Schoolgirl/Glow Images), 31 (Basketball/Image Source), 47 (Table chairs/Design Pics Inc), 51 (Coffee shop/Cultura), 57 (Moon/Radius Images), 61 (Woman turtleneck/Image Source), 69 (Chopsticks bowl/Glow Asia), 84 (Swedish town/Birger Lallo/Nordic Photos), 84 (Coca Cola, Atlanta/Visions LLC), 100 (Japanese woman/Image Source), 103 (Bridge/Britain on View), 152 (Snake/R. Andrew Odum/Peter Arnold Images), 153 (Businesswoman multitasking/Image Source), 153 (Man and flag/Image Source), 153 (Man newspaper/Fancy), 153 (Movie queue/Image100), 153 (Couple TV/Corbis), 153 (Man drinking/Westend61), 154 (Architect/Tetra Images), 154 (Stewardess/Image100), 157 (Wristwatch/Corbis), 158 (Thoughtful man/Fancy), 158 (Happy man/Fancy), 158 (Teenager driving/Blend Images), 158 (Girl bus stop/Brendan O'Sullivan), 158 (Men chess/Imagebroker.net), 158 (Listening/Image Source), 158 (Man woman flowers/Fancy), 159 (Feeling hot/White); Press Association Images p.73 (Pat Gibson/PA/CELADOR/ITV/PA Archive); Rex Features pp.28, 29 (Carla Bruni and Raphael Enthoven/Sipa Press), 73 ('*Who Wants To Be A Millionaire*' TV Series/c.ABC Inc/Everett); Ronald Grant Archive p.96 (*Macbeth*, 1978); p.12 (Roald Dahl/RDNL.Courtesy of The Roald Dahl Museum and Story Centre); V&A Images p.52 (The Duke and Wallis Simpson/Cecil Beaton).

Pronunciation chart artwork: by Ellis Nadler

Illustrations by: Peter Bull Studios: pp.10, 58, 90, 103, 149; Annelie Carlstrom/AgencyRush: p.100; Echo Chernik/IllustrationLtd: p.80/81; Jonathan Burton: pp.65, 66, 161, 162; Mark Duffin: p.17; Dermot Flynn: pp.8, 9, 47, 95. 102, 107; Alex Green/Folio Art: p FolioArt: pp.62, 63; Atsushi Hara/Dutch Uncle agency: pp.4, 5, 55, 126, 127, 133, 134, 135, 142, 143, 156; Satoshi Hashimoto/Dutch Uncle agency: pp: 131, 140, 141, 147, 150; Sophie Joyce: pp.7, 12, 13, 70; Tim Marrs: pp.6, 72, 87; Jerome Mirault/Colagene: p.16; Gaku Nakagawa/Dutch Uncle agency: p.38; Gavin Reece: p.45; James Taylor/Debut Art: p.22

Commissioned photography by: Gareth Boden pp.21(woman in car), 24, 36, 62 (Kim, Leo & Barbara), 63, 69 (cookery contestants), 109 (meals); MM studios pp.12 (books), 68 (food items), 151, 163

Practical English DVD: photography by: Richard Hutchings

Stills photography by: Rob Judges: pp.10, 11, 26, 42, 43, 58, 59, 74, 75, 90, 91